Towards Legal Literacy

Towards Legal Literacy
An Introduction to Law in India

Edited by

KAMALA SANKARAN
UJJWAL KUMAR SINGH

on behalf of the BA Programme Committee
University of Delhi

OXFORD
UNIVERSITY PRESS

OXFORD
UNIVERSITY PRESS

22 Workspace, 2nd Floor, 1/22 Asaf Ali Road, New Delhi 110002, India

Oxford University Press is a department of the University of Oxford. It furthers
the University's objective of excellence in research, scholarship, and education
by publishing worldwide in

Oxford   New York
Auckland   Cape Town   Dar es Salaam   Hong Kong   Karachi
Kuala Lumpur   Madrid   Melbourne   Mexico City   Nairobi
New Delhi   Shanghai   Taipei   Toronto

With offices in
Argentina   Austria   Brazil   Chile   Czech Republic   France   Greece
Guatemala   Hungary   Italy   Japan   Poland   Portugal   Singapore
South Korea   Switzerland   Thailand   Turkey   Ukraine   Vietnam

Oxford is a registered trademark of Oxford University Press
in the UK and in certain other countries

Published in India
by Oxford University Press, New Delhi

First published in India 2008
25th impression 2024

ISBN-13: 978-0-19-569222-8
ISBN-10: 0-19-569222-5

Typeset in Baskerville 10/13
By Jojy Philip
Printed in India by Replika Press Pvt. Ltd.
Published by Oxford University Press
22 Workspace, 2nd Floor, 1/22 Asaf Ali Road, New Delhi 110002, India

Contents

Acknowledgements

We are grateful to our contributors who so readily agreed to write on the complex aspects underlying the different braches of the law, in a concise and easy-to-read form. Our gratitude also to the University of Delhi's BA Programme Committee, in particular, the Chairperson, Prof. Rajiva Verma, the former Chairperson, Prof. Manoranjan Mohanty, and Dr Poornima Roy, who saw the need for such a book to help in the Legal Literacy course, and have helped in many ways in making this book a reality; the Registrar and his colleagues who have been extremely helpful in arranging the publication of the book; our colleagues in the Legal Literacy Sub-Committee, Dr Kavita Sharma, Ms Meera Verma, and Ms Anita Rajpal, for a fruitful and enjoyable time in preparing for this course; our colleagues from various colleges of Delhi University who enthusiastically participated in various workshops and took up the initiative of introducing a legal literacy course in their colleges; Shyam D. Nandan for his help in editing, and to the broader circle of friends and family who have encouraged us in the task of bringing out this book.

Introduction

KAMALA SANKARAN AND UJJWAL KUMAR SINGH

Few will disagree that laws, whether emanating as statutes enacted by parliaments, or existing as overarching constitutional norms, manifest the will of a society to govern itself efficiently and morally. The assumption that the vast and complex array of laws, touching upon all aspects of our personal and social lives has the force of our consent, is not therefore surprising. The question, then, is why people consent to have their lives regulated by laws. If the efficiency argument is taken up, it is clear that people would want to submit themselves to regulatory laws in order to ensure that their lives are conflict-free; which is to say that there is an assumption that if each of us submits to the discipline of the law, we shall all live orderly lives, which is the least we ask for in a world which is bewilderingly complex and chaotic.

Yet, the efficiency argument in favour of laws will work only in a society where all are equal, which is to say, where everyone has access to the same resources in the same measure, and possesses the same capacity to use them. We all know, however, that the real world is highly unequal, and there are almost unbridgeable social and economic gaps. Laws therefore, are more likely to elicit consent of the majority if they reflect an urge towards dismantling hierarchies and ushering in a society where all its members have an equal opportunity to access the common resources of society. Moreover, such a society would need to display an inclination towards equipping those who may be debilitated by unequal social or economic relations to participate as equal members of society. As soon as we talk about laws which discriminate in favour of the disadvantaged we bring in the moral argument, and the justification for consenting to laws that bring in substantive equality.

Thus when we talk about laws, clearly we are not talking only about its punitive character, that is, its power to punish those who step out of its bounds. We are talking also about how they reflect our concern with re-constituting ourselves into a moral society. This basically means that as members of such a society we would not want laws which are indifferent to the contexts in which they unfold, but are actively engaged in creating and interacting with the society in meaningful ways.

Yet, laws have not always been seen as reflecting the will of the people. Historically, laws were considered a manifestation of the sovereign's will and authority, and as dictates to which people submitted out of compulsion.

The transition from viewing law as the command of the sovereign to something born out of a democratically constituted society of equal citizens took place through a series of struggles by different sections of the people at different periods in history. At the base of this transition was a gradual but progressively broadening sphere of the rights of citizens, alongside the development of representative political structures, constitutional norms, the principles of rule of law and notions of substantive justice, and a judicial system which could give effect to them. It is significant that principles of rule of law pledged equal protection and equality through specific and precise legal procedures. Equality, as we discussed earlier, would remain inadequately realized if an account of the rule of law that also created substantive rights was not woven into the formal 'rule-book' version that requires rules to be enforced with an even hand. Over the years, the rights approach to law has assumed importance primarily because of peoples' struggles to promote a more substantive version, that is, the 'rights' (as distinct from 'rules') conception of the rule of law. The rights version of the rule of law is in several ways more ambitious than the rule-book conception. It assumes that citizens have moral rights and duties with respect to one another, and political rights against the state as a whole. It demands that moral and political rights be recognized in positive law so that they may be enforced upon the demand of individual citizens through judicial institutions. This conception of the law is based on the 'best practices' available across different countries and from internationally accepted norms. The rule of law under this conception is the ideal of rule by an accurate public conception of individual rights. It does not distinguish, as the rule-book conception does,

between the rule of law and substantive justice; on the contrary it requires, as a part of the ideal of law, that the rules in the rule book capture and enforce moral rights.

On the other hand, a rights approach to the rule of law can accomplish substantive justice incompletely, if it remains focused on individual rights. For a long time now, the sphere of rights has expanded to include groups and communities, and laws have reflected the need to address contexts of social exclusion, especially those in which entire groups, such as women, the elderly, the disabled, or communities such as cultural, religious, or caste communities, may be collectively subjected to systemic repression.

It follows then, that laws are not merely a set of rules distanced from us, rendered inaccessible by their inscrutability and requiring mediation by those who 'know' or are 'expert practitioners' of the law. Laws are inextricably associated with our lives. A growing consciousness about rights and the need to understand law without expert mediation and to be aware of its empowering potential, has become increasingly evident to more and more people. It is not surprising that a host of new statutes that have recently been enacted, such as the Scheduled Tribes and other Forest Dwellers (Recognition of Forest Rights) Act, 2006 and the National Rural Employment Guarantee Act, 2005 or the proposed laws that are being considered, such as a social security law for workers, have an explicit democratic rights agenda. Again, the fact that laws, in whatever measure, have addressed or responded to citizens' struggles for rights has indeed augmented and democratized the space for citizens to manifest their will in the creation of law discussed earlier. The origins of many of the laws in India can be traced to the legal system introduced by the British to serve their imperial ends. Yet, the laws mentioned above make it evident that democracy allows for the creation of spaces that may be used by citizens to express their will.

This reader is an attempt at reinforcing this space through the creation of an alert citizenry, enhancing rights consciousness and making the law more accessible. This requires not only an adequate knowledge of laws, but also an understanding of how this knowledge may be realized in actual practice. Perhaps the best resource of these rights is the meta-rules and philosophical principles that are embodied in the Constitution. The democratic pre-disposition of the Constitution is evident in both the fundamental rights and directive principles of state policy which together assure basic values of equality, free speech and association, the right to life, and freedom of faith. The Constitution moreover, lays down the framework of the institutional structure and distribution of powers among them, which would be essential for preserving these basic values. The state has been forbidden from making any law, which contradicts the fundamental rights or subverts the structural distribution of power between the different organs of government. Not only is the judiciary empowered to declare void any law that violates these basic norms that the Constitution lays down, but a well-etched out judicial system has been put in place to redress any violation of rights that takes place. Moreover, precise legal and juridical procedures have also been laid down in the penal codes to identity specific crimes of omission and commission, in respect of which punishment may be handed out. Such codes seek to ensure that the mutual commitment among citizens to abide by rules of orderly and conflict-free life is sustained. Further, since these rules of procedures are impersonal in the sense that they apply equally

and in the same measure to all citizens, they also seek to make the constitutional promise of equality before the law and equal protection of the law effective. Moreover, the right of access to justice and to legal aid in the criminal justice system is considered an integral part of fair trial.

Putting in place 'neutral' and 'uniform' laws and procedures, which treat all citizens equally, paves the way for procedural justice, ensuring that no-one is privileged because of his or her status of birth, etc. On the other hand, as mentioned earlier, laws often go beyond a stern adherence to procedure to take into account the specific contexts which shape the ex-periences of disadvantaged groups. In such cases, special protective measures are under-taken in some cases, and exceptions to the normal procedure are allowed in others to facilitate punishment of wrongdoers, and to deter future recurrence. In the case of scheduled castes and scheduled tribes, for example, the law has taken into account the historically entrenched repressive structures which have ritual sanction, leading to social disabilities and indignities like untouchability, and physical violence like rape and murder. Thus while the Constitution has reserved to the state the responsibility of providing special protective measures, laws like the Civil Rights Act, 1955 and the Scheduled Castes and Scheduled Tribes (Prevention of Atrocities) Act, 1989, make these provisions effective. It is significant that in an effort to check struc-tures of oppression and discrimination based on caste/birth, these laws allow for more stringent provisions to ensure speedy trial and punishment of the guilty. However, since laws unfold in social contexts which are deeply hierarchical, the capacity of these laws to check socially sanctioned and enforced disabilities and violence is hampered.

Women have a more ambivalent relationship with the law. Independence brought equal rights to Indian women with constitutional provisions removing gender disqualifications in the exercise of fundamental rights. Yet, in the name of autonomy to religious communities, paradoxically, the Constitution itself curtailed the right to equality that it guaranteed to women as citizens by subjecting women to the personal laws of specific communities. Personal laws of religious communities govern matters relating to marriage, divorce, guardianship of children, and inheritance. By and large, they limit the choices available to women with regard to economic freedom and equality by allotting them a subservient and dependent position in matters of family and finances. Furthermore, protective legislation pertaining to prohibition of dowry and prevention of sexual harassment in the workplace remain inadequately implemented.

While specific social groups may have special relationship with laws, more often than not laws recognize people as individuals, and society as constituted of individuals in a relationship of mutually agreed obligations. It is not surprising that the law of contract which is often considered the most fundamental branch of law is premised on the idea that the individual is an autonomous and rational person, who enters into voluntary and mutually beneficial agreements with other individuals independent of the intervention of the state. The regulatory role of the state, as a non-partisan arbiter becomes important in matters of breach of such a contract, in order to uphold the sanctity of mutual trust and abiding by the self-imposed discipline and rules of a harmonious social life.

The centrality given in law to the rational individual with a free will committed to a society characterised by mutual respect,

notions of common good, friendship and a sense of community, also envisages the individual as a 'public spirited' active citizen. It is not surprising therefore, that law has shown a tendency towards both inculcating and demanding responsible and active citizenship. The development of Public Interest Litigation (PIL), for example, combines the principles of social justice with the idea of people's participation in setting in motion or activating the judiciary for protecting those sections which are most vulnerable to social and political repression. It is interesting how the faith in collective effort to preserve social rights has extended in making space in the judicial process for social activism. The courts have simultaneously articulated an idea of rights which is closely associated with the performance of specific duties. This is perhaps evident in instances such as the right to a clean environment which has been recognized by the Supreme Court as a right encompassed by the fundamental right to life. Simultaneously, the Supreme Court has also upheld the preservation of the environment as a primary fundamental duty which has to be observed collectively.

Apart from the burgeoning environmental crisis which has encouraged the conception of collective responsibility, other new challenges have emerged in recent years, eliciting specific legal responses from the state, which impact upon notions of rights and justice. Notions of 'global risks' in the form of 'terrorism', for example, have resulted in a spate of anti-terror laws, which bypass constitutional safeguards and principles of fair trial as laid down in the Code of Criminal Procedure, 1973. On the other hand, such laws, by spinning a web of suspicion around specific communities, assume a civil society founded on suspicion and distrust. Moreover they squeeze spaces of freedom and liberty and narrow down spaces of public dialogue and democratic deliberation. The communication revolution has introduced yet another set of insecurities, posing the problem of checking cyber crimes, and at the same time maintaining the precarious balance between surveying the nebulous world of cyberspace and respecting the privacy of individuals. Significantly both terrorism and cyber crime have opened up debates on issues of public security and the limits of state action.

This book is an attempt to introduce students to laws that impact our lives in significant ways. The papers in this volume take up themes that have been identified above, to broach issues of both rights and social responsibilities. They aim not only at initiating a person who is not a student or practitioner of law to aspects of law which everyone must be familiar with, but also, to give an insight into ways in which laws are not just punitive measures, but are also protective and affirmative of social justice and responsibility. Perhaps it is these aspects of law that empower and equip people to know and act upon what they consider just, that need to be identified, explained, and emphasised. This book is an effort in that direction.

August 2007   The Editors

Why Legal Literacy?

A Wake-up Call

UPENDRA BAXI

I. GENERAL REMARKS

The 'law' is an enterprise that seeks to rule us all from cradle to the grave, whether as constitution confronting custom, or as custom confronting constitution, and often indeed as the diverse combinatory prowess of both. The very notion of enterprise suggests risk-taking i.e., risk is a site for both opportunity as well as failure for regulation or felicitation of approved social conduct. At the same moment, this coupling of the constitution and the custom is at the outset designed to pluralize the notion of legal literacy, a message yet to be fully constructed and conveyed co-equally to those who govern us and those who would resist domination.[1]

As citizens, we are supposed to know the law made by the state, whether we intend to obey it or break it. As members of cultural and religious communities, we also need to know the norms that define our membership of these collectivities. Often, our identity and obligations as members of a political society and of diverse memberships within cultural and religious communities constitute spheres of peaceful, mutual coexistence. Often, too, these collide. To decide what obligations ought to have precedence, each one of us in collision situations has to know a great deal about the law of the state and that constituting community and identity other than the political. Literacy in state law is important but never enough for an understanding of multiple sources of obligations that constantly press upon us. This invites engagement with many difficult questions including what we may want to mean by literacy, law, domination, and resistance. Further, the question always is: how far do resources of legal literacy endow us with resources of justice for all and care of self and care for others?

II. WHAT MAY IT MEAN TO SPEAK OF ILLITERACY

Illiteracy as the lack of acquisition and retention of skills of reading and writing is a widespread and deeply rooted problem in India, as elsewhere. Quantitative measurements of illiteracy rates are obviously important as

[1] Unfortunately, space constraints prevent me from even a minor elaboration of this aspect, save some side-comments in the footnotes.

these convey a sense of the scale of the situation, and its dimensions across age, gender, race, class, demographic shifts, and related factors. The next steps entail three different sorts of related but distinct concerns: first, understanding the causation of illiteracy; second, the question of ethical evaluation; and third, the relationship between causal facts and ethical judgements about individual, social, and political responsibility.

Causation studies invite attention to a domain of understanding a large number of variables across stretches of historical time and space. Those who would worry about legal literacy of the law of the state, need to more fully to attend to these studies (too voluminous to cite here) because it is largely written and therefore inaccessible in that form to the 'illiterate'.[2] Causation studies indicate that illiteracy and innumeracy rather than describing individual attributes, define aspects of social and political systems as a whole which distribute opportunities of acquiring and retaining literary[3] in terms of systemic discrimination, whether gender, race, caste or class-based. These also demonstrate that the production and persistence of illiteracy depends in part on the cooperative relationship between governmental/state actors on the one hand and civil society actors on the other. Illiteracy is thus socially and politically produced and placed at the service of the ends of the dominant.

Causation studies, under the auspices of the positivistic ('value-neutral') social science traditions of discourse, impose no ethical burdens on the researchers or the reader; no prescription follows out of description and this is precisely what makes description important. Whether you are misogynist or a feminist, for instance, it remains still remains important to know social facts about female illiteracy; one does not have to share the consciousness of the oppressed classes, or their erstwhile world historic revolutionary projects, to provide measures of why and how certain classes are systematically denied access to literacy.

The question then arises: 'What may we do with that which "we" know?' That 'we' constitutes a very diverse category indeed! Very few otherwise literate persons read the causation studies and even when they intuitively understand the causes of illiteracy, they offer some standard evasive responses. One such response simply is that illiteracy is a state of misfortune inviting no more than occasional social compassion and acts of charity.[4] Another response is this: illiteracy is a problem (if that at all in the first place) that individual or social action collectivities on their own can never fully resolve; thus remains largely a function and a task for the politically organized community (the state). Should the state too handle

---

[2] The other of the state law—the community 'law'—of course remains available through communicative means (such as forms of songs and dance. also orders of visual representations) that may not require any recourse to literacy.

[3] Studies about literacy promotion draw our attention to this distinction. Learning imparted is not often retained either because it aggravates their recipients everyday vulnerability or it is felt that such learning does not make them any the better off than before.

[4] See, Sidel, Mark, *New Economy Philanthropy in the High Technology Communities of Bangalore and Hyderabad, India: Partnership with the State and the Ambiguous Search for Social Innovation*, mimeo, University of Iowa College of Law and Obermann Center for Advanced Studies; Sundar, Pushpa, *Charity for Social Change and Development- Essays on Indian Philanthropy*, New Delhi, Indian Centre for Philanthropy, 1997; Sunder, Pushpa, *For God's Sake: Religious Charity and Social Develop Women and Philanthropy in India,* New Delhi, Indian Centre for Philanthropy, 2002; Tandon, Rajesh, *Voluntary Action, Civil Society and the State* New Delhi, Mosaic Books, 2002.

this problem in terms of largess or public/ social philanthropy or as a fundamental constitutional obligation? Most of the 'we' do not have time or inclination to worry much about this. Thus arises what I wish to name here as the illiteracy of the literate; this illiteracy is often paraded as a badge of egotistic civic virtue because ways of living finite 'good life' as individuals caring for their immediate family entails no further solicitude or regard, outside erratic and episodic acts of charity, for the suffering others.

In contrast, a minuscule 'we' regard the question of illiteracy as a question of injustice, not misfortune.[5] Illiteracy stands here perceived as an aspect of the injustice of the basic structure of social arrangements. These 'we' however further sub-divide in terms of the broadly 'liberal' and radically 'revolutionary' folks. For the former, removal of illiteracy may be best attained by working together with the state and international, even international, financial institutions. For the latter, literacy grows out of the barrel of a gun; put another way, for them acquiring literacy is an act of political education which may best be furthered and even achieved by armed struggles that wage a perennial war against the bourgeois/landlord/ globalizing Indian state, and much else beyond.

The liberal response struggles to problematize illiteracy via the languages of human rights, under which it remains axiomatic that persistent illiteracy constitutes a violation of human rights or even the confiscation of the right to be and to remain human. Illiteracy and innumeracy constitute, on this view, constant vulnerability to exploitation and other forms of violent domination and social exclusion. It thrives on the expectation (quite often disappointed) that those endowed with a modicum of responsibility for the other should do their best to contribute to the removal of these obstacles to a fuller human and social development. The violent 'pedagogy of the oppressed' (to invite attention to Frantz Fanon all over again) has, in the Indian experience, often prepared the ground for the liberal endeavour.

Straddling these divides, many leaders of the subaltern struggles in colonial India, thought, far in advance of all the contemporary and voguish human rights talk, that literacy and 'education' furnished the wherewithal for the civil society oriented emancipatory struggles. I have in view here the legacy of Mahatma Jyotibha Phule and Bhim Rao Ambedkar, Pandita Ramabai, Iravati Karve, among magnificent others. Babasaheb Ambedkar articulated the mission of literacy in terms of the maxim: 'Educate, Organize, and Agitate'. For him, literacy and education were ways of achieving radical social change for the Atisudras (the social and economic proletariat.) Learning and education that do not foster capacities for organization (that is, social cooperation to name the production of human rightlesness, degradation, and abuse as a radical evil) and for agitation (that is, discovery and deployment of strategies that effectively lower the intensity and incrementally diminish the scope for social predation).

For Mohandas,[6] literacy and education (his constant use of the Gujarati word–*kelvani*–

---

[5] I here rely on the gifted and troubled distinction offered by Shklar Judith N, *The Faces of Injustice*, New Haven, Yale University Press, 1990.

[6] This is how he must be named because there are now too many Gandhis and his middle name–Karamchand–remains appropriated by mass media entertainment industries).

redefines translation even in terms of lifelong learning, a nearest equivalent) remained an unending, even infinite, task. For Mohandas, kelvani signified at least three things: a continual development of individual moral conscience, the ethic and theology/technology of civil disobedience and a re-education of the *vaishnav-jans* (the literate and educated) to empathize with the *pid-parai* (the sufferings of the impoverished, disadvantaged, and dispossessed).

Many of his followers, including Vinoba Bhave and Jai Prakash Narayan, translated this message into *bunyiadi* or *nai talim* (roughly basic and new forms of learning). This essay does not furnish any scope for any detailed narration of, say, differences (even the chasms) separating the inaugural figurations of Mohandas and Ambedkar and their loyal and not-so-loyal followers.

However, it needs to be said that neither Babasaheb nor Mohandas ever approximated, or anticipated, the lean and mean conception of what now passes under the rubric of massively globally (and at times rather in sinister ways) funded 'empowerment' projects. Literacy and education in these inaugural conceptions was not at all matter of creating new globalized consumer classes but of the ways of profound de-linkages with the forms and methods of advanced or late capitalist globalizing economy.

III. THE CONSTITUTION OF ILLITERACY

The making of the Indian Constitution was a world-historically inaugural event. By establishing a constitutional right to universal adult suffrage, it de-legitimated arguments favouring the thresholds of literacy and property in the constitution of political

representation.[7] And this indeed has served Indian constitutional and political development strikingly well; the success of the Indian democratic experiment owes a very great deal to the literacy of the literate rather than the illiteracy of the illiterate,[8] now constantly on display by Indian middle classes' chorus of celebration of massive Indian-style hyper-globalizing governance.

For the moment, it remains important to note that the Constitution did not make compulsory literacy or education (at least elementary and primary educations) for young persons under the age of fourteen years; rather it consigned this as social right in Part IV of

[7] And fortunately for India, there were few takers of Nani Palkhivala's (ironically also the author of *We, the People*) *repeated* call that some literacy qualifications should be considered by way of a radical constitutional amendment. Nani's forensic contributions to constitutional jurisprudence were immense and we should acknowledge these rather more fully, despite his regrettable advocacy of the Union Carbide Corporation in the *Bhopal Case*. Even so, it must be said that his spirited advocacy of this cause conferred an odious sense to the appellation 'jurist.'.

[8] It is all too often the case, and not just in India, that the more educated one is the less one knows about the plight of the suffering and right-less others. Specialized quotients of knowledge that provide passports for upward social and economic mobility for some, entail the privileging of certain spheres of cultivated ignorance. The less 'legitimacy' one knows about the causes and consequences of human rightlessness and suffering, the better is one's efficiency in the pursuit of 'rational' interests. To be well-educated is indeed to develop a limited capacity for moral altruism and social empathy as limited as humanly possible. There was a time when even official education policy at least talked of secular value-based learning and education. No more so. In these days of hyperglobalizing India, learning and education are indeed presented in terms enhancing India's competitive edge in the world market. The quintessence of education now is summed by how our graduates, specialists, and super-specialists, become front-rank 'global' players.

the Constitution enunciating the Directive Principles of State Policy. Although declared a constitutional obligation fundamental to law and policy-making, nothing much really happened. Even Chacha Nehru as he was fondly called by India's children, and who had a mighty love affair with them, could not overcome the notion that India lacked sufficient resources to tackle the problem of illiteracy on a war footing; neither did his successors to the throne of Indian Prime Minister-ship. In this sense, at least, we may speak of a great promise betrayed, or more precisely regard the great Indian Constitution as furnishing the corpus of the immense constitution of illiteracy.

It remains interesting to note though that an activist Supreme Court is able, 50 years or so after the working of the Constitution, to convert right to literacy and education as a 'fundamental right', the 2002 eighty-sixth constitutional amendment now adding Article 21-A reconverts this into a directive principle. The new right may only be serviced by, and in such manner, 'as the State may, by law, determine'! What the state may thus determine is governed not by any sense of obligation but stands rather determined by considerations of state largess. And the state has, in any event, thus far determined very little indeed. I may only refer to the articulate despair voiced by civil society folks concerning the constitutional femicide/infanticide of this new right.[9]

[9] It is beyond the bounds of this presentation to overview the grounds of this necessitous conclusion or to refer to voluminous policy and activist literature. It should be enough to note that many a distinguished civil servant turned into social and human rights activist upon superannuation while lamenting the present state of affairs, 'help' the state governments to devise literacy and education programmes, with or without the massive World Bank funding.

The structures and operations of the constitution of illiteracy also condition other voluntary social efforts and movements. Those who wield power to make public decisions seem to need greater human rights learning; only adult and continuing education legislators, civil servants, political leaders and cadres can pave some future pathway to progress in the eventual overturning of the constitution of illiteracy.

IV. FORMS OF CONSTITUTIONAL OATHS AND THE TASKS OF LEGAL LITERACY

Let me illustrate this thematic in a first instance in terms of forms of official oaths that fully confront the programschrift of constitutional and legal literacy (hereafter CALL).

Each and every elected official (and even some unelected ones such as the High Court and the Supreme Court justices) has to swear, or solemnly, affirm the oath in the forms prescribed by the Third Schedule of the Indian Constitution. Obviously, this means everything else than performatives of swearing at the Constitution, both in its letter and spirit. Ask any generation of the Indian elected, and some unelected officials, designated by the Third Schedule, why it enunciates so many, on my count as many as ten forms of oath, and not just a single one of the past or actually incumbent constitutional agent/official would have a clue! All, I assure you, that you will find is nothing 'better' than frothing political incoherence!

Why is it that the oath of office for a minister of the Union, Justices of the Supreme and High Courts, and Comptroller and Auditor General of India recites the paramount obligation to perform the 'duties of the office without fear or favour, affection or ill-will' that does not equally rigorously address the official others—including nominated or elected members of parliament and state legislatures, and even those who declare their candidature for legislative offices? Why/how does it to comes to pass that Attorney Generals, Solicitor Generals, and State Advocate Generals, and at grassroots levels, district judiciary, prosecutorial and investigative agencies, the Central Intelligence Bureau, Central Vigilance Commissions, state and union public services commissions, and the national human rights agencies, routine and specialized police, paramilitary, and related security forces, thus remain in existence in an oath free zone, or to use a current sovereign metaphor, constitutionally constituted special economic/security/executive zones? How do we ever understand that union and state planning commissions, the Finance Commission, the law reform commissions, the election commissions, and the commissions of enquiry should also form an integral feature of these zones? Why, further, is it the case that we find some reiteration of oath of secrecy?

To raise these, and related interlocutions, is already to demonstrate the illiteracy of the literate. At least, any well-conceived CALL programmes should attend such vexatious, without at no moment being frivolous, to these concerns. Further, the obligations referring to 'all manner of people' in these recitals must at least entail obligations of determined erasures of forms of gender, race, caste, homophobic, 'disability'-challenged, among other forms, of policy-making and constitutional governance tasks.

To argue that oath-taking is a mere ritual is to undermine the letter and spirit of the Constitution. This is not exactly a James Bond type 007 license! Yet this is precisely how so many managers and actors of Indian ruling classes conceive this. If this is the case, human rights and social activist literacy campaigns must call for a repeal of the Third Schedule; if not they need to struggle to make forms of oath in real-life terms. By this I signify the power of CALL to script an unwritten human right of recall of errant and perfidious elected and other related public officials. This is precisely what the total revolution, under the inaugural leadership of Jai Prakash Narayan, unleashed only to be visited by a draconian emergency rule (1975–7). All this immediately suggests that taking CALL seriously entails some fresh starts for understanding and reframing Indian constitutionalism, 60 years after its adoption.

The CALL in the contemporary Indian 'development' contexts needs to proceed to frame the illiteracy of the literate in many further poignant contexts. The CALL programschrift is rather simple and stark. It has to explain, for example, why the state, law, and apex adjudication remains so effete in terms of answerability to the following.

1. Bhopal disaster violated Indian humanity, and after more than two decades of their suffering there has been no redressal of their injustices.
2. The Gujarat episode in the year 2002, and their precursor communities cruelly constituted by politically organized collective violence ('riots' and 'rape culture') in combating the culture of impunity and genocidal leadership.
3. Bereaved families of the tortured, tormented, 'encountered,' and 'disappeared' peoples.
4. Citizen Public Project–Affected families, to which the Narmada Dam violated so fulsomely testify, after a decade and half of the Apex Court contestation.

Manifestly, the bulk and generality of project–affected citizen/peoples continue to insist on the removal of constitutional illiteracy on the part of the ruling classes, developmental experts, and even some apex adjudicators; all they are saying, in sum, is that they co-equally remain worthy of constitutional and human rights solicitude and respect. On this register, it is the illiteracy of the literate which constitutes the part of the problem, without at all intending to offer, even in a remote implication, any contumacious remark for an otherwise an explosively activist Apex Court! It is the Supreme Court of India that now, after all, vigorously translates the right to literacy and primary and elementary education from directive principles to the status of fundamental rights, partially cancelled by an effete constitutional amendment that now demotes this right to its earlier constitutional status.

The point of the foregoing complex observations, in the context of legal literacy, is rather simple: literacy as human and human rights value consists in what it performs for the amelioration for the worst-off peoples in conjunction where possible with the acts of partnership with enormously better-off, and where necessary, in acts of insurgency/insurrection against these.

V. THE STATE/LAW COMBINE PRODUCTION OF LEGAL ILLITERACY

CALL must further address admittedly complex, combined and uneven forms of the conditions of its production. A crucial dimension of contemporary governance is always that those who govern take the utmost scrupulous care to craft legal rules in ways which render it incomprehensible to those most governed by it. The law is 'public', yet,

as Pratiksha Baxi has reminded us poignantly it also constitutes some enduring forms of obscene ordering of regimes of 'public secret'.

Thus, the state law and languages, in the main, create and sustain myriad orders of legal illiteracy amidst a vast subject populace. To know one's obligations and rights, one has to have access to the 'free' market for legal services which already out-prices a large majority of people. Legal literacy then may be simply thought of as a continual war against forms of power and domination that thrive by the production of legal illiteracy.

In and through this confrontation, subjects constantly seek to convert themselves into active citizens. Citizens are beings, as Aristotle reminded us a long while ago, who possess two faculties: they know how to be ruled and also how to rule. Legal literacy, ideally conceived, at the same moment, fosters the capability of subjection to 'good' governance and the power to question and combat 'bad' governance.

Mohandas Gandhi framed this matter momentously differently when he said that Swaraj meant not just governance, but just governance. In this view, citizens are beings that develop capabilities for defining unjust law and popular habits and forms of conscientious disobedience towards, its processes, and institutions. Legal literacy thus is not merely imparting formal instruction concerning the 'law' but also relates to the development of collective/dialogical social thinking about 'justice'. To understand legal literacy in the contemporary Indian context is to invite a sober and anxious consideration to Jai Prakash Narayan's contingently ill-fated yet at the same time so propitiously future-freighted 'Total Revolution' movement.

In this dynamic view of it, CALL begins its itinerary as a compelling civic virtue; we do not just learn the law instrumentally—in ways that serve the immediate strategic self-interests of the dominant, deploying the languages of human rights for their distinctively carved and crafted ends of domination—but rather as a way of resisting injustices to others. In this dynamic view, legal literacy becomes an art and science of citizenship through which we take not merely our rights seriously, but coequally take other people's sufferings seriously.

True, this is not how the tasks of legal literacy stand conventionally conceived. Yet, it is important to understand that our rights and obligations remain unintelligible outside a first step that underscores a chain-connection with the rights and obligations of all others.[10] To take here as an example the endless confrontation over the politics and pro-grammes of affirmative action, we remain for or against reservation only because we under-stand 'well', for weal or woe, this connectivity between 'our' rights and 'theirs'.

Programmes for legal literacy launched by human rights and social activists preciously accentuate literacy for the rightless peoples, the perennial estate of the constitutional have-nots. This undoubtedly crucial move should not obscure the fact that even the constitutional 'haves' stand in dire need of such literacy. The lawmakers themselves often remain para-doxically mired in legal illiteracy when they think that the laws that they make create obligations for others and none for them. Autonomization of legal and constitutional literacy, now variously fostered, on my view,

remains a part of the problem, not any part of the solution. I say this with very great respect for grassroots activists who produce legal literacy kits ('Know Your Rights', or 'What to When There is No Lawyer to Help You') and indeed I had the happy experience of actively assisting and promoting these ventures. But these can be no more than palliatives when Indian constitutionalism itself stands infected by 'the uses of illiteracy'.[11]

VI. A BRIEF REMARK CONCERNING INDIAN JUDICIAL ACTIVISM

CALL must of course fully acknowledge the gift of judicial activism. Fortunately, for the future of Indian democracy, the judiciary now slowly but surely insists that the political classes also stand in dire need of continuing adult and continuing education concerning their obligations and responsibilities to those they seek to rule. The Supreme Court of India that now wholesomely assumes a new egali-tarian CALL mission suggests powerfully for the rulers and the ruled a road map of difficult tasks ahead.

At one moment, judicial activism best serves the diverse platforms provided by Babasaheb and Mohandas. It fully nurtures and nourishes the imagination of CALL by an unqualified insistence that the rulers need utmost literacy and education. Preserving in

---

[10] To take here a contemporary example the endless confrontation over the politics and programmes of affirmative action, we remain 'for' or 'against' the Indian-style affirmative action/ reservation only because we understand 'well,' for weal or woe, this connectivity between 'our' rights and 'theirs'.

[11] On another and rather difficult terrain the question pertains to the contest between the *oral* and *written* human 'cultures,' or of elevating the primacy of the written over the spoken word. For those hardy souls that may wish to engage this domain, there exists no better guide than Jacques Derrida's three works: *On Grammatology, Writing and Violence*, and *Negotiations*. Difficult as these texts and genre remain, no one seriously interested with the problematic of constitutional and legal literacy may afford to blithely, and with integrity, bypass this discourse.

part, the great legacy of the four musketeers (Justices Krishna Iyer, P.N. Bhagwati, D.A. Desai, and Chinnappa Reddy), the contemporary Indian Apex Justices continue to promote the reinventing of the constitutional conception of the future of Indian human rights and indeed of the spirit animating the enunciation of the basic structure and essential features of the Indian Constitution.

At another dialectical moment, the Apex Justices also tend to fully undermine this legacy. I have fully described this in my Indian Law Institute Golden Jubilee Celebration presentation named as 'structural adjustment of judicial activism'.[12] While I keep hoping that this book will include this analysis as an appendix, I also continue to hope that for those seriously engaged with the enterprise of re-defining legal literacy may still have some independent access to this text.

Regardless, the challenge thus posed is this: CALL programmes need to be read against their grain, as it were! The choice has to be made, as Michael Foucault presciently and memorably named this in terms of the passages from domination to domination as distinct from the passages from domination to liberation. I hope that this precious and precautious monograph work errs, as it were, on the side of the Angles! Amen!

Any constitutional envisioning of legal literacy remains important only so far as it addresses the need for literacy for both citizens and 'super-citizens' alike. Neither may serve their own short and long term interest and cause by entrenching forms and habits of legal illiteracy. When the governors remain constitutionally and legally illiterate, standardless, and rather ungovernable, political violence and insurrection remains a sovereign norm. When citizens turn their face away from public education in rights and obligations, they in turn invite unbridled state repression.

The important message, thus, is stark and poignant: civic education shapes our common dignity and democratic futures, and there exist no halfway houses. On all available evidence unfortunately, yet perhaps not terminally so far, the resistance to social learning now defines for us all the (im)possible futures of legal literacy projects.

---

[12] Baxi, Upendra, 'Access to Justice in a Globalised Economy: Some Reflections', in *Golden Jubilee Volume*, Indian Law Institute, New Delhi, 2007, pp 27–36.

The Basic Structure of the Constitution and 'We, the People of India'

V.R. KRISHNA IYER

I. PROLEGOMENON

Perhaps the world's second longest constitution, the first largest ensemble of civilized values and the noblest articulation of pragmatic comprehension is the great juristic avatar which formally breathed life on 26 January 1950 into the sovereign socialist secular democratic Republic of India. British imperialism, extinguished by a Westminster legislation,[1] enacted a rare wonder: India, that is Bharat, created a glorious tryst with destiny and transformed a colossal colony under the British Crown into the world uniquely won, peacefully wrung, historic democracy with a billion and odd common people and a bevy of billionaires who seek to corner power. On 15 August 1947, the British writ quit Delhi, installed an independent India and resolved to build a Republic by 'We, the People of India' who constitute a sixth of the earth's mankind. The odyssey of victory from the British

Crown, after a 'do or die' struggle and the liberation from Westminster and the Empire made history. Our glorious journey as a free people, each with a free vote, began with a magnificent pledge on behalf of Indian humanity. In Churchill's elegant diction 'the little man, walking into a little booth, with a little pencil, making a little cross on a little bit of paper–no amount of rhetoric or voluminous discussion can possibly diminish the overwhelming importance of the point'.

Our constitution, with universal adult franchise, gender equality and the entitlement to vote at age 18, makes India numerically the foremost nation in global democracy. Decades of parliamentary debate and participation by every political party, uninhibited challenges in the House, authority and impartiality and learned rulings of the presiding Speaker are a constitutional marvel. The constitution is great in its noble foreword and eclectic in its prolix provisions. Our founding fathers have selectively inscribed many features from the world's democratic fundamental laws.

The vision of the architects of the constitution is projected in the Preamble and

---

[1] The British Parliament enacted the Indian Independence Act, 1947 which would grant dominion status to the India and Pakistan on the 'appointed day'. The Constitution of India that declared India a sovereign country repealed the Indian Independence Act, 1947.

illumined lucidly in Part III as inviolable fundamental rights enjoying paramount importance. These great rights are enforceable judicially. But beyond these lofty human rights are Directive Principles of State Policy spelt out in Part IV as provisions which, though not enforceable by any court are, never-the-less, principles 'fundamental in the governance of the country and it shall be the duty of the State to apply these principles in making laws'. The conscience of the constitution is the confluence of Part III and IV and although the highest court has sometimes differed in interpretation, it is now settled semantically that the two parts have a harmonious togetherness. It is fair to hold that a complete understanding of the supreme values of the constitution must include Fundamental Duties added later as Part IV A. Indeed, Part III, IV and IV A have certain integrality. The meaning of meanings while reading these three parts has a cultural humanism and fraternal interaction. So much so, the finer essence of the constitution is missed if the three parts are interpreted in isolation. So, to gain a plenary sense and sensibility of these values, a semantic synthesis is imperative. Then alone the glory to the articles will unfold the vision and mission of the *suprema lex*. If we adopt the method of dialectical materialism in its dynamic dimensions, the soul of the paramount law will be grasped while a grammatical interpretation of the words used in the constitution will fail to disclose the humanist excellence and social justice essence which are the pride of our founding deed. I would, therefore, emphasize that any jurist can do justice to the sovereignty and supremacy of Indian humanity only by adopting a grand perspective, realizing that we are interpreting a majestic constitution, not a mere municipal legislation.

India, governed by the British for long, was a diamond in the Queen's Crown and was exploited as a resource-rich mega-market colony. There were hundreds of maharajahs, petty princes, several languages, wrangling communities, plural cultures, rabid religions and sects—a motley crowd under the sovereign supremacy of the British Viceroy and Governor General from Delhi. Paramountcy of power was with Westminster. The country being large and territorially variegated by mountains and valleys, deserts and plains, Indian humanity could not be a unitary administration. The East India Company, with its aggressive business mission, geographically and politically established itself by battles and treaties. When the Crown took over the reign from the pseudo-imperial Company, provinces came into existence. Governors were made rulers and granted micro-doses of local self-government to Indians. But India has a sublime past, glorious heritage, spiritual profundity, plural literary treasury. Britain, in its imperial arrogance hardly realized the material, social, cultural and political history of Bharat as the storehouse of ancient wisdom whose suppression met with militant resistance. A quote from Max Muller opens the eyes of the west to the magnificence of India of the ages:

If we were to look over the whole world to find out the country most richly endowed with all the wealth, power, and beauty that nature can bestow—in some parts a very paradise on earth—I should point to India. If I were asked under what sky the human mind has most fully developed some of its choicest gifts, has most deeply pondered over the greatest problems of life, and has found solutions of some of them which well deserve the attention even of those who have studied Plato and Kant—I should point to India. And if I were to ask myself from what literature we here in Europe, we who have been nurtured almost exclusively on the thoughts of Greeks and Romans, and of one Semitic race, the Jewish, may draw the corrective which is most wanted in order to make our inner life more perfect, more comprehensive, more universal, in fact more truly human a life, not for this life only, but a transfigured and eternal life—again I should point to India.[2]

Swaraj, as a birthright of every Indian, gained movement. The national movement in India had deep roots and manifested itself organizationally in the Indian National Congress. An Englishman was a formal founder and Dadabai Nauroji was the first prominent President of the National Congress. Of course, when the history of India comes to be written, Mahatma Gandhi will figure as the most revolutionary personality with neither a purse nor a sword but with non-violence, truth and unconquerable will to win *poorna swaraj*. There were other great heroes who had sacrificed their life and career. Of course, Subhash Chandra Bose, Jawaharlal Nehru, Rajaji, Ambedkar, Lokamanya Tilak and Sarojini Naidu, among other illustrious patriots are luminous stars in the national horizon of liberation and democracy.

In England a demand for independence found expression and, after long struggle, the House of Commons responded reluctantly. The Simon Commission and public opinion stirred British politics and eventually the Government of India Act, 1935 was enacted giving a meagre measure of self-government. A constitutional portrait of India in its political, geographical dimension was first presented although with imperial plumage.

[2] Muller, F. Max, *India: What Can It Teach Us?*, New York, John W. Lovell Company, 1883, pp. 14–15; New Delhi, Rupa & Co, 1883/2002; Muller, F. Max, *India: What Can it Teach Us?*, New Delhi, Penguin Books India, 2004.

Indeed, the importance of the 1935 Government of India Act is two-fold. Firstly, it is the result of the unbending battle for independence, partially conceded in the 1935 Act. Secondly, and more importantly, this constitutional enactment played a great role in shaping the basic structure of the constitution of India, its unitary judiciary, its federal political structure and its Westminster model of governance with the crown as a symbol of the sovereignty of the nation and its powers really vested in the cabinet with a bicameral legislature, the legislators themselves being elected on adult franchise basis. Even the subjects for legislation which fell within the jurisdiction of the state and the union were largely conditioned by the 1935 Act. Imperial power remained a terror until 1947 and this long journey was a story of monstrous events of people demanding freedom.

The Simon Commission visited and reported with little success. Two round table conferences were held in England on the subject of Indian independence and eventually the Indian Independence Act, 1947 was passed which came into force on August 15, 1947 making Bharat one of the greatest democratic countries in the world. India, under the British, was a vast geographic glory but when Lord Wavell and Lord Mountbatten became Viceroy and independence was, actualized Pakistan was carved out with communal considerations and consequential carnage. India, with Jawaharlal Nehru as Prime Minister, and Dr Rajendra Prasad as the President of India, started the grand odyssey. A constituent assembly drafted the Constitution of India with Dr Rajendra Prasad as the Chairman. Dr Ambedkar, matchless in constitutional wisdom, chaired the drafting committee. Nehru, in his historic speech on 15 August 1947 spelt out India's democratic tryst with destiny and when after years of deliberation, the draft constitution was completed, Dr Ambedkar made a comprehensive, incomparably erudite address moving the passage of the nation's constitution on 25 November 1949.[3] The bill was approved and became law on 26 November 1949. The Sovereign Democratic Republic came into active existence on 26 January 1950, with Dr Rajendra Prasad as President and Nehru as Prime Minister.

II. FUNDAMENTAL RIGHTS AND DIRECTIVE PRINCIPLES OF STATE POLICY

Part III of the constitution, together with Part IV, constitutes the conscience of the Indian nation. These two parts are a profound foundation of human rights, drawing inspiration from the Magna Carta, the French Revolution and the American Declaration of Independence. Socialist thought was popular in England, and Harold Laski, the great teacher of a new socialist school, influenced intellectuals of the English teaching world. Inevitably, progressive Indian intellectuals had a socialist inclination. Articles 14, 15, 16, 21, 38, 39 and 46 are manifestations of human rights, although broadly speaking, these and other articles can be read together in a wider sense as guaranteeing the basic value of equality, free speech and association and the right to life and freedom of faith as the fundamental essence of dignity and divinity. Article 13 exalts the fundamental rights under Part III as above all ordinary legislation invalidating them if they are inconsistent with the provision of this part. Existing laws contradicting fundamental rights are declared void and the state has been forbidden from

making any law, which obviates or abridges the right concerned under Part III. Thus these rights are judicially enforceable and any statutory provision, which violates the articles of Part III are contrary to the basic structure of the constitution as the *Kesavananda Bharati* case[4] lays down. Although there is no exhaustive definition of the basic structure of our constitution, the courts have, in the *Indira Gandhi* case,[5] laid down the basic structure of the *suprema lex.*[6]

The supreme court, in its majesty and magnanimity, has expounded profoundly the semantic sweep of Article 21, which deals with the right to life. Its extraordinary amplitude includes the right to food and shelter, education, health and other opportunities of development. When read with Article 14, a dimension of equality must be available for the poor as well as the rich, but the truth is that the court itself has spoken in many voices. The rich are treated as a class and the poor as

[3] See http://parliamentofindia.nic.in/ls/debates/vol11p11.htm for the text of the address.

[4] *Kesavananda Bharati* v. *State of Kerala* (1973) 4 SCC 225.

[5] *Indira Gandhi Nehru* v. *Raj Narain* (1975) Supp SCC.

[6] Justice Chadrachud speaking in the *Indira Gandhi* case observed, 'I consider it beyond the pale of reasonable controversy that if there be any unamendable features of the Constitution on the score that they form part of the basic structure of the Constitution, they are that: (i) India is a sovereign democratic republic; (ii) Equality of status and opportunity shall be secured to all its citizens; (iii) The State shall have no religion of its own and all persons shall be equally entitled to freedom of conscience and the right to freely profess, practice and propagate religion and that (iv) the nation shall be governed by a Government of laws, not me. These, in my opinion, are the pillars of our constitutional philosophy, the pillars, therefore, of the basic structure of the Constitution. *Indira Gandhi Nehru* v. *Raj Narain* 1975 Supp SCC 1, p 252, at para 664. Subsequent cases have added to this list of what constitutes the basic structure of the Constitution, such as judicial review, secularism and federalism.

another class. Similarly, where demonstrable differences in categories are seen the court has evaded the imperative nature of article by interpreting equality as meaning equality within a category although category may differ as between palaces and huts. That is why critics have viewed the judges as biased in favour of certain classes depriving equality of its quintessence.

Article 32 makes it a fundamental right for any citizen to move the supreme court for the enforcement of their rights conferred by Part III. But it also happens that in violation of this article the supreme court often directs parties who complain under Article 32 to go to the high court first and then come to the supreme court. This is avoidance of duty and doubling of litigation thus defeating the guarantee of Article 32.

One of the valuable provisions in the constitution is Article 38, which obligates the state to secure a social order for the promotion of welfare of the people effectively so that a social order in which justice, social, economic and political, may prevail in all institutions of national life. But sadly, violent differences mar the social order in the matter of health and education as hospitals and colleges in reality establish. The court blinks at this social injustice and even views commercialization of health and education as permissible. The Preamble speaks of a socialist republic. Article 38 prescribes social and economic justice as a parameter. So much so, the court and the executive have taken a common perspective ignoring the socialist mandate of the constitution. 'If the salt lose their savour wherewith shall they be salted.' Article 39 enunciates certain important principles of policies to be followed by the state. Article 39 runs thus as the best commentary of Article 38. Let us read both as the soul of the *suprema lex.*

38. State to secure a social order for the promotion of welfare of the people.–(1) The State shall strive to promote the welfare of the people by securing and protecting as effectively as it may a social order in which justice, social,

39. Certain principles of policy to be followed by the State.–the State shall, in particular, direct its policy towards securing–

......

(b) that the ownership and control of the material resources of the community are so distributed as best to subserve the common good;

(c) that the operation of the economic system does not result in the concentration of wealth and means of production to the common detriment;

We are a country of plurality of languages, cultures, creeds and races but constitutionally we are all peers, discrimination among people being anathematic. Every person can make representation for redress of grievances in any of the languages used in the Union or the state. This linguistic justice is a valuable facility for a minority. So too freedom of religion and autonomy of their institutions. Weaker sections have special constitutional protection. Our country has many minorities and special provisions for their survival, development and opportunity for education, public offices, economic and socio-political status. Democracy, which discriminates against minorities, robs the essence of its basic structure.

Child rights, gender rights, working class health and welfare of Indian humanity with easy access to justice administrative and judicial shall be not merely guaranteed in the constitution but be available in reality. Women are given equality, but this is on paper only because men dominate in every profession and life's pleasures and wealth. Children are given opportunities and facilities to develop in a healthy manner and in conditions of freedom and dignity guarding the youth against moral and material abandonment. India has ratified an international convention conferring valuable rights on children and agreeing to take legislative action thereon, but nothing has been done until now. This is neglect especially because the UNESCO has presented to the Prime Minister a comprehensive bill and a report which gives full expression to the International Convention. If the state fails in its constitutional obligation and the court blinks at it what shall the people do for re-dressal and accomplishment of their rights. The point is that the great instrumentalities themselves are wanting in reality notwith-standing eloquent articles.

By the Constitution (Forty-Second Amend-ment) Act, 1976, the adjectives 'Socialist, Secular' were added. The idea of socialism and the need for secularism were a part of the ideology of the founding fathers but did not find specific expression in the constitution. Later, during the emergency, these paramount values were added by an amendment and ever after remained integral aspects of the republic. The beauty and truth of our constitutional vision is briefly inscribed in the Preamble but explicitly amplified in Parts III and IV of the constitution.

III. JUDICIARY

The Montesquieuean anatomy of our republic indubitably stresses the judiciary as over-seeing, reviewing, and justicing the functional implementation of the executive and the legislature without of course in any manner encroaching upon the constitutional autonomy of the two great instrumentalities. The vision of India's unity and fraternity is magnificently manifested in the single structure of the judiciary. The trial court, civil and criminal court are at the base. The appellate court is the next higher step. Then comes the high court which has vast powers including the writ jurisdiction, supervisory power like review and revision and lay down the law especially constitutional law so that at the state level finality of litigation is at the high court level but there are several high courts, each state having, one and so the Supreme Court of India is the highest and indeed, under Article 32, access to this great institution itself a fundamental right. The appointment of judges, the code of conduct regarding judges, the enforcement of fundamental duties are subjects of critical importance but the constitution has not specifically provided for them.

The judicature is central to the constitution in action: '...while unconstitutional exercise of power by the executive and legislative branches of the government is subject to judicial restraint, the only check upon our own exercise of power is our own sense of self-restraint'.[7]

The constitution expressly provides, by Article 32, a fundamental right for the enforcement of all rights conferred by Part III which means that the guarantee of the realization of the basic rights which are paramount for the citizen depends on the functional accessibility of the supreme court. The ultimate authority to interpret the con-stitution and the law is the supreme court and what it declares as law is binding on all courts. Article 141 lays down this proposition. It is equally important to realize that the Apex Court in the exercise of its jurisdiction may adjudicate on any cause or matter as is necessary for doing complete justice and such a direction shall be enforceable in such manner as is prescribed by the municipal law. Indeed

[7] Justice Harlan F. Stone, U.S. Supreme Court in *U.S.* v. *Butler* 271 U.S. 1 (1936).

under Article 142 these watch power include capacity inherent in the court as guardian under the Constitution. However, it may be noticed that what is binding, as pronouncement of the court does not include:

(a) *Obiter dicta*, i.e., statements which are not part of the *ratio decidendi*.

(b) A decision per *incurium*, i.e., a decision given in ignorance of the terms of a statute or rule having the force of a statute.

(c) A decision passed *sub-silentio*, i.e., without any argument or debate on the relevant question.

(d) An order made with the consent of the parties, and with the reservation that it should not be treated as a precedent.

Another extraordinary provision is given in Article 143. Whenever an issue of national importance and constitutional implication demands resolution such as between the court and the parliament, the President may seek the jurisdiction of the supreme court to illumine the different aspect of the dispute and find a harmonious solution with the statesmanship and majesty of the highest court in the country. The historic decision rather the advisory opinion given by the supreme court headed by the judicial statesman, as did great Chief Justice Gajendragadkar, is a classic instance in point.[8] It is open to the court to decline to answer the reference, although it will be of supreme national value if the supreme court with its authority and luminosity pronounces an advisory judgment.

One may briefly sum up the central role of the supreme court in exercising its jurisdiction on judicial review. There are many instances where legislation and executive action in their extravaganza or egregious error may render opinions which retard progress or violate socialist secular dimension of the republic. Even so, the supreme court is supreme; it is final, not because it is infallible but is infallible because it is final. If pronouncement of court is found flawed, the only way to set right a grave mistake is to refer the matter to a larger bench or to resort to an appropriate amendment by exercising the constituent power of the Parliament.

The appointment of the judges of the supreme court is of paramount importance because what they decide is law that binds the people of the country. Nevertheless, the people have no voice in their appointment because the supreme court, in a constitutional bench has seized that power from the executive by a majority ruling. To my mind this declaration of law based on the principle of the independence of the judiciary but contrary to half a century of practice and unknown in any other democratic country is wrong.[9] It requires correction either by a large bench or by a constitutional amendment. The performance of the collegium of judges in exercising its new found power has been marred by gross mis-selection and grave delay largely because of absence of judicial business management and tremendous inexperience.

There have been serious complaints about the functional failure of the judiciary and the obnoxious delinquency the bench and the bar have brought out. And yet there is no remedial provision except impeachment by Parliament. Because of its political travesty, impeachment becomes a remedy, which aggravates the malady as, happened in the case of Justice Ramaswamy. The time has come for a commission of empowerment governing

---

[8] *Keshav Singh's* case, AIR 1965 SC 745.

[9] See *In re: Presidential Reference (Reference on the Principles and Procedure regarding appointment of Supreme Court and High Court Judges)* AIR 1999 SC 1.

appointment, performance, censure and removal of superior court judges. Such a commission should include outstanding members of the Bar, great judges sitting or retired, statesmen, whom the nation respects without division. After all, the greatest of a powerful institution like the judicature must be such that people's voice at an enlightened level shall reach the appointing authority.

IV. EMERGENCY

An extraordinary phenomenon which may affect the destiny of the nation, the destination of its development and the human rights of the Indian people may occur in case a state of emergency is declared by the top executive.

No nation, in its long history fails to face causes and emergencies natural or created by causes of internal chaos or internal invasion. Financial emergencies may threaten the security or survival of the people and a multitude of malignant forces; social, economic and political may force emergency situations demanding immediate and extraordinary action by the state lest survival, peace and progress should be diminished or destroyed. The founding fathers of the constitution, anticipating these disasters and disturbances, have provided in Part XVIII, special articles intended to be used in exceptional conditions justifying resort to extraordinary measures suspending the operation of the normal functioning of the governmental processes, even judicial powers.

The sovereignty of the state depends on its authority and power to safeguard its security if threatened by war, armed rebellion or external aggression. In such an event the President may make a declaration to that effect and as required by the Union Cabinet. This emergency power with grave consequences requires affirmation by both the houses of Parliament within a month with important and imperative parameters to make the proclamation valid as set out in Article 352. While an approval by Parliament within the specified period of one month is a *sine qua non* the proclamation perishes if its continuance is disapproved by the President. Likewise, if a written notice signed by not less than 1/10th of the total number of the House of the people demanding the convening of the House of the people disapproving the continuance of the proclamation to the speaker of the House, a special meeting of the House shall be held within 14 days. A resolution passed therein will settle the fate of the proclamation. It need hardly be said that the jural terrorism of a proclamation of emergency vests totalitarian authoritarianism, over the whole country including the state notwithstanding Part III and its paramountcy. Article 355 obligates the Union to protect every state against external aggression and internal disturbance. The experience of the declaration of the emergency during the period beginning with 26 June, 1976 was a grave blow against democracy. Article 356 (imposition of President's Rule) is more often used on the ground or pretext of failure of constitutional machinery of a state if the President receives a report from the governor of a state or otherwise to the effect that a situation has arisen in which the government cannot be carried on in accordance with the provisions of the constitution. Thereupon the President assumes to himself the functioning of the state government and takes over the powers of the legislature of state as exercisable by or under the authority of the Parliament. If this power under article 356, which can nullify state autonomy and federal functionalism can the supreme court demolish the proclamation?

Yes, in my view, if the emergency was an unwarranted monstrosity. A contrary view has also been suggested. Some may be surprised that the great judiciary upheld the terrible emergency (of course, Justice Khanna was an exception),[10] and critics of great stature in India voiced the view about that judgment best expressed by borrowing Winston Churchill's words: 'An extraordinary event, a monstrous event, an event which stands in singular and sinister isolation'. Indeed, any student of the Indian constitution must study the emergency chapter with great care and seriousness in the light of articles 358 and 359 which inflict disaster on the guaranteed fundamental rights.

The glory of constitutional governance ends in a graveyard if the Bench and the Bar and the people at large do not defend this great instrument of liberty and orderly government. I may be pardoned if I conclude this section by a quote from a judgment of the U.S. Supreme Court.

The history of the world had taught them that what was done in the past might be attempted in the future. The Constitution of the United States is a law for rulers and people, equally in war and in peace, and covers with the shield of its protection all classes of men, at all times, and under all circumstances. No doctrine, involving more pernicious consequences, was ever invented by the wit of man than that any of its provisions can be suspended during any of the great exigencies of government. Such a doctrine leads directly to anarchy or despotism, but the theory of necessity on which it is based is false, for the government, within the constitution, has all the powers granted to it, which are necessary to preserve its existence; as has been happily proved by the result of the great effort to throw off its just authority.[11]

It is a fundamental duty, a paramount obligation of the humblest to the highest to defend the democratic conscience and concept of the constitution without allowing internal usurpation by the powerful and external invasion by the imperial war power or arrogant ambitious freebooter nation.

V. PARLIAMENT AND DEMOCRACY

At the outset let me cite the great Oliver Wendell Holmes:

I trust that no one will understand me to be speaking with disrespect of the law, because I criticize it so freely. I venerate the law, and especially our system of law, as one of the vastest products of the human mind. No one knows better than I do the countless number of great intellects that have spent themselves in making some addition or improvement, the greatest of which is trifling when compared with the mighty whole. It has the final title to respect that it exists, that is not a Hegelian dream, but a part of the lives of men. But one may criticize even what one reveres. Law is the business to which my life is devoted, and I should show less than devotion if I did not do what in me lies to improve it, and, when I perceive what seems to me the ideal of its future, if I hesitated to point it out and to press toward it with all my heart. ...In the present state of political economy, indeed, we come again upon history on a larger scale, but there we are called on to consider and weigh the ends of legislation, the means of attaining them, and the cost. We learn that for everything we have we give up something else, and we are taught to set the advantage we gain against the other advantage we lose, and to know what we are doing when we elect.[12]

The parliament is the grand inquest of the nation. In the diction of Edmund Burke:

---

[10] *A.D.M. Jabalpur* v. *S. Shukla* AIR 1976 SC 1207.

[11] (David Davis in *Ex parte Milligan*, 71 U.S 2 (1866), 4 Wall. at 120.

[12] Holmes, Jr., Oliver Wendell, 'The Path of Law', *Harvard Law Review*, no 10, 1897, p. 457.

Parliament is not a congress of ambassadors from different and hostile interests; which interests each must maintain, as an agent and advocate, against other agents and advocates; but parliament is a deliberative assembly of one nation, with one interest, that of the assembly of one nation, with one interest, that of the whole; where, not local purposes, not local prejudices ought to guide, but the general good, resulting from the general reason of the whole. You choose a member indeed; but when you have chosen him, he is not member of Bristol, but he is a member of parliament.[13]

But our parliament in the present generation operates in gross violation of this sublime obligation. The powers, privileges and immunities of legislators are not specifically inscribed in the constitution. We follow what prevails in the British parliament. But the conditions of two countries are different. There is considerable confusion regarding privileges of the House especially because legal erudition is lacking as a matter of profession in the Members of the House or even of the Speaker. *May's Parliament Practice*, Kaul and Shakdher are still our authority.[14] When there is a conflict of views and confrontation of jurisdiction in the matter of privileges and immunities complications are created an unhappy battles between two great institutions are not uncommon. An amendment to the constitution on these matters is a challenge to the creative genius of the country's parliamentary statesmanship. A national conference on all these subjects particularly on the privileges of the House almost like a second constituent assembly is a desideratum. Defection of members from one party to another and losing membership in the House as a consequence is covered partly by the Tenth Schedule but that has created a controversy between the Chairman of the House and the judiciary. Such a situation calls for clarification by appropriate constitutional legislation. Slow locomotion in such legislation aggravates conflicts in constitutional law which is an unhappy situation for the largest democracy in the world.

The Ninth Schedule has been introduced into the constitution with a specific purpose geared to alleviation of the poor who suffer on occasions from fundamental rights which are at times interpreted in such manner that the court strikes down legislation or executive action meant to benefit the weaker classes. Once included in the Ninth Schedule, statutes which are designed to benefit the agrarian community are immunized from judicial jurisdiction to quash the legislation. Two abuses have rendered the Ninth Schedule jejune or impotent. The executive, induced by pusillanimity and lazy illiteracy seeks to avoid the court's examination of the law by easy resort to inclusion in the Ninth Schedule. Thus the Ninth Schedule suffers from reckless profusion which is a vicious misuse. The court retaliates by holding that the Ninth Schedule is itself invalid if fundamental rights are violated by illegitimate legislation. The recent decision in Ninth Schedule is an example in point. On the whole this ambiguous dimension of the Ninth Schedule demands a thorough re-examination. Nothing succeeds like success, especially when it is easy for the legislature to enact and the court to quash.

We are going through a world war of ideas... The extent to which we maintain the spirit of our constitution with its Bill of Rights will in the long run do more to make it both secure and the object

---

[13] Speech to the Electors of Bristol in 1774.
[14] Kaul, M.N., S.L. Shakdher and G.C. Malhotra (eds), *Practice and Procedure of Parliament*, New Delhi, Metropolitan, 2001.

of adulation than the number of hydrogen bombs we stockpile.[15]

Fair is the Preamble because it impregnates the constitution with the sublime values of socialism, secularism and democracy. Foul is the functional experience of the constitution in action despite the oath of office of the President, Prime Minister, Chief Justice of India, Comptroller and Auditor-General and other high office bearers. How contradictory and paradoxical is it, that in practice the engineers and architects of the constitution ignore socialism, shake up secularism with lunatic caste-creed confrontation and division that has mangled our democratic institution from Panchayat to parliament by performances of pathos and bathos and walk out after drawing sumptuous daily allowances instead of purposeful interpellation and debate. Here, listen to Winston Churchill in the Commons defending his position while we criticize for the transitory retrial of these forces:

This long debate has now reached its final stage. What a remarkable example it has been of the unbridled freedom of our Parliamentary institutions in time of war! Everything that could be thought of or raked up has been used to weaken confidence in the Government, has been used to prove that Ministers are incompetent and to weaken their confidence in themselves, to make the Army destruct the backing it is getting from the civil power, to make the workmen lose confidence in the weapons they are striving so hard to make, to present the Government as a set of nonentities over whom the Prime Minister towers, and then to undermine him in his own heart, and, if possible, before the eyes of the nation. All this poured out by cable and radio to all parts of the world, to the distress of all our friends and to the delight of all our foes! I am in favour of this freedom, which no other country would use, or dare to use in times of mortal peril such as those through which we are passing. But the story must not end there, and I make now my appeal to the House of Commons to make sure that it does not end there.[16]

Our country is great because we are the largest democracy but what is democracy? It is a battle, an ideology, a vision and value-set. Two quotes perhaps regarded as redundant best drive home my deep understanding and conceptual philosophy. In his Philadelphia address. Lincoln said that the Declaration of Independence had given 'liberty not alone to the people of this country, but hope to all the world, for all future time. It was that which gave promise that in due time the weights would be lifted from the shoulders of all men, and that all should have an equal chance.'[17]

Democracy is a process, not a static condition. It is becoming, rather than being. It can easily be lost, but never is fully won. Its essence is eternal struggle.[18]

---

[15] Speech of the U.S. Supreme Court Chief Justice Earl Warren, to the American Bar Association in 1954.

[16] Speech by Winston Churchill in the House of Commons, 2 July 1942.

[17] Address by Abraham Lincoln in Independence Hall, Philadelphia, 22 February 1861.

[18] Justice William H. Hastie.

Public Interest Litigation

PARMANAND SINGH

Public Interest Litigation (PIL) is a unique phenomenon in the Indian constitutional jurisprudence which has no parallel in the world. This technique is concerned with the protection of the interests of a class or group of persons who are either the victims of governmental lawlessness, or social oppression, or have been denied their constitutional or legal rights and who are not in a position to approach the court for the redressal of their grievances due to the lack of resources, ignorance, or their disadvantaged social and economic position. Public Interest Litigation has become a byword for judicial involvement for the protection of human rights in India. It is in essence, a movement to involve the judicial process for the creation of norms of a just social order, based upon the principle of justice and humanism. In this movement, people participate in the activation of the judicial power for creating a regime of human rights with the active support of social activists. Judges are asked not only to vindicate governmental commitments to human rights of the poor and the disadvantaged but also to enforce public duties to protect and maintain collective and diffuse social rights, and to prevent the decline in political morality.

The new procedure evolved by the Indian Supreme Court allows any member of public acting in a bona fide manner to espouse the cause of the victims of human rights violations. One can invoke the court's jurisdiction just by writing a letter or sending a telegram. This has been termed epistolary jurisdiction. Only a person acting bona fide and having sufficient interest in the proceedings of PIL *has a locus standi* and can approach the court to wipe out the tears of the poor and the needy, suffering from violation of their fundamental rights. Public Interest Litigation cannot be invoked by a person for personal gain, private profit, political motive, or any oblique consideration. Public Interest Litigation proceedings entail new forms of fact finding such as appointment of socio-legal commissions of inquiry and handing over the investigation to the National Human Rights Commission or the Central Bureau of Investigation. The court has taken the help of journalists, lawyers, district judges, bureaucrats, and expert bodies for ascertaining the facts alleged in PIL proceedings. This has been called investigative litigation. In dealing with these cases, the courts have fashioned new kinds of relief for the victims of state lawlessness—compensatory, rehabilitative, restitutive, preventive, and curative. For example, the court can award interim compensation to the victims of governmental lawlessness. This stands in sharp contrast to the Anglo-Saxon mode of adjudication where interim relief is limited to preserving status quo, pending final decision. The grant of interim relief in PIL cases does not preclude the aggrieved person from claiming damages in a civil court.

Hussainara Khatoon v State of Bihar was the first reported case of PIL seeking relief to the undertrial prisoners languishing in jails.[1] The PIL proceedings in this case resulted in the release of nearly 40,000 undertrial prisoners languishing in Bihar jails. *Anil Yadav v State of Bihar*[2] revealed police brutalities. About 33 suspected criminals were blinded by the police in Bhagalpur jail in Bihar, when their eyes were burnt by putting acid into them. The supreme court quashed the trial of blinded persons, condemned the police barbarity in strongest terms and directed the Bihar Government to bring the blinded persons to Delhi for medical treatment at the state's expense. The court declared free legal aid as a fundamental right as an aspect of right to life and personal liberty. The human rights of prisoners subjected to torture,[3] victims of police excesses,[4] inmates of protective homes[5] and mental asylums,[6] bonded[7] and child labour,[8] victims of sexual harassment,[9] and earthquake victims,[10] and many others have been protected by the supreme court. In environmental cases the court has addressed issues of environmental degradation such as vehicular pollution,[11] leakage of oleum gas from a factory,[12] danger to the Taj Mahal from the Mathura Refinery,[13] degradation of the Ridge area in Delhi,[14] pollution caused by shrimp farming,[15] tanneries,[16] chemical industries,[17] and so on. The court has taken several activist measures to ensure compliance of pollution standards.

The most abiding contribution of PIL has been the emergence of new human rights such

---

to death as the patients could not escape the blaze as they had been chained to poles or beds, the Supreme Court in *In re Death of 25 Chained Inmates in Asylum Fire in Tamil Nadu* AIR 2002 SC 979 took *suo moto* action by way of PIL and issued several directions to every state and union territory to implement the Mental Health Act, 1987.

[7] *Bandhua Mukti Morcha* v. *Union of India* AIR 1984 SC 802. See Singh Parmanand, 'Bandhua Mukti Morcha: Social Action and the Indian Supreme Court', 12 *Indian Bar Review* 228 (1985).

[8] *M.C. Mehta* v. *Union of India* (1986) Supp SCC 553.

[9] *Vishaka* v. *State of Rajasthan* (1997) 6 SCC 241.

[10] In *Bipinchandra* v. *State of Gujarat* AIR 2002 Guj 99: the High Court of Gujarat applied the doctrine of parents patriae for providing relief to earthquake victims of Gujarat , holding that under the constitution, the state has an obligation to help people in distress. Article 21 was the repository of all human rights. The court gave directions for the relief and rehabilitation of earthquake victims.

[11] *M.C. Mehta* v. *Union Of India* 1996 (1) SCALE 42.

[12] *M.C. Mehta* v. *Union Of India* (1987) 1 SCC 395.

[13] *M.C. Mehta* v. *Union of India* (1996) 4 SCC 351.

[14] *M.C. Mehta* v. *Union of India* (1996) 1 SCALE SP – 22; *MC Mehta* v *Union of India* (1996) 6 SCC 756.

[15] *S. Jagannath* v. *Union of India* (1997) 2 SCC 87.

[16] *Citizens Welfare Forum* v. *Union of India* (1996) 5 SCC 647.

[17] *In re Bhavani River Sakti Sugar Ltd* (1998) 6 SCC 335

---

[1] *Hussainara Khatoon* v. *State of Bihar* (I to V) AIR 1979 SC 1360 (right to speedy trial recognized as a fundamental right under article 21 of the Constitution of India).

[2] (1981) 1 SCC 622.

[3] *Khatri* v. *State of Bihar* (1981) 1 SCC 627, at p 635; *Veena Sethi* v. *State of Bihar* (1982) 2 SCC 583 (right to legal aid declared an aspect of article 21).

[4] *Nilabati Behera* v *State of Orissa* AIR 1993 SC 1961.

[5] *Upendra Baxi* v. *State of Uttar Pradesh* 1981 (3) SCALE 1136.

[6] *R.C. Narain* v. *State of Bihar* (1986) Supp SCC 576; *B.R. Kapoor* v. *of India* AIR 1990 SC 752. On the basis of a newspaper report that more than 25 mentally challenged patients housed in mental asylum in Ervadi in Ramanathpuram district of Tamil Nadu were charred

as right to speedy trial, right against torture, right against bondage, right against sexual harassment, right to shelter and housing, right to dignity, right to clean environment, right to education, right to legal aid, right to health care, and so on. It creates a new jurisprudence of accountability of the state for constitutional and legal obligations towards the interest of the weaker sections of the society. It reminds and alerts the political executive of its failings and lapses. In exposing such lapses, the judges remind the governmental functionaries to perform their public duties and maintain rule of law. Public Interest Litigation seeks to hold the government and its agencies within the leading strings of egalitarianism, humanism and fairness and correct by judicial admonition episodes of governmental lawlessness, excesses of power or abuse of authority or lapses.[18]

Women's issues have increasingly been brought before the supreme court with the growth of women's movement and investigative journalism exposing cases of dowry, rape, sexual harassment and gender based discrimination. In *Delhi Domestic Working Women's Forum v Union of India,*[19] the PIL arose out of indecent sexual assault by seven army personnel against six domestic servants travelling in train from Ranchi to Delhi. The supreme court, with a view to assisting rape victims, has laid down various broad guidelines. These guidelines include legal assistance, anonymity, compensation and rehabilitation for rape victims. The National Commission for Women was directed to evolve a scheme for providing adequate safeguards to these victims. In another significant pronouncement in *Vishaka v State of Rajasthan,*[20] the supreme court declared that sexual harassment of women at workplace constitutes violation of gender equality and right to dignity, which are fundamental rights. Taking note of the fact that the existing civil and penal laws in India did not provide adequate safeguards against sexual harassment at work place, the court laid down 12 guidelines to be followed by every employer to ensure prevention of sexual harassment. Most importantly, the court ruled that all courts in India must construe the contents of fundamental rights in the light of international conventions so long as such conventions were not inconsistent with fundamental rights.

In India, the bonded labour system continues to be the most pernicious form of human servitude. Under such system, a worker continues to serve his master in consideration of a debt obtained by him or his ancestors. Bondage can be inter-generational, child bondage, loyalty bondage or bondage through land allotment. According to an early study there were 26,17,000 bonded labourers in 10 states in India.[21] Most of these labourers come from the lowest strata of society, such as the untouchables, *adivasis* or agricultural labourers. It occurred to the Indian government only in

---

[18] In *Bipin Chandra* v. *State of Gujarat* AIR 2002 Guj 99, a PIL was filed for a direction to the government to provide relief to the earthquake victims in Gujarat. On the morning of 26 January 2001, an earthquake of high magnitude had shook the whole of Gujarat, leaving thousands dead, injured, crippled, orphaned and homeless. The PIL was filed on the basis of newspaper reports that the government had failed to meet the situation arising from the calamity and had no adequate infrastructure to satisfactorily perform the stupendous task of providing relief and rehabilitation to the earthquake victims.

[19] (1995) 1 SCC 14.

[20] *Supra,* note 9. This principle was reiterated in *Apparel Export Promotion Council* v. *A.K. Chopra* AIR 1999 SC 634.

[21] Sharma M, 'Bonded Labour in India: A National Survey on the Incidence of Bonded Labour Final Report', Hyderabad, Academy of Gandhian Studies, 1981.

1976 to pass a central legislation, the Bonded Labour System (Abolition) Act, 1976. After this Act came into force, bonded labour system has been abolished at least on paper and the practice of bonded labour has been made punishable.

Most of the PIL proceedings on bonded labour seek to implement the Act. The first major PIL on this issue was *Bandhua Mukti Morcha v Union of India*,[22] filed in 1981 and decided on 16 December 1983. The action was brought for the identification, release and rehabilitation of hundreds of bonded labour working in the stone quarries of Haryana. The court issued 21 directions to the Haryana Government. During the proceedings, the court monitored its own directions and appointed a number of commissions of inquiry. Unfortunately most of the directions remained unimplemented for many years. The court acknowledged its limited capacity in monitoring the schemes of rehabilitation. In 1992, the court recounted the history of the case and was shocked to note that there had not been the slightest improvement in the conditions of the workers of the stone quarries. The litigation ended up with one more warning to the government to be responsive to judicial directions.[23] Despite the initial failure of the *Bandhua Mukti Morcha* case in terms of effectiveness, PILs were brought before the courts for the liberation of bonded labourer in Madhya Pradesh,[24] Tamil Nadu,[25] Bihar[26] and other states.

Public interest actions concerning children have sought the implementation of existing constitutional and statutory obligations.[27] Early PIL cases focused on children in prisons. In 1981, the supreme court's attention was drawn to a news report about sexual exploitation of children by hardened criminals in Kanpur jail.[28] The court directed the District Judge, Kanpur, to visit the jail and report on the matter. The District Judge's report confirmed the crime of sodomy committed against the children. The court directed that the children be released from jail and shifted to a children's home. No punishment was given, however, to the administrators of the jail. Another PIL exposed the inhuman conditions in which children lived in Tihar Jail, Delhi.[29] Sexual exploitation of children in Orissa jails also formed the subject matter of another PIL.[30]

A major PIL on juveniles in jails was filed by a journalist in 1985. The petition asked for release of children below the age of 16 and for information on the number of such children housed in jails. The court was also asked to ensure that adequate facilities were provided for the children in the form of juvenile courts, homes and schools, that district judges should be directed to visit jails and so on. There were many orders from 1985 onwards which remained unimplemented for a long time.[31] In the meantime, Parliament passed the Juvenile Justice Act, 1986. The

[22] Supra, note 7. Also see *Bandhua Mukti Morcha* v. *Union of India* (2000) 10 SCC 104.

[23] *Bandhua Mukti Morcha* v. *Union of India* AIR 1992 SC 38.

[24] *Mukesh Advani* v. *State of Madhya Pradesh* AIR 1985 SC 1363.

[25] *H P Sivaswamy* v. *State of Tamil Nadu,* 1983 (2) SCALE 45.

[26] *T. Chakkachal* v. *State of Bihar,* JT 1992 (1) SC 106.

[27] Articles 15(3), 21(A) 24, 39(e), 39(f) and 45 of the Constitution of India; Juvenile Justice Act, 1986; Child Labour (Prohibition and Regulation) Act, 1986.

[28] *Munna* v. *State of Uttar Pradesh* (1982) 1 SCC 545.

[29] *Sanjay Suri* v. *Delhi Administration* 1987 (2) SCALE 276.

[30] *M.C. Mehta* v. *State of Orissa* W.P. (Cr) 1504 of 1984 (Unreported).

[31] *Sheela Barse* v. *Union of India,* AIR 1986 SC 1773.

court's attention was now diverted to the implementation of the Act. The Supreme Court Legal Aid Committee pursued the case. In its final order in 1989, the supreme court stressed the need to create juvenile courts, homes and schools. A committee of advocates was appointed to prepare a draft scheme for the proper implementation of Act. Thus, the PIL in this case was ultimately effective as today the country has no juvenile delinquents in jails.[32]

Public Interest Litigation on child labour began in early 1980s in response to a large number of news reports exposing the exploitation of children in fire works and match factories of Sivakasi in Tamil Nadu and in carpet industries in Mirzapur, Uttar Pradesh. In response to a PIL, the supreme court appointed a commission of inquiry on child labour in carpet industries in Uttar Pradesh. The commission's report indicated high incidence of child labour. The children were released with the help of local administration.[33] In 1986 a major PIL was brought before the supreme court complaining that thousands of children were employed in match factories in Sivakasi, Tamil Nadu.[34] These children were exposed to fatal accidents occurring frequently in the manufacturing process of matches and fire works. The court directed the state government to enforce the Factories Act, 1948 and to provide facilities for recreation, medical care and basic diet to the children during working hours and facilities for education. The court also advocated a scheme of compulsory insurance for both adults and children employed in hazardous industries. Every employee had to be insured for a sum of Rs 50,000. A committee was appointed to monitor the judicial directions. It is rather surprising that although the Child Labour (Prohibition and Regulation) Act, 1986 has banned the employment of children in manufacture of matches yet the court in this case permitted child labour in the process of packing, holding that tender hands of the young workers were more suitable to the task. In its final judgment delivered in 1996, the supreme court directed that the offending employer of child labour in match factories will pay Rs 20,000 which would then be deposited in a Child-Labour-Rehabilitation-Cum-Welfare-Fund.[35] The illegally employed children would receive education at the cost of the employer. This is indeed a happy development.

In *People's Union For Civil Liberties* v *Union Of India,*[36] the petitioners sought a direction for the enforcement of the Famine Code and immediate release of food grains lying in the stocks of the Government of India. Directions were also sought requiring the Government to frame fresh schemes of public distribution for the scientific and reasonable distribution of food grains. The court expressed its deep concern that despite the fact that plenty of surplus food grain was lying in the stocks of the Union of India or drought affected areas, people were dying of starvation. The court recalled that between 2001 and 2003 it had passed various directions to see that food was provided to the aged, infirm, disabled and

[32] *SCLAC* v. *Union of India,* (1989) 2 SCC 325. On 17 March 1989, the court again issued directions to every district judge to report to the court as to the exact position of juveniles in jails, setting up of juvenile homes, special homes and observation homes. In *SCLAC* v. *Union of India* (1989) 4 SCC 738, the court expressed its satisfaction that except in Andaman and Nicobar, a Union Territory, no state had kept the children in jails.

[33] *Bandhua Mukti Morcha* v. *Union of India* 1986 (Supp) SCC 553.

[34] *M.C. Mehta* v *State of Tamil Nadu* AIR 1991 SC 417.

[35] *M.C. Mehta* v. *State of Tamil Nadu,* 1996 (1) SCALE 42.

[36] 2003(9) SCALE 835, at p 840.

destitute men and women who were in danger of starvation, pregnant and lactating women and destitute children, especially in cases where they or members of their family did not have sufficient funds to provide food. It was unfortunate that plenty of food was available but its distribution among the very poor and destitute was scarce, leading to starvation, malnutrition and other related problems. Mere schemes without implementation was of no use.

Today PIL is less utilised as a medium of social empowerment and is being increasingly used to raise issues of political governance or to espouse the interests of middle class Indians. The concept of justiciability has been expanded to such an extent that one can easily invoke article 32 jurisdiction (which is intended to be used to enforce fundamental rights) to challenge the constitutional validity of a law setting up private universities[37] or a law dealing with deportation of illegal migrants,[38] or the legality of the dissolution of State Assembly under President's Rule,[39] or questioning the induction of tainted ministers in the Union Cabinet,[40] protesting the rise in the price of onions or strikes by the workers or the issue of disproportionate wealth owned by a Chief Minister, and so on.

Public Interest Litigation has produced astonishing results which were unthinkable two decades ago. Degraded bonded labourers, tortured under-trials and women prisoners, humiliated inmates of protective women's home, blinded prisoners, exploited children,

beggars, and many others have been given relief through judicial intervention. The greatest contribution of PIL has been to enhance the accountability of the governments towards the human rights of the poor. Although judges acting alone cannot provide effective responses to state lawlessness or inaction, they can surely seek to produce a culture where political power becomes increasingly sensitive to human rights. When people's rights are invaded by dominant elements, PIL emerges as a medium of struggle for protection of their human rights. The legitimacy PIL enjoys in the Indian legal system is unprecedented. PIL activism interrogates dominant power structures and transforms the courts into people's court. PIL today constitutes a significant segment of the expanding judicial repertoire and has acquired legitimacy. Through their new jurisdiction, the judges have undertaken expanded responsibilities as critics and monitors of the governments and its agencies

Ideologically, PIL activism performs a formidable task of addressing and confronting dominant formations in civil society and activates public discourse on practices of power. The significance of this movement lies in the creation of norms for a just and equal society. In performing the function of exposing the ills perpetrated upon the helpless, the judges remind and alert the executive of its failings and lapses and give the public functionaries an opportunity to right the wrong. Public Interest Litigation activism creates a new jurisprudence of state accountability and seeks culture formations sensitive to human values and human rights. However, to expect that PIL will automatically bring about legal and social change is a delusion. One should always bear in mind the limits of judicial action in bringing about social change.

---

[37] *Professor Yashpal* v. *State of Chhattisgarh* AIR 2005 SC 2026.

[38] *Sarbananda Sonowal* v. *Union of India* AIR 2005 SC 2920.

[39] *Rameshwar Prasad* v. *Union of India* (2005) 7 SCC 625.

[40] *Manoj Narula* v. *Union of India* 2005(6) SCALE 23.

The Indian Judicial System

I. INTRODUCTION

The administration of justice is the primary task of the judiciary, which is one of the essential organs of the state. Justice has been universally considered to be a sovereign function. Specialised institutions such as courts were not present in early societies for the settlement of disputes. In fact, the earliest modes of justice took the form of 'revenge', which was a private matter. In course of time, kings acquired the powers to maintain law and order and likewise assumed the responsibility of punishing those that committed crimes against what the British called the 'king's peace'. With the emergence and consolidation of state power, the administration of justice came to be regarded as exclusively falling within the domain of the state.

II. BRIEF HISTORY OF THE JUDICIAL SYSTEM IN INDIA

Ancient India acknowledged the importance of the king as one who dispensed justice through the practice of *Danda* or punishment. In the Vedic and pre-Mauryan times, the king presided over the law courts and was guided in his duties by the law codes or Smritis. Gradually a hierarchy of courts evolved with the highest court, the Sasita that was presided over by the king. The laws of Manu and the writings of Indian jurists refer to the existence of peoples' courts at the village level. There were laws of procedure and evidence as well as a code of conduct for judges. Justice was dispensed according to the norms laid down in the scriptures–the Vedas, Dharmasutras, Vedangas. Puranas as well as the customs and usages of communities. During the Mauryan period the influence of Kautilya's *Arthasastra* could clearly be seen. Two kinds of courts existed during the Mauryan period, one for civil cases, the *Dharmasthiya* and the other *Kantakasodhana*, for criminal cases. This system continued during the reign of Asoka. The rock edicts of Asoka throw light on the evolved judicial system prevalent. The city judges were the *Mahamatyas* who administered justice according to *niti* (justice). Ancient India had a gradation of courts. There is sufficient reference to this in the Manusmriti and the *Naradiya Dharmasastra*.

The Mughal period saw the predominance of Islamic jurisprudence which drew heavily from the Quran and the Muslim law of the

Shariat. Akbar made some attempts to establish one uniform system of justice for all. There were three kinds of courts: courts of religious law, courts of secular cases and courts dealing with political cases. The panchayat system also finds mention in the writings of the period.

The British came as merchants and remained as such for quite some time. The three presidency towns of Madras, Bombay and Calcutta had some form of adjudication of disputes set up by the East India Company. The Charter of 1726 set up uniform judicial institutions in these three towns. Subsequently, once the East India Company became the *Diwan* of Bengal, Bihar and Orissa, the British set up an *adalat* system under the judicial plan of Warren Hastings of 1772. Diwani adalats dealt with civil matters while Faujdari adalats handled criminal disputes. A Supreme Court was set up in Calcutta in 1774; similar courts were later set up in the other two Presidency towns. Warren Hastings, set up *Faujdari* Adalats in Bengal, followed by Madras. By the middle of the nineteenth century a uniform system of law was established. Codification of criminal law was a tremendous achievement. The Code of Civil Procedure was passed in 1859, followed by the Code of Criminal Procedure in 1861. The Indian High Court Act, 1861, empowered the Crown to establish by Letters Patent three High Courts at Madras, Bombay and Fort William (Calcutta). Subsequently, the Government of India Act, 1935 brought with it provisional autonomy and a federal system was put in place. The Federal Court was established by the Government of India Act, 1935. This court was the forerunner of the Supreme Court of India.[1]

---

[1] For details see Jain, M.P., *Outlines of Indian Legal History*, New Delhi, Wadhwa, fifth edn, 1990, reprint 2003.

III. JUDICIARY TODAY

The courts in India are arranged in a three-tier structure. This hierarchy, however, is nowhere expressly recognised by the Constitution. It is only through subsequent judicial and academic interpretations that this hierarchy became a convention. The Supreme Court is the highest court in the hierarchy. It has original as well as appellate jurisdictions. The high courts at the state level also have similar powers. The third tier is occupied by courts at the trial level. Even among these courts there is a hierarchy; this is not a constitutional creation, but laid down by the Code of Civil Procedure, 1908 and the Code of Criminal Procedure, 1973 as well as some other statutes.

The role of the judiciary assumes great significance in a federal set up where it has to not only interpret and uphold the Constitution, but also decide controversies between the constituent states inter se, as well as between the centre and the states. The judiciary has the important task of interpreting and adjudicating on the meaning of law and in a sense, 'judges interpret and construct law'.[2]

India has a unified judicial system with the Supreme Court at its apex, unlike the United States which has a dual system of courts.[3] India has a hierarchy of courts in a pyramid-like structure with the Supreme Court standing like a sentinel on the *qui vive* (on guard/alert) at

---

[2] Heywood, Andrew, *Politics*, New York, Palgrave Macmillan, 2002, p. 304.

[3] The United States has a perfectly federal legal system. There is a judicial hierarchy at the state level, which has a State Supreme Court at its top. To deal with matters relating to federal law, there is a separate hierarchy of courts. The US Supreme Court is the highest court in this framework. There is a clear cut separation in the jurisdiction of each system, with the US Supreme Court interfering with the state legal system only in extreme circumstances.

the apex. Below the Supreme Court are the High Courts in the states and below the High Courts is a vast network of subordinate courts.

In 1977 there were 6,266 courts in the country which increased to 10, 638 courts in 1996.[4] The pendency of cases in the courts have also been rising, from 2.1 million cases pending all-India in 195623 million cases pending in 2001.[5] There is a need for increase in the number of courts in the country to decrease the pendency of cases and also a need increase the number of judges. The population to judge ratio is one of the lowest in India. According to the Law Commission of India, there is a need to increase to 50 judges per 10 lakh persons.[6]

Delays in the disposal of cases is a violation of the fundamental right to life under Article 21 of the Constitution.[7] In *Hussainara Khatoon v Home Secretary, State of Bihar*,[8] the Supreme Court observed: 'Now obviously procedure prescribed by law for depriving a person of his liberty can not be "reasonable, fair, or just" unless that procedure ensures a speedy trial for determination of guilt of such person. No procedure which does not ensure a reasonably quick trial, can be regarded as "reasonable, fair or just" and it would fall foul of Article 21.'

Thus, the judiciary in India has an important responsibility in ensuring the dispensation of justice in the most speedy, efficient and fair manner.

THE SUPREME COURT

The Supreme Court is the supreme interpreter of the Constitution. It is also the final court of appeal in all civil and criminal matters and the final interpreter of the law of the land and thus helps in maintaining a regularity of law throughout the country.[9] India has a federal Constitution that provides for the distribution of power with regard to the administration of justice between the Centre and the States. Under List I of the Seventh Schedule of the Constitution, Parliament alone can legislate with respect to: the Constitution, organisation, jurisdiction and powers of the Supreme Court and High Court (except as to employees of the High Courts). The Centre has authority to set up courts with respect to matters in the Union List without ousting the jurisdiction of the Supreme Court and High Courts. The powers of the administration of justice, i.e., the power over the constitution and organization of all courts except Supreme Court and the High Court, has now been transferred from the State List to the Concurrent List. The states can set up courts with respect to any matter in the State List.[10]

Article 124 (1) establishes the Supreme Court of India. The Chief Justice of the Court is designated the Chief Justice of India. In 1950 there were only seven judges apart from the Chief Justice. But with the increase in the work of the judiciary, the Parliament increased the number of judges to the present number, i.e., the Chief Justice of India and the 25 justices of the court.[11]

[4] Dr Justice GC Bharuka, *Rejuvenating Judicial System Through E-Governance & Attitudinal Change,* New Delhi, Wadhwa, 2003, p. 62.

[5] Ibid., p. 64.

[6] Ibid., p. 70.

[7] *A.R. Antulay* v. *R.S. Nayak* (1988) 2 SCC 602.

[8] (1980) 1 SCC 93.

[9] Jain, M.P., *Indian Constitutional Law*, Nagpur, Wadhwa, 2006, p. 191.

[10] Constitution of India, Seventh Schedule, List I, Entries 77-79, 95; List II, Entry 65; List III, Entry IIA.

[11] Supreme Court (Number of Judges Act), 1956, raised the number of judges from seven to ten. This was subsequently raised to 13 vide Act 17 of 1960, later to 17 by the Supreme Court (Number of Judges) Amendment Act, 1977, again to 25 judges and one Chief Justice in 1986, vide Act 22 of 1986.

COMPOSITION

Under article 124 (2) the President appoints the judges of the Supreme Court after consultation with such of the judges of the Supreme Court and of the High Court in the States as the President may deem necessary for the purpose. The judges hold office till the age of 65. In the appointment of a judge other than the Chief Justice, the Chief Justice of India shall always be consulted.[12]

In July 1998, the President sought clarification on issues concerning the appointment of Apex Court judges and the transfer of High Court Judges. A nine-judge Bench of the Supreme Court in *Re Presidential Reference* in 1999 reaffirmed the primacy of the Chief Justice in the appointment of judges of the Supreme Court.[13] The court has declared that the Chief Justice of India should consult a collegium of the four senior-most judges of the Apex Court in the matter of appointment of judges to the Supreme Court. The collegium must make the decision by consensus as far as possible. Even if two judges were to give an adverse opinion, the Chief Justice of India should not send the recommendation to the government.

A person is not qualified for appointment as a judge of the Supreme Court unless he is a citizen of India and: (i) has been for at least five years a judge of a High Court or of two or more such courts in succession; or (ii) has been for at least ten years an advocate of a High Court or of two or more such courts in successions, or; (iii) is, in the opinion of the President, a distinguished jurist.[14]

The Constitution does not make any provisions regarding the appointment of the Chief Justice of India. The senior-most judge of the Supreme Court is normally appointed the Chief Justice. This precedent was broken in 1973 where the government appointed Justice A.N. Ray as the Chief Justice, superseding three senior judges of the court. This was a significant departure from the earlier practice and needless to say, the appointment was challenged in the Delhi High Court through a petition for *quo warranto* under Article 226, but it was quashed by the High Court. Two other important aberrations in the seniority rule were the appointments of Justice Beg in 1976 as Chief Justice of India superseding Justice Khanna, and that of Justice Y.V. Chandrachud in 1978 as the Chief Justice. After 1978, the seniority principle has been observed.

One of the defining characteristics of a liberal democratic system is the independence of its judiciary and this depends on the manner of selection, appointment and tenure of the judges. The Indian Constitution guarantees 'security of tenure' to the judges. According to Article 124(4), a judge of the Supreme Court shall not be removed from his office except by an order of the President passed after an address by each House of Parliament, supported by a majority of the total membership

---

[12] In the United States, the. President appoints the Supreme Court judges with the consent of the Senate. In practice, party affiliations influence judicial appointments. In Great Britain, judges are appointed by the Crown, i.e., the government of the day. Senior judges are appointed the Prime Minister on the advice of the Lord Chancellor. Political considerations rule the day. In *France* – the French President and the Presidents of the National Assembly and the Senate selects one-third of the members of the court. Again we can see the intrusion of party affiliations. In India, the Constitution makers wished to avoid the glaring drawbacks in the British and American methods of appointment. The Indian Constitution neither gives absolute authority to the executive nor does it permit Parliament to influence appointment of judges: article 124 (2).

[13] *In re Presidential Reference* AIR 1999 SC 1.

[14] Constitution of India, article 124 (3).

of that House and by a majority of not less than two-thirds of the members of that House present and voting, has been presented to the President in the same session for such removal on the ground of proved misbehaviour or incapacity. It is not easy to remove a Judge of the Supreme Court under Article 124(4) as was seen in the case of Justice V. Ramaswami, when for the first time, steps were taken in 1991 to remove a judge on grounds of financial irregularities committed by him during his tenure as Chief Justice of Punjab and Haryana High Court. Since the requisite minimum votes for the succession of the motion against Justice Ramaswami could not be achieved in Parliament, he could not be impeached.

The salaries of the judges and their allowances are fixed by the Constitution and cannot be put to vote by the legislature. The administrative expenses of the Supreme Court, including salaries, pensions, allowances payable to the officials are all charged on the Consolidated Fund of India. Once appointed the privileges, rights and allowances of the judges cannot be altered to their disadvantage.

The Constitution provides for the appointment of ad hoc judges by the Chief Justice of India if at any time there should not be a quorum of the judges of the Supreme Court available to hold or continue any session of the court. A High Court Judge who is duly qualified for appointment as a judge of the Supreme Court can be appointed ad hoc judge by the Chief Justice of India.

The Supreme Court sits in Benches of at least five to decide a case involving a sub-stantial question of law as to the interpretation of the Constitution or for hearing a reference by the President under Article 143. The concurrence of a majority of judges present at the hearing of a case is necessary for any judgement or order. When the Bench consists of two judges and they differ, the matter is referred to the Chief Justice for constituting a larger bench. Dissenting judgments can be given. The law declared by the Supreme Court shall be binding on all the courts within the territory of India. The law declared by the Supreme Court is the law of the land and judgments of the Supreme Court are sources of law. Its decisions are binding on all courts within the territory of India. All courts are bound to follow the decision of the Supreme Court. The law declared by the Supreme Court is the law of land. Indian legal system adheres to the principle of binding precedent (stare decisis). This principle is necessary in order to achieve consistency in judicial pronouncements. Article 141 gives a constitutional status to this doctrine.

Court of Record

The Supreme Court is a court of record and has all the powers of such a court, including the power to punish contempt of itself. A court of record is one where of the acts and judicial proceedings are enrolled for perpetual memory and testimony and which has authority to fine and imprison for contempt of itself and of subordinate courts.[15] The Supreme Court has held that its power to punish for contempt under article 129 is not confined to its own contempt but that it extends to all courts and tribunals subordinate to it in the country.[16] This constitutional power of the Supreme Court can neither be curtailed nor be taken away by any legislation.

Jurisdiction of the Supreme Court

The Supreme Court enjoys a wide range of powers as an Apex Court.

[15] Constitution of India, article 129.
[16] *Delhi Judicial Service* v. *State of Gujarat* (1991) 4 SCC 406.

(a) Writ Jurisdiction

The Supreme Court is a guardian of the fundamental rights and it is empowered to issue writs under Article 32.[17] It has the power to issue writs for the enforcement of fundamental rights under Article 32. This is a concurrent original jurisdiction which High Courts also possess under Article 226.

(b) Original Jurisdiction

When a court has the authority to hear and determine a case in the first instance we can say that it has original jurisdiction. The Supreme Court has original and exclusive jurisdiction in inter-governmental disputes, i.e., in any dispute: (1) between the Government of India and one or more states, or; (2) between the Government of India and any state or states on one side and one or more states on the other; (3) between two or more states, if and in so far as the dispute involves any question (whether of law or of fact) on which the existence or extent of a legal right depends. This jurisdiction does not extend to treaties signed before the commencement of the Constitution.

This jurisdiction given to the Supreme Court is extremely important in a federal structure where powers have been clearly delineated between the Centre and the states and an impartial authority is needed to adjudicate if disputes arise. Article 131 imposes two limitations on the exercise of this power: (1) one as to the nature of the party concerned. Supreme Court cannot entertain suits brought by private individuals against the Government of India under its original jurisdiction, and; (2) as to the subject matter—the dispute must involve any question on which the existence

or extent of a legal right depends.[18] Justice Bhagwati observed that this article (131), 'is a necessary concomitant of a federal or a quasi-federal form of government'.[19] The Supreme Court has original jurisdiction on matters relating to the elections of the President and Vice-President and its decision is final.

(c) Appellate Jurisdiction

The Supreme Court is also the final court of appeal having constitutional and criminal jurisdiction under articles 132–136. All appeals from the High Court lie with the Supreme Court if a substantial question of interpretation of the Constitution is involved, and also if the High Court grants a certificate to the effect. Article 133 provides for appeals from the decision of the High Court in civil proceedings if the High Court certifies that the case involves a substantial question of law of general importance or, if in the opinion of the High Court, the subject matter needs to be decided by the Supreme Court. The decision appealed against must be a judgement or final order of a High Court in the territory of India and such judgement or final order should be given in a civil suit, i.e., proceedings affecting civil rights.

Article 134 is important because it gives the Supreme Court limited criminal jurisdiction in exceptional cases, only where the demand of justice requires interference by the highest court in the land.[20] Appeals can be brought before the Supreme Court from any judgment, order or sentence in a criminal proceedings of a High Court if the High

---

[17] For further details see section on High Courts below.

[18] Shukla, V.N., *Constitution of India,* as revised by Mahendra P. Singh, Lucknow, Eastern Book Company, 2001, p. 424.

[19] *State of Karnataka* v. *Union of India* AIR 1978 SC 68.

[20] Ibid., p. 435.

Court: (a) has on appeal reversed an order of acquittal of an accused person and sentenced him to death, or; (b) has withdrawn for trial before itself any case from any court subordinate to its authority and has in such trial convicted the accused person and sentenced him to death, or; (c) certifies under Article 134 that the case is a fit one for appeal to the Supreme Court.[21] The parliament may by law confer on the Supreme Court, any further power to appeal from any judgement final order or sentence in a criminal proceedings of a High Court in the territory of India subject to such conditions and limitations as may be specified in such law. If the High Court has applied the correct principles in reversing an order of acquittal, the Supreme Court does not interfere with the High Court's orders of conviction or reassess the evidence.

Besides the above jurisdiction, the Constitution provides for special leave to appeal by the Supreme Court under Article 136. Articles 132–133 of the Constitution deal with appeal to the Supreme Court which a person may avail of as a matter of right. But under Article 136, appeals to the Supreme Court may be made only with its permission. The Supreme Court has very wide and general power in the matter of hearing appeal by granting special leave against any judgement, decision, determination or order (it is not confined to judgements, decision or final order of the High Court alone) or in any cause or matter. This special appellate power is used by the Supreme Court where grave injustice has been done by disregard of legal process or violation of the principles of natural justice.[22] The Supreme Court observed in *Pritam Singh* v *State*[23] that the power under Article 136 is to be exercised sparingly and only in exceptional cases.

(d) Advisory Jurisdiction

Under Article 143, the President can refer to the Supreme Court a question of law or fact which in his opinion is of such a nature and of such public importance, that it is expedient to obtain its opinion upon it. The advisory opinion given by the Supreme Court is not binding on the President but the precedent is that he normally honours it. The Supreme Court too, has discretion in the matter and may decline to express any opinion on the question submitted to it. The Supreme Court has advised the President on several important cases–Kerala Education Bill 1958,[24] Special Courts Bill 1978,[25] and the matter of the Cauvery Water Disputes Tribunal 1992.[26]

(e) Review Jurisdiction

The Supreme Court has the power to review its own judgment or order. This special power is exercised in accordance with and subject to any Parliamentary legislation and rules made by the court itself under its rule making power.[27] In civil cases, review of a court decision will lie if there is the discovery of new and important matter of evidence or there is a mistake or error apparent on the face of the record or any other sufficient reason. Review is a serious matter. A judgment once

---

[21] Inserted by the Constitution (Forty-fourth Amendment) Act, 1978.

[22] The law recognizes two principles of natural justice:

(1) *Audi alteram partem,* i.e., hear the other side; thus no one can be punished without being given a fair and equal opportunity to state their case, and; (2) Rule against bias, i.e., you cannot be a judge in your own case.

[23] AIR 1950 SC 169.

[24] AIR 1958 SC 996.

[25] AIR 1979 SC 478.

[26] AIR 1992 SC 522.

[27] Constitution of India, article 145.

given is final and a review is justified only if circumstances are of a compelling nature.

Power of Judicial Review

This is the power of the court to enquire whether a law or executive order is in violation of the written Constitution and if the court concludes that it is so, the said law or executive order can be declared unconstitutional and void. This is a unique power given to the Supreme Court due to which it can review the legislative enactments both of Parliament and of state legislature as well as the actions of the executive and administrative arms of the government. The power of judicial review of legislation is mentioned in articles 13, 32, 131–136, 143, 226, 245, 246, 251, 254 and 372. This power of judicial review is considered part of the basic structure of the Constitution; the court as the final interpreter of the Constitution can determine if the other two organs, viz., the legislature and the executive are functioning within their constitutional limits.

Power to do Complete Justice

Article 142 confers a plenary power on the Supreme Court which is free of statutory limitation and has wide implications. Article 142 (i) enables the Supreme Court to pass in the exercise of its jurisdiction any decree/order as is necessary for doing complete justice in any cause or matter pending before it. The court has emphasized that the power given to it under Article 142 is conceived to meet situations which cannot effectively and appropriately be tackled by the existing legal provisions.[28] This power is of a supplementary nature and it cannot be exercised against a fundamental right, nor can it contravene a Constitutional provision.

In *Delhi Judicial Service Association v. State of Gujarat*,[29] the Supreme Court observed that its power under Article 142 (1) to do complete justice 'is at an entirely different level and of a different quality'. The Supreme Court has left the power under Article 142 'undefined and uncatalogued' so that it remains 'elastic enough to be moulded to suit the given situation'.[30] The court's observation is that the plenary jurisdiction under Article 142 'exists as a separate and independent basis of jurisdiction apart from the Statutes'. But the court has cautioned time and again that this power should be used with the utmost restraint so that there is no interference with the performance of duties of other authorities in accordance with the law.[31]

Articles 129, 136 and 141 and 142 highlight the supremacy of the Supreme Court. It is a court of record and it has vested upon itself the power to even hear contempt matters of lower courts and tribunals. Its decisions are binding on all courts and tribunals below it. The power to entertain Special Leave Petitions (SLPs) under Article 136, though the court has emphasized repeatedly that this power is to be used sparingly and in extreme circumstances, it is used to discipline the courts below. Apart from all these powers, it is perhaps the power to do 'complete justice' derived from Article 142, which makes the Supreme Court truly supreme.

The word 'justice' appears only twice in the Constitution—the first time being in the Preamble. This guardianship of 'justice' gives the apex court unabated powers. Though there are many detractors to the superior role of

---

[28] Jain, M.P., *Indian Constitutional Law*, Nagpur, Wadhwa, fifth edn, 2003, reprint 2006, p 264.

[29] AIR 1991 SC 2176.

[30] *Delhi Development Authority* v. *Skipper Construction Co.* AIR 1996 SC 2005.

[31] Jain, M.P., *Indian Constitutional Law*, Nagpur, Wadhwa, fifth edn, 2003, reprint 2006, p. 267.

the Supreme Court, recent incidents have reasserted that other courts largely restrict themselves to being 'courts of law'; while the justice component is supplied by the Supreme Court.

THE HIGH COURTS

The Constitution provides for High Courts and an elaborate system of subordinate courts. Each of the states in the First Schedule of the Constitution has a High Court as defined by Article 215. The jurisdiction of a High Court is coterminous with the territorial limits of the state concerned.[32] Parliament may by law establish a common High Court for two or more states. Thus the High Court of Assam was made a common one for all the north-eastern states. This High Court is called the Gauhati High Court.

Parliament may by law create a new High Court for a union territory or exclude a union territory from the jurisdiction of a High Court or even extend the jurisdiction of a High Court over a union territory. Delhi acquired its own High Court in 1966. The Madras High Court exercises jurisdiction over the union territories of Pondicherry, Kerala High Court has jurisdiction over Lakshadweep, Bombay High Court over Dadra and Nagar Haveli, Calcutta High Court over Andaman and Nicobar Islands and Punjab and Haryana High Court over Chandigarh. The State of Goa comes under the jurisdiction of the Bombay High Court.

High Courts in India can trace their history back to 1862, when under the Indian High Courts Act, 1861, the Crown established by Letters Patent, the High Courts of Calcutta, Madras and Bombay. In 1866, the fourth High

Court was set up at Allahabad. The same year the Imperial Legislative Council passed an Act constituting a Chief Court in the Punjab on the same pattern as the High Court at Allahabad. The Indian High Court Act, 1911 provided for the establishment of additional High Courts in British India. All High Courts are parts of a single judicial system with separate territorial jurisdictions.[33]

Composition

Article 216 provides that every High Court shall consist of a Chief Justice and such other judges as the President may from time to time deem it necessary to appoint. The Constitution thus, does not fix the number of judges. However the Supreme Court has declared that that Chief Justice of India and the Chief Justice of the concerned High Court can make recommendations to the President regarding the strength of the judges in the High Court, which the President needs act upon.[34]

Appointments

High Court judges are appointed by the President after consulting the Chief Justice of India, the Governor of the State concerned and in the case of the appointment of judges other than the Chief Justice, the Chief Justice of the High Court. Where there is a common High Court for two or more states, the Governors of all the States concerned are consulted.[35]

After 1999 it has been categorically established that consultation with the Chief Justice of India requires consultation with a collegium of judges consisting of the Chief Justice of India and any two senior-most judges

---

[32] Agarwala, B.R., *Our Judiciary*, New Delhi, National Book Trust, 2004, p. 87.

[33] Ibid., p.84.
[34] *Supreme Court Advocate-on-Records Association* v. *Union of India* AIR 1994 SC 268.
[35] Constitution of India, article 231(2).

of the Supreme Court.[36] The individual opinion of the Chief Justice of India does not constitute 'consultation'. In the matter of transfer of judges too, the collegium was enlarged to include the Chief Justice of the two High Courts concerned—one from where the transfer was being affected and one from the High Court to which the transfer was being made. Any recommendation made by the Chief Justice of India without complying with the required norms of consultation would not be binding or the Government of India. The court has declared that transfers should not be politically motivated.[37]

To be appointed a High Court judge a person should be: (1) a citizen of India; (2) should be one who has held a judicial office for at least ten years, or; (3) been an advocate of a High Court of at least ten years standing. As in the case of Supreme Court judges, in order to ensure and protect the independence of the judiciary, the Constitution has provided for the security of the salaries of judges. The salaries mentioned cannot be varied unless the Constitution is amended. The Constitution was amended in 1986, conferring power on Parliament to determine such salaries. The salaries and allowances of the judges are charged on the Consolidated Fund of India. High Court judges enjoy security of tenure. A judge of the High Court holds office until (s)he attains the age of 62 and can be removed from office only by impeachment for which the procedure is the same as that for the Supreme Court judges.

Jurisdiction

The High Court is the highest court in the state on questions of law and for the adjudication of disputes. It is the only court apart from the Supreme Court which has been vested with the jurisdiction to interpret the Constitution.[38] The pre-Constitution jurisdiction of the High Court has been preserved and there is a continuity in the laws administered by the High Court. Every High Court is a court of record and has all the powers of such a court including the power to punish for contempt of itself as well as the power to determine questions of its own jurisdiction.

High Courts Enjoy Original and Appellate Jurisdiction

The powers given to the High Court under Article 226 are very extensive. Article 226 empowers the High Court to issue to any person or authority, including in appropriate cases, any government orders or writs including writs in the nature of *habeas corpus, mandamus, prohibition, quo warranto* and *certiorari* for the enforcement of any of the rights conferred by Part III and for any other purpose, i.e., for the enforcement of any other legal right.

These five writs are called prerogative writs and the concept has been borrowed from English law. There is a two-fold limitation on the power of the High Court to issue writs: (1) this power is to be exercised within the territories subject to the jurisdiction of the High Court, and; (2) The person or authority to whom such a writ can be issued must reside within those territories.[39]

The Constitution (Forty-second Amendment) Act, 1976 sought to restrict the High Courts' power to issue writs. But the

---

[36] *In re Presidential Reference* AIR 1999 SC 1.

[37] *Subhash Sharma* v. *Union of India* AIR 1991 SC 631; *In re Presidential Reference* AIR 1999 SC 1.

[38] Agarwala, B.R., *Our Judiciary*, New Delhi, National Book Trust, 2004, p. 83.

[39] Shukla, V.N., *Constitution of India* as revised by Mahendra P. Singh, Lucknow, Eastern Book Company, 2001, p. 545.

Constitution (Forty-fourth Amendment) Act, 1978 restored the original power. The power of the High Court under Article 226 is a supervisory power not an appellate power. It is only when an action is challenged that the court examines the legality/illegality of it. The legal remedy provided under Article 226 is at the discretion of the High Court and if it is satisfied that an alternative remedy exists or that certain crucial facts have been deliberately suppressed by the petitioner, it can reject the application.

Appellate Jurisdiction: High Courts function as the highest court for appeal and revision in both civil and criminal matters in the state. Appeals are made to the High Court in civil cases if a substantial question of law is involved. In criminal matter, appeals to the High Court lie from the Court of Sessions. A sentence of death by a Sessions Court must be confirmed by a High Court.

Supervisory Jurisdiction: Article 227 (1) gives the High Courts power of superintendence over all courts and tribunals throughout the territories in relation to which it exercises jurisdiction. It can make and issue general rules and prescribe forms for regulating the practice and proceedings of such courts. This power is both administrative and judicial in nature, for not only does it empower the High Court to ensure that the subordinate tribunals do not exceed the limits of their jurisdiction, but it also has to ensure that the principles of natural justice are not disregarded. However, as the Supreme Court has observed in *Waryam Singh v Amar Nath*,[40] 'This power should be exercised sparingly and only in appropriate cases'.

[40] AIR 1954 SC 215.

Under Article 228, if the High Court is satisfied that a case pending in a subordinate court involves a substantial question of law as to the interpretation of the Constitution the determination of which is necessary for the disposal of the case, it shall withdraw the case and may: (1) either dispose of the case itself, or; (2) determine the said question of law and return the case to the court concerned along with a copy of its judgment on the question. The said court can then proceed to dispose of the case in conformity with such judgement.

SUBORDINATE JUDICIARY

Often called the 'lower courts' in common parlance, these courts constitute the very backbone of the Indian judicial system. They have a history dating back to the eighteenth century; from an era when the Supreme Court and High Court were merely visions for the future. These courts were the early cradles for common law in India. In these courts, Anglo-Saxon law was modified on the principles of 'equity, justice and good conscience' to suit the Indian social landscape.

Before 1862, the presidency courts—courts in the three presidency towns of Calcutta, Bombay and Madras—followed the modified common law. At the same time courts in the *mofussil* towns (towns outside the presidency towns)—dispensed justice according to customary laws of Hindus and Muslims. In 1862, the High Courts were formed and these two jurisdictions were merged.

The setting up of the High Courts was another step in the creation of the modern Indian judicial system. Through the proverbial doctrine of 'justice, equity and good conscience', these courts merged traditional Indian law and common law. In a vast and diverse country like India common law could not have asserted itself as judge-made law. As the first step, for purposes of certainty and uniformity, the legal machinery had to be codified. This was attained through the three great codes—The Code of Civil Procedure, 1859, the Code of Criminal Procedure, 1861, and the Indian Penal Code, 1861. The first two codes, in particular, laid down the framework for the courts system in the country, to be hierarchically linked to the High Courts with the Privy Council in London as the final appellate authority. Thus, one can see how the 'lower judiciary' formed the 'basic structure' of the Indian legal system way before the Federal Court and the Supreme Court came into existence.

Structure of the Subordinate Judiciary

The administration of justice of all courts except the Supreme Court and High Courts is now a Concurrent subject.[41] The constitution and organization of the High Court is a Central subject and Parliament alone can set up a High Court. So there is certain uniformity throughout the territory of India as far as the constitution and organization of High Courts are concerned. But state legislatures can create other courts and invest them with power and jurisdiction to try a wide range of matters whether civil or criminal. They can enlarge their jurisdiction or alter and amend it.

Given the variation across states in the designations of the subordinate judiciary, an important Supreme Court decision has sought to bring about uniformity.[42] On the civil side, the posts are now designated District/Additional District Judges, Civil Judges Senior Division and Civil Judges Junior Division. On the criminal side, they are Sessions Judge /

Additional Sessions Judge and Chief Judicial Magistrate and Judicial Magistrate.[43] In the Metropolitan areas they are Chief Metropolitan Magistrate/Additional Chief Metropolitan Magistrate and Metropolitan Magistrate.

Subordinate Civil Judiciary

There is a three tier system of Civil Courts in every state. For the purpose of the civil judiciary the Civil Courts Act divides each state into districts. Each district has a District Court which is the highest court. In matters in which original jurisdiction has not been conferred upon the High Court, all suits are to be filed in the District Court, which is presided over by the District Judge.

The court of the District Judge is the appellate court which hears appeals from the orders and judgements of the subordinate judges.

Article 236 states that the expression 'District Judge' includes a judge of a Civil Court, Additional District Judge, Joint District Judge, Assistant District Judge, Chief Judge of a Small Cause Court, Chief Presiding Magistrate, Additional Chief Presiding Magistrate, Sessions Judge, Additional Sessions Judge and Assistant Sessions Judge. The term 'District Judge' also includes a hierarchy of specialized civil courts such as Labour Courts and Industrial Courts.

Under section 9 of the Code of Civil Procedure, 1908, every right of a civil nature can be enforced in a civil court. Limits on the jurisdiction of a civil court are: (1) pecuniary or monetary limits; (2) limits regarding subject matter, and; (3) territorial or local limits. Suits relating to immovable property can only be filed in that court within whose jurisdiction the property is situated. Other suits of a civil

[41] Constitution of India, List III, Entry 11A.

[42] *All India Judges' Association* v. *Union of India* AIR 1992 SC 165.

[43] Ibid., p. 603.

nature can be filed in the court within whose jurisdiction the defendant lives or where he is employed or has business. Civil suits can be filed by or against a corporation or association if these bodies have been given legal recognition. The state can also be a party if a civil right is claimed by or against the state.

Appointments to the subordinate judiciary are made by the governor in consultation with the High Court. Under Article 234, appointments of persons to the judicial service of the state other than the District Judge are made by the governor of the state in accordance with the rules made by him in consultation with the High Court of the state and the state public service commission. The government's control over the subordinate judiciary ceases after the appointment.

It is the High Court which exercises extensive administrative control over District Courts and courts subordinate to it in all matters concerning posting, promotion, transfer, grant of leave etc.[44] This control has been vested in the High Court in order to preserve the independence of the subordinate judiciary from executive interference. The power of the High Courts extends to imposing punishments over judicial officers short of 'dismissal' or removal or reduction in rank. These major punishments lie with the governor, but action can be taken by the governor only on the recommendation of the High Court, which is binding.

The District Judge exercises administrative control over all civil courts within the territorial limits of his jurisdiction. (S)he can hear appeals from the orders/decrees of the subordinate judges. There are disputes which have been kept out of the purview of civil courts and instead decided by tribunals (see below).

Below the District Court are courts which are termed differently in the different states. The Supreme Court has now sought to bring about uniformity in their nomenclature.[45] The pecuniary valuation of suits that are filed is made with reference to the rules under the Suits Valuation Act. Suits exceeding the pecuniary limit go to the High Court and so the High Court has original civil jurisdiction in such cases. Appeals from all decrees/order of the subordinate courts lie with the District Court. If the case involves a higher amount (varying in each state) then the appeal lies directly to the High Court. Appeals from the original orders and judgements of the District Courts lie to the High Court. The procedure in civil courts is governed by the Code of Civil Procedure, 1908, which provides for the institution of all suits in civil courts.

Section 115 of the Code of Civil Procedure, 1908 provides that the High Court may call for the record of any case which has been decided by a subordinate court in which no appeal lies if the High Court is satisfied that the subordinate court has: (a) exercised a jurisdiction not available to it, or; (b) failed to exercise a jurisdiction vested in it, or; (c) acted in an illegal or irregular manner in the exercise of its jurisdiction.

Courts of Small Causes: These courts exist in Presidency towns like Bombay, Delhi, Calcutta and Madras and are governed by the Presidency Small Causes Courts Act, 1887. They are vested with jurisdiction to deal with claims for small monetary amounts.

---

[44] Constitution of India, article 235.

[45] Supra note 38. Also see *All-India Judges Association* v. *Union of India (II)* AIR 1993 SC 2493 and *All-India Judges Association* v. *Union of India(III)* (2002) 4 SCC 247.

Subordinate Criminal Judiciary

The Code of Criminal Procedure, 1973, deals with the various categories of criminal courts of special jurisdiction. It provides machinery to deal with offences under criminal laws in order to ensure fair, speedy and effective justice. The Code provides not only a general procedural law but also gives a detailed structure of criminal courts. Law in India has been neatly delineated into the two categories of civil procedures and criminal procedures with a separate hierarchy of courts for each set of offences.

Criminal Courts are structured on three separate levels:

(1) Courts of Session: Presided over by a Sessions Judge. There is a Court of Sessions for every Sessions Division. The Sessions Judge is assisted by the Additional Sessions Judge or Assistant Sessions Judge. Court of Session is the highest criminal court which has both appellate and original jurisdiction. The District Court acts as a Sessions Court. When the District Court deals with criminal cases we term it a Sessions Court. That is why it is termed as the Districts and Sessions Court.

The Sessions Court can try any offence and impose any sentence authorized by law for the particular offence. But if the Court of Sessions passes a death sentence it must be confirmed by the High Court. A Sessions Court has jurisdiction to try only serious offences requiring severe sentence, like sedition, dacoities, homicide, war against the State, etc. Such offences are not tried by the Magistrates.

(2) The Chief Judicial Magistrate and Additional Chief Judicial Magistrate are appointed by the High Court. The Chief Judicial Magistrate defines the local jurisdiction of Judicial Magistrates and exercises control and supervision over their work. The Additional Chief Judicial Magistrate has all the powers of a Chief Judicial Magistrate. The Chief Judicial Magistrate and Chief Metropolitan Magistrate can pass any sentence authorized by law, other than a sentence of death or imprisonment for life or imprisonment for a term exceeding seven years.

Every Chief Judicial Magistrate is subordinate to the Sessions Judge and other Judicial Magistrates are subordinate to the Chief Judicial Magistrate.

(3) Courts of Judicial Magistrates function under the Chief Judicial Magistrate. In Metropolitan areas there are the courts of the Metropolitan Magistrates and one of the Metropolitan Magistrates is appointed as the Chief Metropolitan Magistrate. He presides over the court and has the power of the Chief Judicial Magistrate. In addition, there are Special Metropolitan Magistrates. Courts of Judicial Magistrates First Class and Second Class can be established in every District by the State Government after consultation with the High Court. The First Schedule of the Code of Criminal Procedure, 1973, indicates whether an offence can be tried by a Magistrate of the First or Second Class.

A Metropolitan area is an area declared to be one by the State Government under section 8 of the Code of Criminal Procedure, 1908. A town whose population exceeds one million qualifies to be termed a 'metropolitan area'. Every metropolitan area constitutes a separate Sessions Division and district and every state can have several Sessions' divisions. The former Presidency towns of Bombay, Calcuttta, Madras are metropolitan areas along with the city of Ahmedabad and Delhi.

If a person is convicted on a trial held by a Sessions Judge or Additional Sessions Judge he can appeal to the High Court. A person convicted on a trial held by a Metropolitan Magistrate or Assistant Sessions Judge or Judicial Magistrate can appeal to the Court of Sessions. There is no appeal if an accused has pleaded guilty and has been convicted by the appropriate court.[46]

THE EXECUTIVE MAGISTRATE

The Executive Magistrates (as distinct from the Judicial Magistrate) in every District and Metropolitan areas are appointed by the State Government and one of them is made the District Magistrate. The District Magistrate has all the powers designated by the state government. He defines all the local limits of the areas in the district within which the Executive Magistrates can exercise their power. The power of the Executive Magistrates are administrative and quasi-judicial in nature.

ALTERNATIVE MECHANISMS— THE WAY FORWARD

Traditional courts in India have today become infamous for delays and rigid procedural rules. Though we have historically known many other modes of dispute resolution, it was only during the British Raj that many of these methods got institutionalised. Out of these arbitration and conciliation (mediation) occupy a place of prime importance. Settlement of disputes is subject to the parties' choice and the role of the courts is very limited (though the recent attempts by the Supreme Court to change this cannot be ignored).[47]

Some other modes are not as removed from the courts as arbitration is. They include the various tribunals, Lok Adalats, Nyaya Panchayats etc. These are largely judicial or

quasi-judicial bodies which do not use strict procedural techniques and gathering of evidence as traditional courts would do. They are mostly informal, with an implied or explicit appeal option to the High Courts. Many of them, like Central Administrative Tribunal (CAT), Telecom Disputes Settlement Appellate Authority (TDSAT) and Motor Accidents Claims Tribunal (MACT) have specialized functions.

On the other hand, Lok Adalats handle most disputes. They are formed under the National Legal Services Authority Act (NALSA), 1987. As on 31 March 2005, 4,57,510 Lok Adalats were held in India, during which time over, 1,70,00,000 cases were settled out of court and 8,54,529 were motor accidents cases.[48] The large number of motor accident cases settled in Lok Adalats indicates that there is a bright possibility of using Lok Adalats to arrive at an amicable settlement of disputes in other areas of litigation also.

NYAYA PANCHAYATS

A Brief History of the Panchayat System

The history of the panchayat system goes back to the vedic times when at the village level members or *Panchas* were elected and a head was appointed from amongst them. These institutions of local self government enjoyed a certain amount of independence and non-interference from the king in their functioning. Our ancient Smritis and Kautilya's Arthashastra mentions the existence of panchayats. Panchayats were effective in dealing with local causes concerning distribution of land among the villagers, collection of taxes from the procedure of the land, punishment of offences,

[46] Code of Criminal Procedure, 1973, sections 375 and 325.

[47] Refer to the chapter on Alternate Dispute Redressal Mechanisms in this volume.

[48] Nariman, Fali. S., *Indian Legal System: Can it be Saved?*, New Delhi, Penguin Books, 2006, p. 48.

etc. Panchayats fell into disuse during British rule. In 1882, the British under Lord Rippon established some semblance of local self government under the Local Self Government Act, 1889. The Bombay Village Panchayat Act, 1920 constituted the Panchayat into an elected body with power to levy taxes.

After independence, the Government of India took steps to give local self government real meaning. Article 40 of the Constitution expressly provides that the states shall take steps to organize village panchayats to enable them to function as units of self government. Different states had enacted legislation for this purpose. Panchayats are set up at the village, intermediate and district level. The Constitution (Seventy-third Amendment) Act, 1993 has now given a constitutional basis to the panchayat system, and the Eleventh Schedule of the Constitution details their functions.

Nyaya Panchayats deal with settlement of disputes, but have unfortunately not been uniformly established throughout the country. The village panchayat elects members of the Nyaya Panchayat from among themselves or the entire village. The members are lay persons with no legal or even basic educational qualification. They deal with civil and criminal offences of a petty nature. The maximum fine that they can impose ranges from Rs. 15 to Rs. 250. Generally, they cannot pass any sentence of imprisonment. The quorum for each bench of the panchayat is usually three persons. Criminal cases can be transferred from a Nyaya Panchayat to a criminal court if the facts warrant it.[49] Panchas can be removed by the executive or grounds of misconduct, corruption, neglect in the performance of duties.

[49] Jain, S.N., 'Judicial System and Legal Remedies', in *Indian Legal System,* ed. Indian Law Institute, pp. 148-149, 2006.

TRIBUNALS

The large number of cases dealing with a variety of technical matters has resulted in the setting up of tribunals to deal with certain specialized matters exclusively. Traditional courts proved inadequate to deal with technical issues. Besides, disputes in these areas needed speedy and effective adjudication which the courts already over burdened, could not do. Thus it was decided to set up tribunals. Examples of tribunals are Administrative Tribunals, Industrial Tribunals, Debt Recovery Tribunals, Railway Rates Tribunals.

Tribunals are not, strictly speaking, courts, although they do resemble the traditional court system. Both are created by the legislature and have specific judicial power. Both adjudicate disputes between parties. Yet, there are significant differences between them. Courts of law are a part of the traditional judicial system. Their powers are derived from the state and they deal with justice. A tribunal is an agency created by a statute and invested with judicial power in specific matters. A court of law is presided over by a judge but a tribunal need not be presided over by a person trained in law. A court of law is bound by rules of evidence and Code of Civil Procedure, 1908, but a tribunal is not. They can summon witnesses and requisition documents. Some tribunals are composed of technical experts who are better equipped and trained to deal with specialized problems, relating to, for e.g., monopolistic trade practices. We now examine one of these tribunals, viz., administrative tribunals in detail.

The large numbers of government employees has seen greater frequency of disputes between government employees regarding recruitment, service conditions, transfers, promotions, etc. It was felt that ordinary courts of law with their procedural limitations were not ideally suited to settle such disputes amicably. The jurisdiction of an Administrative Tribunal constituted under the Administration Tribunals Act, 1985, extends to service matters which mean appointment, tenure, pension retirement benefits, disciplinary matters, leave, seniority, etc. It also covers disputes relating to pay interest or delayed payment of GPF, pension or gratuity government accommodation, etc. The services covered by the CAT are All India Services, Civil Services of the Union, and civil posts, except those which have been specifically excluded. The Administrative Tribunals Act does not apply to armed forces, staff of the Supreme Court, High Court and subordinate courts. There is a Central Administrative Tribunal and a State Administrative Tribunal covered by the Administrative Tribunals Act 1985. The Act was passed in pursuance of Article 323 A of the Constitution, which empowered Parliament to set up service tribunals. Under Article 323A, Central Administrative Tribunals (CAT) with branches in specified cities have been set up for adjudication of disputes. These administrative tribunals adjudicate or conduct trials of dispute and complaints with respect to recruitment and conditions of service of persons appointed to the public service and posts in connection with the affairs of the Union or of any local or other authority within the territory of India which is under the control of the Government of India or of any corporation or society owned or controlled by the Government of India.[50]

Some other important tribunals are the industrial tribunal (under the Industrial Disputes Act, 1947) and the motor accidents claim tribunal. The industrial tribunal is constituted by the Central Government if an industrial dispute relates in any way to the Central Government. The motor accidents claim tribunal was established under the Motor Vehicles Act 1988. Appeals against the award of the tribunal can be made to the High Court within 90 days from the date of the award. The Railway Rates Tribunal was established under the Indian Railways Act, 1989.

FAMILY COURTS

The family is the first of all social forms and is the bedrock of civil society. The maintenance of harmony and equilibrium at the level of the family is essential for the health and progress of any society. It is therefore important to ensure that if and when family disputes of a serious nature take place, justice should be done in a manner in which the basic values of family life are preserved. The ordinary judicial machinery is considered unsuitable and so special Family Courts have been set up in several countries. The movement towards establishment of Family Courts began in the west and today countries like the United States of America, Japan Australia and New Zealand have all recognized and accepted the utility of family courts. The Law Commission of India recommended the establishment of Family Courts in its 59th report.

Family Courts are established under the Family Courts Act, 1984. The Central Government notifies the setting up of Family Courts in a particular state.[51] After that, the state government, after consulting the High Court establishes such courts within the

---

[50] Agarwala, B.R., *Our Judiciary*, New Delhi, National Book Trust, 2004, p. 105.

[51] For instance, Family Courts have not yet been established in Delhi.

state.[52] Family Courts are set up for every area in the state comprising a city or town whose population exceeds one million.[53] A Family Court consists of one judge appointed by the state government with the concurrence of the High Court.

Purpose of a Family Court

Family Courts are a specialized type of courts entrusted with the disposal of cases concerning disputes related to the family, e.g., marriage, divorce, maintenance, guardianship and property of the spouses. The purpose is to promote conciliation and secure speedy settlement of disputes without disturbing the very fabric of family life. Social welfare agencies and counsellors can assist the Family Courts. It is felt that counselling can prove to be quite effective in settling marital discord. If necessary, the help of a medical expert is also taken.

Jurisdiction of the Family Courts

This has been described in the Family Courts Act, 1984. Its jurisdiction covers suits and proceedings concerning varied matters such as nullity of marriage, restitution of conjugal rights, judicial separation or dissolution of marriage; the validity of matrimonial status; property of the spouses or either of them; guardianship of a minor, etc. Legal practitioners cannot represent any party to a suit. The Family Courts are not bound by the Indian Evidence Act, 1872 and under section 9 of the Family Courts Act, 1984, they can follow such procedure as it (they) deem fit. Proceedings of the court may be held in camera, i.e., behind closed doors. The judgements of the Family Court are required to be precise and concise. The decision or order passed by the Family Court shall have the same force and effect as the decision of any civil court. No appeal lies from the decision of a Family Court if the decree / order was passed with the consent of both parties. An appeal can lie otherwise only on grounds of facts and on law.

The Family Courts Act is not a self contained Act. It has to be read along with other laws, such as personal laws, and can award only such interim relief as is provided for in the law under which the petition has been filed. Family Courts also have no jurisdiction to try offences against women under the Dowry Prohibition Act, 1961.

IV. CONCLUSION

The horizon of courts and that of judicial review has slowly expanded to cover the vast and hitherto neglected areas of social and economic justice. The principle of social justice is duly enshrined in the Indian Constitution and in particular, in the Directives Principles of State Policy, which aim at removing social and economic anomalies from our system; yet the bitter truth is that it is the educated elite, 'the governing and non-governing elite' (Pareto) that has deprived millions of a life of equality, of dignity and of economic justice. The credit for transforming judicial attitudes towards the administration, for making the state truly accountable for its apathy towards the plight of the underprivileged and for upholding the rights of the common man must be given to the judiciary, and its creative use of public interest litigation.

At the same time, it is apparent that the judicial arteries are getting clogged with the burgeoning number of court cases. The time has come to look outside court-based systems

[52] Mathew, P.D., P.M. Bakshi, 'Family Courts', in *Legal Education: Personal Laws-2*, New Delhi, Indian Social Institute, p. 4.

[53] Ibid., p. 4.

of dispute resolution. This calls for a change in the attitude of the people towards disputes. The judiciary and the law makers should not only improve the fairness and efficiency of the existing judicial system; they must also promote alternative mechanisms of dispute resolution. This would be a very modest beginning for the long journey from a legal system to a 'justice system'.

Access to Criminal Justice
Towards an Effective Right*

S. MURALIDHAR

The right of access to justice and to legal aid in the criminal justice system is considered non-derogable and an essential fair trial standard both in international human rights law and in domestic law. This chapter focuses on the relevance of legal aid in providing access to justice within the criminal justice system and suggests what could be the essentials of a workable legal services programme in the criminal justice system in India. The contexts in which this study has been undertaken include economic incapacity, social vulnerability and the loss of liberty—each of which prevents an equal access to justice. A position that emerges is that legal aid which is a tool for ensuring processual justice also has to address itself to law and institutional reform.

The chapter takes a comprehensive view of legal aid and the criminal justice system in India, revisiting the conceptual and programmatic content of legal aid. This is followed by setting out certain issues critical to the understanding of the domain of legal aid which require to be recapitulated in order to complete the picture. The paper concludes by attempting an outline of a plan of action for legal aid in the criminal justice system in India.

I. ACCESS TO LEGAL AID: AN OVERVIEW

NATURE OF THE RIGHT OF ACCESS TO JUSTICE

The nature and scope of the right of access to justice and the framework of the legal services programme were delineated with clarity in the reports of the expert committees on legal aid. The 1971 Gujarat Committee Report,[1] the 1973

* This paper is a slightly modified version of chapter 8 from the book *Law, Poverty and Legal Aid: Access to Criminal Justice* by the author published by LexisNexis Butterworths, New Delhi, 2004.

[1] On 22 June 1970, the Government of Gujarat constituted a committee under the chairmanship of Justice P.N. Bhagwati 'to consider the question of grant of legal aid in civil, criminal, revenue, labour and other proceedings to poor persons, to persons of limited means and to persons belonging to backward classes, and to make such recommendations as may be desirable so as to render legal advice more easily available and make justice more easily accessible to such persons, including

Expert Committee Report[2] and the 1977 *Judicare Committee Report,*[3] were unanimous and consistent in the position that:

1. Legal aid was primarily a responsibility of the state.

2. A concerted shift had to be made from confining the legal services programme to its remedial role of dealing with individual problems to a preventive and rehabilitative legal services programme that would tackle the reasons for the economic and social marginalisation of the people; legal aid was not confined to providing legal representation but included legal advice, counselling and rehabilitation.

3. In the criminal justice system, legal aid would be available at every stage from the point of arrest and custody to the disposal of the judicial proceedings at all levels including appeal, review or revision; legal aid would have to be made available in jails and other custodial institutions.

4. Legal aid was part of the larger agenda of reformation of the legal system, which had to take place simultaneously acknowledging the linkage between crime and poverty and the law's criminalization of the activities of the poor; the system of monetary bails and bonds had to be reformed to account for the difficulties faced by the indigent person brought into the criminal justice system.

(e) Consistent with this reorientation, law and institutional reform was to be a part of the legal aid agenda; legal aid committees and lawyers' cooperatives were expected to initiate test cases and PILs to challenge arbitrary laws and practices that discriminated against the poor.

(f) The role of the lawyer would be more than that of the authorised representative of a client in an adversarial proceeding; legal services had to reach the poor rather than the other way round; a public sector in the legal profession was envisaged where salaried lawyers would be engaged whole time in legal aid offices located within and in proximity to communities.

(g) Legal aid institutions created at different administrative levels were expected to be autonomous and independent of executive control or interference; and

(h) The right to legal aid was not a measure of welfare or charity but a manifestation of an enforceable fundamental right to equal access to justice.

JUDICIAL RESPONSE

Much of this vision of access to justice was carried forward into the judgments handed down in the post-1974 phase by the Supreme

---

recommendation on the question of encouragement and financial assistance to institutions engaged in the work of such legal aid'. The term of the Committee was extended till 31 August 1971, the date on which it submitted its report.

[2] By a notification dated 27 October 1972, the Ministry of Law and Justice, Government of India, appointed an Expert Committee on Legal Aid with Justice Krishna Iyer as chairman to examine the matter of making legal aid and advice available to the community.

[3] On May 1976, the Government of India appointed a two-member Committee consisting of Justice P.N. Bhagwati as Chairman and Justice V.R. Krishna Iyer as member. One of the purposes for setting up the Committee was that the Central Government felt the need for establishing 'an adequate and vigorous legal service programme in all the states in the country on a uniform basis.' The terms of reference of the Judicare Committee included making 'recommendations for establishing and operating a comprehensive and dynamic legal service programme for effective implementation of the socio-economic measures taken or to be taken by the Government, including formulation of scheme or schemes for legal service.' See Annexure-1, Terms of Reference, 'Report on National Judicare: Equal Justice-Social Justice', Ministry of Law and Justice and Company Affairs, 1977, p. 87.

Court and followed by the High Courts. Further, the courts developed PIL jurisdiction as a strategic arm of the legal aid movement. It facilitated the tackling of issues concerning the criminal justice system—particularly the problems of under trials in accessing courts and getting legal assistance, overcrowding of prisons, speedy trial and legal aid to victims of crime. While this may have helped bring the issue centre stage and present it in a constitutional conspectus, it was slow to influence the essential approach of the state to the issue of access to justice. For one, the judiciary itself was inconsistent in the application of the judicially evolved rules in individual cases. There was a lack of clarity on whether the denial of the right of legal representation vitiated a criminal trial. Secondly, the focus of the PIL cases in later years shifted from the concerns of the accused to those of the victim and more importantly to those of the institution. For instance, the right of the accused to speedy trial was, contrary to the initial approach, addressed from the point of view of the legitimacy of the judicial system in the eyes of the victims of crime. The uncertainty about the status and enforcement of the right to criminal legal aid only under-scored the need for the Constitution and the statutes to make explicit the law that had been declared by the judiciary.

THE CONSTITUTION AND THE STATUTES

The Constitution still treats free legal aid as a non-enforceable directive principle of state policy under Article 39-A. It denies the right to legal representation, and therefore legal aid, to a person preventively detained. The statute governing criminal procedure too recognises only a limited right of criminal legal aid. Section 304 of the Code of Criminal Procedure 1973 provides for a statutory, procedural right to legal representation in trials before the Sessions Court. It does not give the assisted person the choice of counsel and does not visit the violation of the right with serious consequences. The Code of Criminal Procedure 1973, does not provide for the right to legal aid in other criminal proceedings or at any of the other stages of the criminal justice process including arrest and pre-trial detention. The prison manuals too do not reflect any such right of the incarcerated person to legal aid either by way of representation, advice, or assistance at different stages. This failure to acknowledge the right of an indigent person to legal aid at all the stages of the criminal justice process as an enforceable fundamental right results in the denial of an effective access to justice.

In criminal proceedings, where the person accused is in danger of losing life and liberty; where the procedures of evidence and rules of practice are mystifying and make it imperative for the person to be represented by a competent lawyer; and where the economically and socially marginalized person may be unable to engage a lawyer and thus be placed in an unequal position against the state; the denial of the right to legal aid by way of representa-tion may tantamount to a conviction without trial, a position that is anathema to the fundamental norm of the rule of law. This gets further compounded by the denial of legal aid to persons who are preventively detained or charged with economic offences or with offences like gambling, dealing in alcohol or offences that are punishable only with fine. This irrational exclusion militates against another norm of criminal law—the pre-sumption of innocence.

The principal statute concerning legal aid, the Legal Services Authorities Act 1987 (LSAA), and the rules and regulations there under, do not also provide an effective right of legal aid in the criminal justice system.

LEGAL SERVICES AUTHORITIES ACT, 1987

By confining the entitlement of a person to legal aid to filing or defending a case, the emphasis in the Legal Services Authorities Act, 1987 (LSAA), has remained on litigation-oriented assistance.[4] The LSAA creates a network of legal services institutions at the state, district and *taluk* levels. However, the institutional model of legal services delivery envisioned by the LSAA has its limitations.

(a) The manner of their constitution, the structure, the funding and the functioning of the legal aid institutions involve a pervasive control by the executive and a co-optation of the judiciary for a collaborative venture. The lack of autonomy of the legal aid institutions challenges their ability to mount a credible challenge to the laws, policies and practices of the state that may result in deprivation or violation of fundamental rights including the right of access to justice. This also questions the ability to maintain the independence of the judiciary vis-à-vis the executive.

(b) This also has a negative fallout from the point of view of the assisted person. Legal aid institutions are part of the institutions of the state and subject to state control. In effect, those requiring legal assistance have little participation in designing the legal services programme or in overseeing its implementation. As in many similar state administered welfare programmes, the 'consumers' are disabled from demanding quality of services or accountability of the legal aid bureaucracy. This explains, in part, the reluctance on the

---

[4] Legal Services Authorities Act, 1987, section 12, confines entitlement to legal assistance to those filing or defending a case.

part of the indigent person to look to legal aid for a reliable defence in a criminal trial.

The Rules and Regulations under the LSAA, which detail the structure and contents of the legal aid schemes in the different states, fail to account for the factors that led to the failure of the earlier schemes. For instance:

(a) they do not recognize the facets peculiar to the criminal justice system that require a different approach to the question of providing legal aid; barring a few exceptions, there is no system in the states and union territories for making legal assistance available at police stations, magistrates' courts and prisons;

(b) the preventive and rehabilitative aspects of legal aid are not built into the programme; legal aid invariably begins and ends with court proceedings and is not made available at the pre-trial and post-trial stages; further, the legal aid needs of the victims of crime are not accounted for;

(c) the problems of the criminal justice system are not addressed in a composite manner; the present schemes do not view the need for legal reforms as having to be simultaneously undertaken with the implementation of the programme for legal services;

(d) legal aid committees are not charged with the responsibility of initiating moves to reform the system of monetary bail, to question arbitrary laws and procedures that discriminate against the poor, or to provide legal aid at all stages of the criminal process from the point of arrest till after the person exits the system;

(e) they offer few incentives to the competent lawyer to participate in the legal services programme—whether in the matter of preparation of panels of lawyers, or in fixing of fees payable for legal aid work or in developing certain measurable minimum standards of performance—they also do not encourage the participation of a wider base of legal service providers like paralegals, law academics and students;

(f) there is hardly any mechanism for evaluating the scheme with a view to examining its relevance to the needs of the people requiring legal assistance.

Thus, we have a situation where despite the existence of the LSAA and the network of legal aid institutions:

(a) a large number of persons get routinely arrested, including those who are arrested for keeping peace and good behaviour, others for activities unconnected with crime such as those picked up as the wandering mentally ill and vagrants; and having thus entered the system are unable to exit it for want of legal assistance;

(b) custodial violence, including deaths, torture, disappearances and encounter killings are on the increase;

(c) a substantial number of indigent defendants are unable to post bail or furnish monetary bonds and sureties and therefore, languish in jail despite being arrested for bailable offences or even after grant of bail in non-bailable ones;

(d) defendants in criminal trials involving loss of life or liberty go unrepresented; this position continues in the further stages of appeal, revision and review;

(e) an indigent defendant is not always assigned a competent lawyer; nor when she is assigned a lawyer have a choice of lawyer; further, she cannot repudiate the services of an ineffective or incompetent lawyer; legal aid is generally not available in prisons and other custodial institutions; meanwhile the number of deaths in prisons is on the increase; prisons are overcrowded and inmates subjected to continuing violations of human rights; and

(f) many jail inmates are unaware about the status of their case, the availability of legal aid; about their right to receive legal assistance at all stages of their case and for preparing mercy petitions, seeking remissions and parole.

In their operation, the legal services programmes under the LSAA and its subordinate legislation have been unable to envision effective access to justice.

STATE INTERVENTION AND DIVERSION OF PURPOSE

State intervention in legal aid through the LSAA has shifted the focus of the legal aid programmes from the persons in need of assistance to the institutions in which they are located. Two features, relevant to the criminal justice system, demonstrate this. The first is the principal activity of the legal aid institutions under the LSAA—organizing *lok adalat* for both civil and criminal cases pending in courts. The term 'lok' adalat is perhaps a misnomer since there is little involvement of the people in the actual decision-making process. This distinguishes lok adalats from the traditional modes of mediation and informal dispute resolution mechanisms. The reasons offered for persuading the litigant to participate in the lok adalat—delay, prohibitive costs and uncertain result—acknowledge the failure of the justice delivery system.

A second feature has been the co-option of legal aid institutions and legal aid lawyers in holding criminal courts inside jail premises. In sittings held periodically as part of the legal aid programme, petty criminal cases involving offences punishable with short sentences of three years and less are sought to be disposed of in bulk. At the hearing, legal aid lawyers appear for the accused but go along with the object of quick disposal of the cases by encouraging guilty pleas. The prospect of immediate release after being sentenced to the period of detention already undergone, is enough of an incentive to an accused to admit to guilt. The institutions of the LSAA thus help deal with the problem of pendency of criminal cases where the period of detention undergone by the accused without a trial can exceed the maximum sentence that would normally be awarded if the accused was convicted at the end of a trial. This manner of disposal does not answer the demand of the accused for a fair just and reasonable procedure but perhaps answers the need to preserve the legitimacy of the legal system that is beleaguered by lack of infrastructure and resources.

Therefore, it does not come as a surprise that the legal services that are presently available are poorly utilized. The reasons could be general lack of awareness of the availability of legal aid, the belief that a person who gets help for 'free' is disabled from demanding quality service and thirdly, the disinterestedness of lawyers and legal aid administrators in providing competent legal assistance. Resultantly, there has been a poor utilization of the funds available for legal aid.

Unlike the committees that examined the issue in 1973 and 1977, the state no longer views legal aid as constituting a tool for reform of the legal system and as being integral to it. Neither in the planning for improving the substantive and procedural content of criminal laws[5] nor in the efficient working of the

courts[6] does the need to provide legal services to the poor form an important component. Legal aid is seen as a welfare measure to which the recipient has no 'right'.

On the other hand, there has been a failure by the state to reconcile the conflicting approaches to the problem of controlling the increasing crime rate while at the same time ensuring fair trial standards. The concern with the former has led to enactment of more criminal laws that hand out severe punishments, and make it impossible to obtain bail. The consequent increase in the under trial population strains the judicial and prison systems and further increases the scope for human rights violations of those incarcerated. While this imposes a disproportionate burden on the legal services programme, it increases the workload of legal aid institutions to initiate law reform (by challenging harsh laws that violate fundamental rights) and institutional reform (by making penal custodial institutions accessible and accountable in their functioning). Ironically, the state does not see the need for legal aid as being essential to preserving the legitimacy of the coercive legal regime of the state. Nor does it acknowledge that legal aid is itself a human right, which in turn is the tool for enforcement of other human rights. The delineation by the Expert Committee in its 1973 Report of the core principles that comprise the concept of legal aid need to be recapitulated and revisited:

The *spiritual essence* of a legal aid movement

---

[5] The questionnaire issued by the Malimath Committee had only one, open-ended, query on legal aid that asks the respondent to suggest improvements. The Committee, in its Report, expressed an unrealistic expectation that the Bar would 'voluntarily extend free legal services in criminal cases to prevent the indigent accused being made the exclusive responsibility of the government', 'Report of the Committee on Reforms of the Criminal Justice System', March 2003, p. 251. It

also recommended provision of legal services to victims of crime, ibid., p 271.

[6] Appendix 1, for the note of the member of the Eleventh Finance Commission on the scheme for fast-track courts. There is no mention in the scheme about providing lawyers to indigent accused and how cases of unrepresented accused would be dealt with. The emphasis is evidently on 'fast' trial and not 'fair' trial.

consists in investing law with a human soul; its *constitutional core* is the provision of equal legal service as much to the weak and in want as to the strong and affluent, and the dispensation of social justice through the legal order. The *political thrust* of the movement is that if legality lets down the masses and protects, in actual working, only the upper bracket, anti-law will become a way of life of the numerous poor, the people being prone to seek justice in the streets in preference to the law in the courts.[7]

HUMAN RIGHTS AND LEGAL AID

The annual reports of the National Human Rights Commission (NHRC) as well as the statistics brought out every year by the government in the form of 'Crime in India' reports, point to the increasing state violence including deaths in custody, torture in custody, illegal detentions, disappearances and encounter killings. The process of enforcing accountability for crimes by the agents of state is cumbersome and unsatisfactory. A combination of 'good faith' clauses in statutes that empower the state to curtail the liberty of the citizen[8] and the requirement of prior sanction of the government for prosecuting a delinquent public servant[9] has meant that policemen enjoy impunity in the way they deal with suspects. The extraordinary laws that have been enacted to purportedly deal with serious crimes dispense with basic protections built into the Code of Criminal Procedure, 1973–the presumption of innocence, the right of silence, the right against self-incrimination. While on the one hand, they acknowledge the inability of the regular criminal laws to deal with the situation they also encourage state

violence without accountability. These situations also imperil the independent functioning of courts and lawyers. This calls for greater need for legal assistance in invoking the legal processes and to question state action. Legal aid institutions, clothed with powers and obligated to perform their statutory duties, can play a critical role in providing avenues to access the justice processes, which are otherwise beyond reach in such extraordinary situations.

PIL AND LEGAL AID

PIL was evolved as a tool by the judiciary in response to, *inter alia*, the large scale denial of access to justice to the under trials jailed for a long time of years. PIL facilitated the transcending of the legal aid programmes from providing procedural rights to ensuring the protection and enforcement of substantive rights. PIL was in this sense, a non-conventional response to the failure of legal aid in the formal legal system. In the later years, however, PIL shifted its focus from those requiring legal aid to the problems of the judiciary as an institution. Absent a challenge to the laws and processes that deny effective access to justice, legal aid might well be a legitimation of the coercive criminal justice regime by merely providing procedural, formal, justice. There is then a need to bring the focus of the PIL movement to where it originated–the problems of access to justice within the criminal justice system. PIL can help to focus on the problems of access to justice in the area of interaction of law and poverty.

POVERTY, LAW, AND LEGAL AID

Beggars, the wandering mentally ill and sex workers continue to be governed by laws that criminalise their activities. They are viewed as 'status offenders' and brought within the

---

[7] 1973 Report, p. 10 (emphasis added).

[8] Prevention of Terrorism Act, 2002, section 57, is one instance.

[9] Code of Criminal Procedure, 1973, section 197.

criminal justice system from which they find it impossible to exit. Many of them are incarcerated for reasons wholly extraneous to the purpose of the laws that are used to govern them. That many of them are socially rejected and economically disabled, compounds the problem. The non-availability of legal aid to this constituency at each of the stages that they traverse in the criminal justice system exacerbates the denial of access to justice.

The problems of these constituencies of the law being brought within the criminal justice system do not end with their being released from it. Since they have already been rejected by their families and the society, they find it impossible to reintegrate into society. Long years of incarceration have also denuded them of their ability to survive. The impossibility of performance of conditions placed on the status offenders before they can remain free of the long arm of the law is evident. For a vagrant to be asked to find regular employment as a condition for release is to impose an unbearable burden.

For women, the rules of the prisons and places of custody refuse to recognize their autonomy and make their rehabilitation depend upon acceptance by their families. The rehabilitation potential of women in prostitution in any occupation that is both remunerative and beyond the twilight zone of illegality and immorality that is represented in the ITPA, is unquestionably low. This problem is properly within the domain of legal aid since it is the failure by the state to provide it that leads to the successive violations of the law and the rights and liberties of the individual. The legal services programmes have not begun even to acknowledge this constituency as being in need of legal assistance. This constitutes a large unmet area of legal services.

LAWYERS AND LEGAL AID

Unlike civil litigation that lends itself to a variety of dispute resolution mechanisms that can dispense with the role of a lawyer, criminal law litigation continues to be rooted, except marginally, in the adversarial mould, involving forensic abilities and complex rules of evidence. The presence of the lawyer is integral to a just fair and reasonable procedure in the criminal justice system.

The impetus to get lawyers to participate in legal aid has had to come, not from the legal profession, but from the state. Over the years, the legal aid programmes in several states have experimented with providing counselling by lawyers, visits by them to jails and prisons and providing legal representation in courts. Nevertheless, the working of the schemes has not encouraged participation of lawyers with any degree of commitment. The fees payable to lawyers have also been unrealistically low and have dissuaded competent counsel from offering legal aid.

The legal services programmes have been largely structured without accounting for the realities concerning the position of the lawyer in the criminal justice system. The role of the lawyer, outside of the state sponsored programme, in providing legal aid in cases involving human rights violations has not been adequately accounted for. Their role in bringing forth PIL, in the early years of its development, on behalf of under trials and convicts has also not merited sufficient acknowledgment. It may not therefore be right in attributing the lack of involvement of lawyers in the state sponsored programmes only to lack of motivation.

What was perhaps required was to provide for more than one model of legal services delivery involving the participation of lawyers.

In other words, legal services programmes could employ a combination of the duty solicitor and public defender models, along with the judicare model in seeking to reach the large 'unmet area' in need of legal services. The experiences in other countries where such a combination has been tried out can be usefully adapted to Indian conditions.

II. MODELS OF LEGAL SERVICES DELIVERY: LESSONS FROM OTHER COUNTRIES

Providing legal representation in criminal cases continues to be the principal form of legal aid. The types of representation that are prevalent in the Indian criminal justice system, and which are common to the four countries surveyed, are:

(a)   the judicare model,
(b)   the *pro bono* system, and
(c)   the *amicus curiae* system.[10]

Given the extent of the 'uncovered' area and 'unmet' need of legal services, a combination of these models, as is being mooted in the UK, requires to be tried out. For instance, in serious cases involving offences punishable with imprisonment of over seven years, the judicare model could be adopted. For cases involving capital sentence, a combination of a senior and a less experienced counsel may have to be provided.

What has not yet been tried, except once (and that unsuccessfully) in Kerala in 1978, is the public defender or salaried lawyer model. Under this system, lawyers work full-time as legal aid counsel and are paid a fixed sum as salary. The public defender model has been tried and tested in the USA and is being sought to be introduced in the UK largely on account of its cost efficiency. Although concerns have been expressed in the USA about the institution of public defender, in terms of effectiveness and independence, it may be a mode worth emulating since the Indian situation would require a combination of approaches. The salaried model may work well in the disposal of petty cases involving large numbers of individual defendants, involving similar circumstances and not requiring complex trials. It may also work well in cases that may be disposed of by a summary procedure. Care should be taken to ensure that competent and committed persons are chosen and that they should be paid salaries on par with government advocates.

The questions of quality and of choice require to be addressed. This lends assurance to the person assisted that the right of access to justice is not a formal but a substantive right. It should be possible, in consultation with the legal profession, to evolve standards on the lines of those developed by the American Bar Association in the context of the public defender programme. The criticism, that standards need to be evolved in advance and not wait to be evolved on a case by case basis, holds good for the Indian scene as well.

On the lines of the proposals now mooted in the UK, it should be possible to offer the indigent defendant a choice of counsel at least in those cases involving serious consequences for life and liberty, e.g., cases involving the death penalty.

The duty solicitor scheme, which has been tried and tested in the UK can also be adapted. It may serve the criminal legal aid system in India well, particularly in the areas of poverty law and legal aid. The reasons for the failure

---

[10] For details of the judicare system see below; *pro bono* is work done by the advocates voluntarily for the public good; *amicus curiae* or friends of the court are advocates appointed by the courts in individual cases.

of the earlier attempts need to be analysed in order to design a model that would suit the present needs. The presence of duty counsel at police stations might serve a dual purpose. It could act as a deterrent to custodial violence and it might also help in enforcing accountability for state action. Thus, it could perform a crucial preventive role.

With a view to expanding the legal service provider base, the South African model which accommodates paralegals, law academics and law students is capable of being adapted to the Indian context. In the area of poverty, law and legal aid, this could provide the necessary back-up service to the legal aid lawyer. Thus, paralegals and students could be deputed to visit custodial institutions to ascertain the details of the inmates in need of legal assistance and provide inputs to the lawyer for the case in the court.

The overview of legal aid and the criminal justice system in India points to the lack of an effective right of access to justice. Nevertheless, it offers opportunities and challenges to push for that elusive transformation.

III. OTHER ISSUES

The push for the transition from a formal declaration of the right of access to justice to an effective right has to account for certain other factors as well. Some of these are set out below.

STATE SPONSORED LEGAL AID

The debate on state intervention in the area of legal aid requires to be noticed only to reiterate the continued need for it in the context of criminal legal aid. The principal criticism in the USA of the concept of free legal aid to the poor has been from the law and economics school of which the principal exponent is Richard A Posner. He argues that the value that people place on legal services is in fact far less than they do on other essentials like food and clothing and that the state would rather not 'waste' the money involved in providing free legal services.

According to Posner, many poor people may be able to get along well enough without a lawyer, either because they are fortunate enough to cope with them unaided by a lawyer. But since the lawyer is free, they will use him unless the value of his service exceeds the (often-slight) value of their time in dealing with him. Faced with an excess demand for his time, the lawyer will try to limit his services to those whose needs for legal service seem most acute. Since this requires a difficult judgment, there are bound to be many cases where a poor person receives legal services that cost $100 but are worth only $50 to him. The waste involved in the use of the lawyer in these circumstances would be avoided if poor people were given $100 instead of free lawyers. They would use the $100 to hire a lawyer rather than to buy food, medicine, education, or housing only when the value of legal services to them was at least $100.[11]

This criticism ignores the fact that intangible benefits accrue to an indeterminate class of persons on account of class action litigation brought on their behalf. It drastically reduces the costs of litigation that would be involved if each one of them were to individually litigate the same cause.

According to Roger Cramton, arguments concerning the efficiency of the program fail to reflect the benefits provided to poor people when small claims, uneconomical to litigate individually by any claimant, are pursued

[11] Posner, Richard A, *Economic Analysis of Law*, Little Brown and Company, second edn, 1977, p. 355.

systematically on behalf of several persons as a class. One of the great advantages of the program is that substantial benefits accrue even to those who are not represented. To the extent that legal rules and procedures are modified in favour of welfare recipients, consumers, tenants, and other classes, everyone in the class, even those not eligible for free legal services, is benefited.[12]

Another criticism is directed at prison condition class action suits by legal services programmes which, it is alleged, 'pit the interests of the law-breaking against the law-abiding poor'.[13] It is also alleged that legal aid in reality benefits the lawyers and not the poor.[14] The counter to this is that 'access to courts is not just another social or welfare benefit, but an issue that goes to the moral tone of a society and the legitimacy of its institutions. Belief in the priority of the rule of law is a view not confined to lawyers'.[15]

While acknowledging that one should not over-estimate the capacity of legal aid to the poor to produce changes in the general social or economic status, Roger Cramton points out that there are both political reasons (increased respect for the law) and economic reasons (improved efficiency in the dispute-resolution process) that justify provision of services whose cost may often exceed what a middle-class litigant would pay for the services.[16]

He points out that 'representation of the poor often reduces the workload of government agencies by putting the claims of poor people into a comprehensive form so that they may be handled easily and cheaply'. Even if the increased costs exceed the savings, the government's compliance with the rule of law enhances its legitimacy, which is itself of substantial value. Further, 'in a society that values the dignity of the individual, the role of legal services in helping the poor to help themselves must remain the basic justification'.[17]

An even more powerful justification, rooted in the very legitimacy of the legal system, was provided in 1963 in the USA by the Allen Committee which studied poverty and the administration of criminal justice. It pointed out that:

...the survival of our system of criminal justice and the values which it advances depends upon constant, searching, and creative questioning of official decisions and assertions of authority at all stages of the process. It follows that insofar as the financial status of the accused impedes vigorous and proper challenges, it constitutes a threat to the viability of the adversary system.[18]

---

[12] Cramton, Roger C, 'Why Legal Services for the Poor?', *Journal of the American Bar Association,* vol 68, May 1982, pp. 550, 553.

[13] Isaac, Rael Jean , 'War on the Poor', *National Review,* 15 May 1995, pp. 32, 36: 'This is because the costs of implementing the improvements imposed by the courts are extremely high, absorbing scarce city and state dollars that could otherwise go to public services benefiting the law-abiding poor. Worse, these suits dump large numbers of felons back into the community, where the poor become their chief prey.'

[14] Attributed to Stephen Chapman as quoted in Cramton, Roger C, 'Why Legal Services for the Poor?', *Journal of the American Bar Association,* vol. 68, May 1982, pp. 550, 553.

[15] Ibid., p. 553.

[16] Ibid., p. 554. This is echoed by Richard Abel who argues that: 'Just as the criminal justice system finds it far easier to process accused who are represented by counsel, so legal aid lawyers serve to weed out unqualified welfare claimants, remonstrate with those who cause trouble, and get all the papers in order'; Abel, Richard, 'The Paradoxes of Legal Aid', in *Public Interest Law,* Jeremy Cooper and Rajeev Dhavan (eds), Basil Blackwell, 1986, pp. 379, 384.

[17] Ibid, p. 554.

[18] 'Report of the Attorney General's Committee on Poverty and the Administration of Criminal Justice',

The issue of legitimacy of the system touches upon the question of the relevance of legal aid for the poor. They are reluctant to engage with the system, much less avail of legal aid, for a variety of reasons, some of which require recounting.

'HIDDEN' AND OTHER COSTS

One disincentive for a person to avail of legal aid offered is the problem of uncompensated costs that have to be incurred. Legal aid schemes do not account for the 'hidden' costs incurred by those brought involuntarily into the system either as victims or as accused. While the legal aid programme may pay for court fees, cost of legal representation, obtaining certified copies and the like, it usually does not account for the bribes paid to the court staff,[19] the extra fees to the legal aid lawyer,[20] the cost of transport to the court, the bribes paid to the policemen for obtaining documents, copies of depositions and the like or to prison officials for small favours.[21] Legal aid beneficiaries do not get services for 'free' after all.[22]

At the end of a long litigation, where the person emerges innocent, he is not awarded the costs of the litigation.[23] Thus, the amount of time and money spent on establishing

---

cited in Solomon, Harold, 'This New Fetish for Indigency: Justice and Poverty in an Affluent Society', *Columbia Law Review*, no 66, 1966, pp. 248, 252; Cohn, EJ, 'Legal Aid for the Poor', *Law Quarterly Review*, no 59, p. 256 who argues: 'the state is responsible for the law. That law again is made for the protection of all the citizens poor and rich alike. It is, therefore, the duty of the state to make the machinery work alike for the rich and the poor'.

[19] For a study pointing to corruption prevalent in the district and subordinate courts in Delhi, see Rajan, VN, and MZ Khan, 'Delay in Disposal of Criminal Cases in the Sessions and Lower Courts in Delhi', New Delhi, Institute of Criminology and Forensic Science, 1982. The authors point out (p. 42): 'It was seen that those who greased the palm of the readers and peons were able to get adjournments readily while others waited outside the court helplessly to those who were unwilling to part with money, these court officials were not prepared even to tell whether the presiding officer would come and the cases would be heard or not'.

[20] Sait, Siraj, 'Save the legal aid movement', the *Hindu*, 29 June 1997, 'What is galling is that many sleazy lawyers who get legal aid cases tell the poor victims that if they want result they must pay them extra over what the Tamil Nadu Legal Aid Board pays them'.

[21] Chadha, Kumkum, *The Indian Jail: A Contemporary Document,* New Delhi, Vikas Publishing Pvt. Ltd., 1983, p. 31, where she talks of the system of a 'setting' for various tasks involving the prisoner having to depend on the jail official in Tihar Jail in Delhi: "A minimum 'setting' even for the official to *consider* the request is Rs 500." (emphasis in original); Chambliss, William, 'Epilogue: Notes on Law, Justice and Society', in *Crime and the Legal Process,* William Chambliss (ed.), New York, McGraw Hill Book Co, 1969, points out at p. 421: 'When a police force or an entire legal system is found to be engaged in a symbiotic relationship with professional criminals, the cause of this unfortunate circumstance is seen as residing in the inherent corruptibility of the individuals involved.'

[22] Singh Sujan, *Legal Aid: Human Right to Equality,* New Delhi, Deep and Deep, 1998, p. 272. An empirical study of the working of legal aid schemes in Punjab showed that beneficiaries of legal aid complained that 'they were provided only the services of a counsel and nothing beyond' and that they 'had to spend amounts varying between Rs. 100 to 900 for their cases in lower courts'.

[23] This is certainly an anomaly in the Code of Criminal Procedure, 1973, which remains unrectified. Even where the acquittal is in the Supreme Court, before which the prisoner has been in custody for over ten years, the court does not award the appellant the costs of the litigation: eg, *Arjun Marik* v. *State of Bihar* (1994) 2 Supp SCC 372; *State* v. *Nalini* (1999) 5 SCC 253. The latter case saw 19 of the 26 accused acquitted of all the serious charges by the Supreme Court eight years after they had been arrested and kept in custody throughout without a single day's bail and a part of the time on death row with the sentence of death hanging over them. No costs were awarded.

innocence remains unrecoverable and non-compensable. Equally, it is a loss to the victim of the crime and to the taxpayer whose money has gone into funding the entire prosecution exercise. There are other disincentives too.

LEGAL SYSTEM AS OPPRESSOR

Even an ideal mix of a legal aid programme may have to overcome obstacles before it can attract consumers. This may be on account of a variety of factors: distrust of the legal system including its processes and institutions which are mystifying, alienating and intimidating; distaste of lawyers and courts as they seem imposing and authoritarian; seeing the whole legal process as of nuisance value resulting in irreversible consequences, an uninvited 'trouble' that has to be got rid of.

There is a need to acknowledge that those who are economically and socially disadvantaged regard the entire legal system as irrelevant to them as a tool of empowerment and survival. Since it operates to oppress and disempower them, they have to devise ways of avoiding it rather than engage with it. Without fundamental systemic changes, if legal aid attempts at getting people to engage with the system, however promising the results may seem, it is bound to be viewed with suspicion.

The economic stakes for those currently working the system to suit their ends is too high to permit any meaningful change that can threaten their source of living. As demonstrated by Hernando de Soto in the context of Lima, the parallel system, which started as a by-product of the formal system, has for long been the only system with which the police, the lawyers, the judiciary and the litigant are prepared to readily engage.[24] For the last of the groups mentioned, the engagement with the criminal justice system as an accused is not a matter of choice. For others, it becomes a source of additional means of livelihood. The attitude towards maintaining the status quo, therefore, gets firmly entrenched. This constituency has also managed to use the existing system for their own benefit. There exists a system of pre-paid legal services for those involved in organized crime rackets and other 'criminalized' trades. Professional beggars are able to engage lawyers and obtain bail for those made by them to beg in the streets; they are also able to arrange for sureties and bonds through professional bondsmen. Likewise, brothel owners have a set of lawyers who appear for the girls picked up from a brothel, obtain bail and arrange for bonds. Those who remain in the penal custodial institutions are invariably the ones who are not part of the established trade and therefore, cannot afford the cost of engaging professional legal services or arranging for sureties. This indeed demonstrates how 'violators' are able to organize themselves better and engage with the system to the mutual benefit of the police, the court staff, the lawyers and themselves.[25]

Thus, the mere provision of legal services may not alter the way in which the poor are treated within the criminal justice system, without fundamental changes in the behaviour of the personnel manning the institutions that

---

[24] de Soto, Hernando, *The Other Path,* New York, Harper & Row, 1989. This seminal work could form a model for initiating a study of the working of the criminal justice system. This might reveal the actual costs involved in several stages of the system.

[25] Interviews with Jaishree Suryanarayanan, lawyer working with AAA on 25 November 2001 (in relation to the practice of the professional beggars) and S Vallinayagam, advocate, on 26 November 2001 (in relation to the practice by the brothel owners in Chennai).

comprise the criminal justice system.[26] It must be noticed in this context that although non-state legal systems may not be the most appropriate to deal with complex criminal law issues, they continue to be relevant to a majority of the rural masses in the country, to whom the formal legal system remains alien and oppressive.[27]

The need for law reform as an integral part of the larger legal aid agenda, particularly in the law and poverty context, cannot be over-emphasised. While legal aid cannot claim to solve the problems of the legal system or of the poor, it can initiate law and institutional reform, prevent abuse of power and violations of rights and ensure equal access to justice.[28]

It can 'make the rule of law a dependable ally of the weak and liaison between the statute book and the deprived'.[29]

The general apathy towards the poor, and the problems of providing legal aid to them, is perhaps rooted in the perception that, "those who fail deserve condemnation for their failure rather than assistance from its consequences. Aid, if granted, is merely a matter of 'grace' or 'charity', dispensable welfare which also serves the giver's psychic needs".[30]

The continued criminalization of activities of the poor only exemplifies the truism that 'law is an important mode of symbolic communication of community value judgments'.[31] While it certainly poses challenges to those who believe in equality of the law and equal protection of the law, it provides an opportunity to demonstrate that 'adequate resources allocated to the entire defence of impoverished accused persons-from the station house to final release - may well lead to greater realism and less mythology about crime and criminals'.[32] Legal aid schemes will require to pay special attention to persons brought

[26] Chambliss, William, 'Epilogue: Notes on Law, Justice and Society', in *Crime and the Legal Process,* supra n. 21, p. 422: 'So long as the agencies and individuals who administer the criminal law must enter into extralegal relationships with criminal and non-criminal segments of the population in order to function efficiently as organisations, and to the extent that these relationships interfere with the operation of the law as it is supposed to function, then the hiatus between the legal process and the expressed goals of the criminal law must persist. An alteration of these circumstances can only be brought about by changing those features of the legal system which lie at the root of the problem.'

[27] For an illuminating account of the conflict between the state and non-state mechanisms in the context of a criminal trial arising out of the death of a young woman in a village in Gujarat, see Baxi, Upendra, 'Popular justice, participatory development and power politics: The *Lok Adalat* in turmoil' in *From People's Law and State Law: The Bellagio Papers,* A Allot and G R Woodman (eds), Foru Publications, 1985, p. 171.

[28] 1973 Report, p. 16, 'Legal aid cannot be a substitute or a panacea for the ills of our system of justice. It can be a watchdog, it can be a catalyst, it can spur research and reform but it cannot reach every injustice, every client, every cause. Nevertheless we believe that a commitment to legal and procedural reform is a key element of legal aid, as is its commitment to assistance in litigation and advice, and machinery for both must be implemented.

It must dedicate itself to being a movement of reformation'.

[29] Ibid., p 10.

[30] Solomon, Harold W, 'This New Fetish for Indigency: Justice and Poverty in an Affluent Society', *Columbia Law Review,* no 66, 1966, p. 256.

[31] *Ibid,* p. 269

[32] Ibid., p. 271. The Allen Committee on poverty and administration of justice in the United States, in its report made a strong case for research on an inter-disciplinary basis in order to 'reflect increasing concern for the operative context of criminal and anti-criminal behaviour, the means by which social values are perceived by legal institutions, the open confrontation of the theoretical ingredients of the functional system, and the need for supplying the principles for rational decisions in both the promulgation and administration of sanctions'.

within the criminal justice system not for committing crimes, but for being poor.

IV. OUTLINE OF A PLAN OF ACTION FOR LEGAL AID IN THE CRIMINAL JUSTICE SYSTEM IN INDIA

To begin with, a few caveats would be in order. The outline is based on information that is available, which is essentially about the main parameters of the criminal justice system. A critical input that is not however available is the costs involved in the exercise. Hence, suggestions are not attempted regarding the possible funding pattern of legal services.

The breakdown scenario of the criminal justice system may be recapitulated. On an average, 50 lakh crimes, are registered every year which are sought to be investigated by a police force of 13.2 lakh. The pendency of criminal cases in the subordinate courts is in the region of 1.32 crore and the effective strength of judges is 12,177. The number of undertrials whose criminal cases are pending is 1.44 crore and of these, over 2 lakh are in prisons. Around 63 lakh persons get arrested every year, and over 2500 are victims of custodial violence including deaths and torture in police custody. On an average, the courts are able to dispose of only 19 per cent of the pending cases every year. The budget for legal services is in the region of three crore a year for all the sates and union territories and other legal services committees in the country. Much of this amount remains unutilized. Of what is utilized, no accounts of expenditure are yet available.

CONSTITUTIONAL AND LEGISLATIVE CHANGES

The right of an indigent person to legal aid at all stages in the criminal justice system still awaits declaration as an enforceable fundamental right. The statutes, including the Code of Criminal Procedure, 1973, the LSAA and the prison manuals will then require amendment to reflect this declaration.

In investing the right to equal treatment before the law with meaning, Article 22(1) of the Constitution would need to be amended to provide for the right of a person preventively detained to legal assistance of his choice, and of an indigent person so detained to free legal aid in all legal proceedings including those before the advisory board.

The LSAA will have to incorporate the entitlement of all indigent persons, including those in custody, complainants and victims of crime, witnesses, claimants for maintenance and those having to file or defend a case, to legal aid-not only by way of representation but by advice, counselling and other forms of assistance. Legal aid needs to be expanded to be made available to inmates of all custodial institutions including prisons, protective homes and corrective institutions under the ITPA, juvenile homes, beggar homes and mental asylums. Criminal cases, should not be required to satisfy the *prima facie* test, if the rule of presumption of innocence is to be preserved and the right to equality fostered.

PROVIDING LEGAL SERVICES AT ALL STAGES

The core of the legal services programme would have to be the provision of legal services at all stages of criminal proceedings. Inevitably, lawyers would be at the epicentre of the programme. The systems of *pro bono* and *amicus curiae* require to be supplemented by a combination of the following systems.

Judicare System

Private lawyers would be hired by legal services committees in individual cases, as happens at present. They would be engaged in serious cases, i.e., where the offence is punishable with imprisonment of more than seven years. Where the offence is punishable with death, a combination of a senior and junior lawyers would have to be assigned to the case. However, the principle of equality and equal representation of the accused, would mean that they be paid fees on par with government lawyers. They should be empanelled after satisfying qualifications of a certain minimum years of experience in dealing with criminal cases.

The defendant ought to be permitted a choice of lawyer from among those empanelled, and be permitted to change counsel on showing sufficient cause. No defendant in a criminal case ought to be convicted or sentenced without being represented by a lawyer.

Public Defender System

It could be experimented with in the form of pilot projects in the magistrates' courts. The system could be extended elsewhere if the pilot shows encouraging results. It would be important to develop, in consultation with the legal profession, standards for evaluating the performance of legal aid lawyers.

Duty Solicitor System

It could be implemented to begin with, as a pilot project, in a few select police stations and magistrates courts. Duty solicitors will also be required to visit prisons and other custodial institutions. The evaluation of these pilot experiments should decide the adoption of the system to cover all police stations, magistrates' courts and prisons.

AWARENESS, RESEARCH AND EVALUATION

The experience with the legislation criminalizing the offence of untouchability demonstrates how the existence of the law need not result in a change in social equations.[33] The inability of those whom the law is meant to empower to invoke its processes for a variety of reasons, principally the fear of reprisal from the upper castes, has underscored the need to spread awareness of the existence of the law as well as provide legal assistance in invoking its processes.[34] This manner of awareness generation must form one of the principal tasks of the legal services committees established at various levels of administration.

Research is required to be undertaken, on the lines of the Manhattan Bail Project, into the impact that the criminal justice system, its practices and institutions have on the lives of the poor. There is very little feedback on how the poor perceive the laws, the legal system and the personnel they encounter within it. This will help examining the relevance that the system has to the lives of the poor. It would be a vital input in any attempt at law and institutional reform. An important part of this effort would be to try and simplify the language of the law, demystify its processes, enable people to understand and question the law and reconstruct it in a manner that would subserve their purpose.

OTHER PRINCIPAL ACTIVITIES OF THE LEGAL SERVICES COMMITTEES

One of the key activities of the legal services committees which has remained unrecognized and lain neglected, is the initiation of law and institutional reform litigation, particularly in the context of laws that criminalise the activities of the poor. Thus, it is important to question the validity of vagrancy laws, the

---

[33] Naval, TR, *Law of Prevention of Atrocities on the Scheduled Castes and the Scheduled Tribes*, New Delhi, Concept Publishing, 2001.

[34] Scheduled Caste and Scheduled Tribes (Prevention of Atrocities) Rules 1995, rule 9.

justification for the insistence on monetary bail bonds and sureties irrespective of the capacity of the accused, the functioning of penal custodial institutions that hold vagrants, mentally ill, sex workers and women and children in prison-like conditions. PIL and test litigation would continue to be a strategic arm of the legal aid movement.

Legal services committees could experiment with working on the pattern of neighbourhood law offices. They would be located in the community and employ a few lawyers as well as other legal service providers belonging to different disciplines on a full time basis. Such offices would coordinate with other agencies including the police, the courts and the human rights institutions. They would depute panel lawyers or paralegals or law students to visit police stations, prisons and other custodial institutions to ascertain the details of those in need of legal assistance and help set the legal processes in motion. They would also act as advice centres that could be accessed at anytime of the day.

In the context of the marginalized sections whose activities are criminalized, including the wandering mentally ill, the vagrants and the sex workers, the committees would have to assist in devising schemes for rehabilitation and lobby with the government for their implementation.

In the context of the legal aid needs of convicts including those on death row, the committees would need to depute lawyers to assist in the preparation of petitions of appeal, remission and pardon as well as follow up with the courts and other authorities. Legal aid for questioning the decisions of prison authorities regarding discipline and punishment also

needs to be acknowledged within the programme, and be made available.

TRANSPARENCY AND ACCOUNTABILITY

The structure and functioning of legal aid bodies must encourage their being approached by those in need of legal assistance. There should be a constant review and assessment of the programmes and plans to ensure their continued relevance to those they are meant to serve. The committees should have members who would represent the interests of those being assisted and participate in the devising and administration of legal services programmes. There ought to be an audit of the working of the committees to ensure transparency and accountability.

V. CONCLUSION

The import of a legal aid programme will have to stand its test against the constitutional imperative of equality before the law and equal protection of the laws. Where yawning economic and social disparities segregate the disadvantaged sections into areas of criminality and illegality and further disable them from engaging with the processes that enmesh the criminal justice system, legal aid can provide the buffer that, at least, in part, mitigates the consequences of such inequalities. By expanding its reach to include informed challenges to discriminatory laws and practices, legal aid asserts itself as an ally of the poor and creates for them a vested interest in the law. Legal aid attempts to make the law work for the poor and not against them. It remains an essential instrument in the transformation of equal access to justice from a formal to an effective right.

Laws Relating to Crimes in India

B.B. PANDE

I. INTRODUCTION

Criminal procedure law is integrally related to deviance/crime and the existence of a predictable and pre-determined substantive criminal law system that lays down the precise elements of liability and diverse sanctions ordained by the law. However, all crimes, whether petty or serious, are required to be processed through certain legally ordained procedure, right from the initial move of lodging information about crime down to determination of guilt and the imposition of appropriate sentence. Thus, every crime passes through distinct stages, technically known as investigation stage, prosecution stage, trial stage, sentencing stage and post-sentence prisonization/correction age. The functions of different stages are performed by exclusive criminal justice functionaries such as the police, prosecutors, judges, defence lawyers, prison and correctional officials. In addition to the aforesaid functionaries, the witness, the accused and the victim also play a vital role in constituting the criminal justice system.

The criminal procedure laws can be grouped under either of the two major systems, namely, the adversarial/accusatorial system (prevalent in common law countries) and the inquisitorial system (prevalent in continental countries). The adversarial system treats the accusing party (the prosecution) and the defending party (the accused) as adversaries and the judge as a neutral umpire, who hands down a verdict after examining the evidence and ensuring the pleas of both the parties. The judge is bound by strict rules of relevancy/admissibility, presumptions and burden of proof provided by the evidence law. Unlike this, the inquisitional system that aims at 'search for truth' treats the prosecution, the defence and the judge as three parties to the 'search' or inquest. Here the finding of the judge is not a verdict but a revelation of truth in the matter. The judge enjoys much greater freedom to take into account social facts coming from formal or informal sources to arrive at a conclusion of 'guilt'. The Indian adversarial system is characterized by a presumption of innocence of the accused, a clear-cut separation of investigative, prosecutorial and judicial powers and a heavier burden of proof on the prosecution. Equally significant is the reliance placed on the rules of evidence, which on non-compliance can read to inadmissibility of evidence or the vitiation of the trial itself. In view of special relevance for the present discussion we propose to discuss the three key issues, namely: (i) the concept of crime in the substantive law; (ii) criminal procedure-salient factures, and; (iii) evidence law in criminal trials in the following pages.

II. CONCEPT OF CRIME UNDER SUBSTANTIVE AND PROCEDURAL LAWS

CRIME

There is no word in the whole lexicon of legal and criminological terms which is so elusive of definition as the word 'crime'. Yet an understanding of the meaning of the word is of central importance to the study of the making and breaking of law and to the justification and measurement of punishment.

CRIME ACCORDING TO LAW

One way of exploring the resonances of the word is to consider the different contexts in which it has been used. In law and jurisprudence, for example, crime is defined as those acts or omissions which are specifically proscribed by law. This proscription, however, always involves sanctions or punishments and it is this connection between crime and its punishment that has remained the key element in the lawyers' concept of crime.

For Sir James Stephen (1829-1894), whose *History of Criminal Law* (1883) gave the standard legal view of the time, crime was, 'some act or omission in respect of which, legal punishment may be inflicted'. From this definition we must infer that the criminality of an act is defined in an important way by the punishment which follows it. It is for this reason that the age and state of mind of the offender must be taken into consideration. If, for example, a person is killed or injured by another, the killing or injury would not be criminal if the aggressor were too young, too deranged or too weak-minded to form the kind of evil intention that would render him liable to punishment. For lawyers, then, crime is a concept whose necessary elements are proscribed action, evil intention, and prescribed punishment. This is the stuff of legal argument and decision-making in the courts. It also fixes the definition of crime firmly in the person and the intention of the criminal. There is no crime without a willing criminal.

There are certain acts which the large majority of civilized people look upon with disapprobation, as tending to reduce the sum total of human happiness, which is the ultimate aim of all laws. These we call wrongs, such, for instance, as lying, gambling, cheating, stealing, homicide, etc. The evil tendencies of these acts widely differ in degree. Some of them are not considered sufficiently serious for law's notice. These we only disapprove. We call them mere moral wrongs. Moral wrongs are checked to a great extent by social laws and laws of religion. There are other more serious wrongs which the law takes notice of, either:

(a) for punishment, i.e., infliction of pain upon the wrong-doer, or;

(b) for indemnification, i.e., for making good the loss to the person injured by the wrong.

Wrongs dealt with under the first head are called crimes, those under the first head are called civil injuries.

According to Blackstone, crimes are public wrongs and affect the whole community; Civil injuries are private wrongs and concern individuals. Public and private wrongs are, however, not exclusive of one another, for what concerns individuals, must necessarily concern the community of which the individual is a unit, and similarly everything that affects or concerns the community, must also concern and, affect the individuals that form that community.

According to Austin, an offence which is pursued at the discretion of the injured party and his representatives is a civil injury; an offence which is pursued by the sovereign and his subordinates is a crime. This is a distinction not of substance but of procedure, and so far as the Indian criminal lawyer is concerned, there are a number of offences which cannot be pursued except by the injured party. These lie on the borderline between crimes and civil injuries. For the true basic distinction between crimes and civil injuries we must look to the principles upon which civilized communities have selected some wrongs for retributive and others for remedial justice. I do not think in any country any principles were definitely laid down before making the selection, but this itself does not negative the existence of the principles. We often act in accordance with principles without being conscious that we are so acting. The general agreement of civilized countries, as shown by the result of the selection, strongly points to the existence of common principles leading to common results. It is only by a process of analytical reasoning that we can get at these principles.

CRIME AND SIN

Among moralists there has been some attempt to construct a relationship between acts or omissions which are contrary to accepted religious or moral teaching and acts or omissions which are proscribed by secular law. From this attempt there has grown up a huge and confusing literature on 'crime and sin'. This is an important aspect of any study of the meaning of crime but its interest is historical rather than epistemological. The evolution of moral feeling and moral systems

is on a different historical time-scale from that of any system of secular legislation. It is easy to chart the passage from crime to non-crime of attempted suicide, homosexual acts or adultery; it is also possible to give some social explanation for the change. We cannot synchronize with these short-term movements the long sweeps of continuity and evolution in whole systems of religion or morality. For some time now, the arguments on this matter have been regarded as of interest only to philosophers and therefore, largely academic.

CRIME AS DISEASE

The late 19th and early 20th century saw the development of a new theory of criminal behaviour and thus a new definition of crime. It was thought of as a disease, not in the body politic, but in those who committed criminal acts as they were legally defined. Murders, thefts and robberies were committed by men and women who were abnormal in body and in mind. Crime was a function of their 'diseased' or 'defective' condition.[1] This theory, although it began as an explanation of criminal behaviour, provided an analogy that was comforting and easy to assimilate. Crime was like a disease. It appeared non-randomly among the weaker, more defective of the human race, but its threat could be contained because disease was curable or at least treatable. Such a definition need not incorporate the legal niceties of intention and malice. It could accommodate the notion that the very commission of a wrongful act itself justified intervention—a notion that lawyers call 'strict liability' and apply to a few, very special offences. Therefore the connection between crime and punishment, so vital to legal rationalizations, need not be made.

[1] Lombroso, 1836-1909.

CRIME IN THE CONTEXT OF SOCIAL ORGANISATION

The consideration of crime as a function—or a malfunction—of social organization itself allows for many different kinds of definitions which can be tailored to suit the needs of Marxists, Durkheimians, the Chicago School, followers of Edwin Sutherland and many others. These definitions, however, are vague about the phenomenon of criminal behaviour itself. Is it any breach of the law which attracts punishment? Is it an attempt, deliberate or unintentional, it frustrates the social and political rules that others accept? Is it any kind of behaviour that can be used as an excuse for excluding certain classes and kinds of people from participation in the social activity of the community? Whatever the contention of these definitions, the notions that they describe do not separate the ideas of crime and punishment. If anything, they emphasise the importance of punishment in the same way that lawyers do. It is the sanction which lays bare and defines the crime.

CRIME AS A SOCIAL PROCESS

One of the many other attempts to unravel the strands that are woven into the notion of crime begins with a consideration of the whole process of definition. Here it may be helpful to return to the analogy of crime as disease, if only to see how the process of crime-making begins. Disease has no existence until it is complained about or discovered. Many people may be suffering from kidney disease, bilharzias or fibrositis, but until they complain about their symptoms or are recognised to be exhibiting symptoms, their disease does not exist.

So it is with crime. Victims of offences which have the characteristics of robbery, rape or burglary may not wish to make any complaint of what they have suffered. If these incidents do not come to light in any other way, by police activity, for example, or by the reports of witnesses, they remain without formal definition as crime. In effect, crime does not exist. Calculations of the extent of this non-existent crime can be made where there are studies of victim response to what might be called criminal behaviour. A further stage in the process of crime creation is the acceptance or rejection by law-enforcement agencies (mostly the police) of reports of crime. There is extensive evidence in the USA and some evidence in this country that a sizeable proportion of reported offences never reach the official statistics.

This last notion of crime, therefore, has to do with a series of interactions—the reaction of the victim to the assault upon him or upon his property and the reaction of the police both to reports of what may be criminal acts and to offences they may discover for themselves. There is a final stage in this process which may be of less importance—it is the decision of magistrates, judges or juries that there are not the ingredients of crime in the offence that is described to them.

All these definitions of crime are part of the texture of the complex social and political organizations within which such human activity is devised, organised, controlled and defined. Legal definitions are neither so restrictive nor so inapposite as they seem, for they find a place for sanctions and limit their use. Moral definitions point to deep and long-held beliefs that may colour some of our perspectives on crime and punishment. Medical and social explanations and analogies contribute to the definition of crime. They also point forward to the consideration of criminal activity as a social process by which its existence and recognition depend upon the reactions of victims and law enforcement agencies almost as much as upon the perpetrator of the act which comes to be labelled a crime.

III. ANALYSIS OF CRIMES AS DEFINED IN THE INDIAN PENAL CODE, 1860

The Indian Penal Code, 1860 (hereinafter 'the Code') gives full effect to the doctrine of *mens rea* in two ways. In the first place, the chapter on General Exceptions, which controls all the offences defined in the Code as well as all offences under special and local laws, deals with the general conditions which negative *mens rea*, and thereby exclude criminal responsibility. Under section 6, "throughout this Code every definition of an offence, every penal provision and every illustration of every such definition or penal provision, shall be understood subject to the exceptions contained in the chapter entitled 'General Exceptions', though those exceptions are not repeated in such definition, penal provision or illustration".

A large number of cases having thus been excluded from the category of crimes, every offence is carefully defined so as to include in the definitions the precise evil intent which is the essence of a particular offence, as well as the other necessary elements of it. If these definitions are analysed they generally comprise the following principal elements:

(a) A human being.
(b) An intention on the part of such a human being to cause a certain consequence considered injurious to individuals or to society, and which for the sake of brevity we call an evil intent (*mens rea*).
(c) A willed human action (*actus reus*).
(d) The resultant evil consequence.

In cases where the intended consequence is not injurious by itself, but is injurious in conjunction with certain other facts, a further element is added, viz.,

(e) A knowledge of the existence of such facts.

As to (a)—a human being—it is indicated by the use of the word 'whoever' with which the definition of every offence begins.

As to (b)—the evil intent—it is indicated generally by the use of such words as intentionally, voluntarily, fraudulently, dishonestly, malignantly, wantonly, maliciously, etc. As already mentioned, intention has reference to consequences of acts rather than to acts themselves. A question that naturally follows is how it is then that these words denoting different intentions are generally used as adverbs qualifying verbs which are supposed to indicate acts viz., intentionally joining an unlawful assembly (section 142), intentionally preventing service of summons (section 173), intentionally omitting to attend in obedience to summons (section 174), intentionally omitting to produce a document (section 175), intentionally obstructing sale of property (section 184), intentionally omitting to assist a public servant (section 187), intentionally giving false evidence (section 193), intentionally omitting to give information of an offence (section 202), intentionally omitting to apprehend an offender (sections 221 and 222), intentionally offering resistance to lawful apprehension (sections 224, 225, 225A and 225B), intentionally offering insult (section 228), intentionally causing to be returned as a juryman (section 229). This mode of expression at first creates the impression that 'intentionally', 'dishonestly' and other words of the same class have not been used as they ought to be, to refer to consequences of acts. This impression is mainly due to the fact that we are accustomed to regard verbs as indicating merely acts. But most verbs, whilst indicating acts also indicate the consequence of those acts. Transitive verbs from their very nature cannot be confined to mere acts, for they are defined to be verbs expressing actions which pass from the agent to an object. To explain what I have said: obstructing sale of property, intentionally offering insult, is equivalent to doing an act with the intention of causing the consequence indicated by the words 'obstruction' or 'insult'. Intentionally causing hurt is to do an act, the effect of which is to cause hurt. Intentionally to kill a person is to do an act, the effect of which is to cause death. Death is, therefore, the consequence of that act. It is hardly necessary to multiply these instances. Intentionally joining an unlawful assembly, intentionally omitting to attend in obedience to summons, intentionally omitting to assist a public servant, intentionally giving false evidence, are all susceptible of the same explanation

There are a few cases where words indicating intention are not used in defining an offence. But these are either cases where the acts with their consequences are so hurtful to the state or to society that it has been deemed just and expedient to punish them irrespective of any intention to cause those consequences, or cases where the acts themselves are of such a character that they raise a violent presumption that whoever willed the act must have intended the consequences. Waging war against the Queen (section 121), sedition (section 124A), kidnapping and abduction (sections 359-363) are examples of the former, counterfeiting Queen's coin (section 232) is an example of latter.

There is, as mentioned earlier, between the intention and the act, a will which determines the movements that constitute the act. It is a subconscious mental process assumed in every definition and in most cases a necessary inference from the act itself. The inference is only negatived where the act is shown to be caused by force, compulsion or accident, or under other circumstances indicating the absence of this will and these special cases are among others excluded by the provisions of the chapter of General Exceptions, and are consequently not repeated in the definition.

As to (c)—the act willed—this is an essential element in every offence even where it is an incomplete offence such as an attempt. It is with the commencement of the act that the offence emerges from mind to matter. If the act willed has not taken place completely or partially there is no offence, for, as noted earlier, the law does not punish a mere evil intent so long as it has not led to some overt act. Whilst it is an offence to hurt a person or to forge a document, it is not an offence merely to intend to cause hurt or to commit forgery. There are, however, some offences which do not seem to contemplate any particular acts but merely punish an existing state of things, but these are special cases, and if closely examined, are not exceptions to the general rule. The existing state of things in such cases only indicates an antecedent criminal act where we reason from effect to cause, e.g., possession of an instrument for counterfeiting coin or possession of stolen articles, all indicate an antecedent criminal act.

As to (d)—the resultant consequence—it is not always necessary that the 'intended consequence should take place. Sections 216A, 217 and 263 are instances in point. The man who harbours a robber or dacoit with the intention of facilitating the commission of a robbery or dacoity (section 216A) cannot plead in defence, that as a matter of fact, no robbery or dacoity took place or that his action did not facilitate such robbery or dacoity. Where, however, the happening of the intended consequence is an essence of an offence, the non-happening of it would reduce the offence to a mere attempt to commit it.

The intended consequence is sometimes innocent by itself and becomes nocent only by reason of the existence of other circumstances. Sometimes the existence of these other circumstances only aggravates the offence. In these cases the definition after describing the act adds 'knowing or having reason to believe, etc.' These special cases bring in the element referred to under (e).

Sometimes the immediate consequence of an act is either not harmful or is less harmful than the remote consequence, and the happening of the latter is either a necessary condition of an offence or is only an aggravation.

IV. CRIMINAL PROCEDURE— SALIENT FEATURES

The criminal procedure law sets out standards for pre-trial processes, such as receiving information about crime, interrogation, arrest, remand, bail, recording of vital evidence during investigation and charge-sheet, and trial processes, such as taking cognizance by courts, framing of charges, summoning witnesses, recording evidence, hearing arguments, judgement, pre-sentence hearing and passing of sentence.

The current law of criminal procedure is based on the new Code of Criminal Procedure, 1973, which was enacted with the following three considerations in mind:

(i) 'Due process' consideration;
(ii) 'Speedy disposal' consideration;
(iii) 'Fair deal to poorer sections' consideration.

The new code has incorporated several

provisions that aim at achieving the aforesaid considerations. However, despite this new and progressive code, there are several aspects on which our criminal procedure is found lacking, both in matters of the normative framework as well as their implementation. There are several apex court rulings that have to some extent offset the shortcomings of our criminal procedure and raise the implementation to the constitutionally ordained standards. These need to be closely studied as an important aspect of criminal procedure text.

Certain vital aspects of criminal procedure can be highlighted in terms of the significant stages in the formal journey of a criminal case that are commonly described as: (a) the stage of investigation, (b) the stage of trial (c) the stage of sentencing and (d) the post-sentence stage of prisonization.

THE STAGE OF INVESTIGATION

The raw reality of crime comes within the ambit of formal criminal justice system only when some aggrieved party conveys information about it (under section 154 in case of cognizable offence and section 155 in case of non-cognizable offence) or the police coming to know about crime through their own sources (section 157). On receiving information regarding crime the police is empowered to undertake investigation in case of cognizable offences straight away, but it has to wait for a direction from the magistrate in cases of non-cognizable offences.

In the course of investigation, a police officer can examine witnesses[2] and take statements from them.[3] But no person would be bound to answer questions that can expose him to a criminal charge or to a penalty and

[2] Indian Penal Code, 1860, sections 160 and 161.
[3] Ibid., section 162 .

no statement made to police is required to be signed,[4] or used in any way in the trial stage.[5] The only evidence recorded in the investigation stage that can validly go to the trial stage is the confession or statements recorded in terms of section 164. Where the investigation cannot be completed within 24 hours, the law provides that the person can be remanded in police custody (maximum for 15 days) and judicial custody under section 167 of the Code. On completion of investigation, the police submit a charge sheet in terms of section 173, with which investigation stage comes to an end. Since investigation is treated as purely an executive or police stage, the law favours total non-interference by other agencies. The highest courts have repeatedly upheld the executive's discretion in their rulings on the point.[6]

(i) The Power to Search, Seize and Arrest

A significant attribute of the power to investigate is the power to search premises, seize incriminating material and to interrogate and arrest suspected offenders. Indian law accords very wide powers of arrest to police in cases of cognizable offences and in other situations that the officer deems fit.[7] Such wide powers are largely responsible for many cases of abuse and excesses.[8] The Supreme Court has recently declared that every incident of arrest may involve justified or unjustified interference with the liberty of the citizen,

therefore, certain safeguards like right of the arrested person to have at least one relative or friend be informed about his arrest and place of detention, recording of date and other details of arrest in the diary of arrest be enforced.[9]

(ii) Anticipatory Bail and Bail after Arrest

The law guarantees to every arrested person the right to be informed about the grounds of arrest and the right to bail.[10] There is also a right to get medically examined (section 54) and produced before a superior officer and a magistrate within 24 hours of arrest (sections 56 and 57).

Bail is a remedy that is available to a person to be set at liberty pending trial. The law classified for this purpose offences in the bailable and non-bailable categories. (The first Schedule to the Code provides a list of such categorizations). In cases of bailable offences bail is a matter of right (section 436), and the arrested person or his relative has to seek this right before the appropriate court. In the cases of non-bailable offences (section 437) bail is strictly a matter of discretion of the court and whenever the court is convinced that the grant of bail would not affect the administration of justice adversely it can grant bail.

Under Indian laws, a person having reasonable apprehension of being arrested shortly can seek bail in anticipation or an anticipatory bail, which is the outcome of judicial creativity. The Code of Criminal Procedure 1973 has accorded statutory recognition to anticipatory bail under section 438, which has been recognized as a powerful

[4] *State* v. *Teja Ram* (1999) 3 SCC 507.

[5] Indian Penal Code, 1860, sections 161(2) and 162.

[6] *Assistant Director Enforcement* v. *A.K. Bajoria* (1998) 1 SCC 52; *M.C. Abraham* v. *State of Maharashtra* (2003) 2SCC 649.

[7] Indian Penal Code, 1860, sections 41, 42, 43, 44 and 151.

[8] Dunkel, *et al.*, *Waiting for Trial.*

[9] *Joginder Kumar* v. *State* (1994) 4 SCC 260; *D.K. Basu* v. *State* AIR 1997 SC 610.

[10] Indian Penal Code, 1860, section 50.

tool for fighting political vendetta through the process of law. But in view of the possibilities of its serious interference with the power to investigate and control crime, many states have preferred to suspend the application of this provision in their jurisdictions.

(iii) Release on Remand and Limitation on Pre-trial Detention

Section 167(1) confers power to remand on the production of the production of the accused person within 24 hours after arrest before the magistrate. The power, on the one hand, enables the executive to get the accused on remand for the purposes of investigation, and protects the accused by his physical presence before the magistrate and limiting the period of remand detention to 60 days (for minor offences) and 90 days (for serious offences), on the other. Thus, where investigation in not complete (filing of charge sheet) within the specified aforesaid periods the detained accused has a right to be released on bail.

THE STAGE OF TRIAL

The second important stage in the criminal procedure is the trial or judicial proceedings in which the important function of guilt determination is performed by a magistrate or court. For the purposes of trial the Code has classified offences into summons case and warrant case (a warrant case is a case relating to an offence punishable with death, imprisonment for life or a term exceeding two years). Equally crucial for trial purposes is the hierarchy of criminal court constituted in terms of the Code (section 6 of the Code) in each state as follows:

(i)   Court of Sessions;
(ii) Judicial Magistrates of the First Class or Metropolitan Magistrates;

(iii) Judicial Magistrates of Second Class; and
(iv) Executive Magistrates.

The aforesaid courts function within assigned territorial divisions and commensurate, their sentencing powers. The Court of Sessions can pass any sentence authorized by law, but sentence of death passed by it is subject to confirmation by the High Court. The Chief Judicial Magistrate can pass a sentence up to seven years imprisonment. A Magistrate of First Class can pass a sentence not exceeding three years and fine up to Rs. 5000. A Magistrate of Second Class can pass a sentence up to one year and fine up to Rs. 1000.

Criminal proceedings in each case have to be initiated in the Court of Magistrate of First Class only and even in respect of offences for which the Court of Sessions has original jurisdiction, the case will reach the court after committal proceeding in the Magistrate Court.[11] On forming an opinion that there is sufficient ground to proceed, the Magistrate shall commence proceedings by issuing summons or warrants to the accused to attend the appropriate court.[12] The criminal cases can be subject to either of the four kinds of trials, namely: (a) sessions trial; (b) warrants case–trial by Magistrate (d) aummons case–trial by Magistrate (d) summary trial. At the trial stage the following two rights of the accused deserve special mention.

(i) Right Against Double Jeopardy

Section 300 of the Code provides that a person once tried by a competent court for an offence or convicted or acquitted of such offence shall, while such conviction or acquittal remains in force, not be liable to be tried again for the same offence nor on the same fact for another

---

[11] Ibid., sections 190 and 193.
[12] Ibid., s 204.

offence for which charge could have been framed at the time of first prosecution. The provision is somewhat similar to constitutional guarantee contained in Article 20(2) that reads: 'No person shall be prosecuted and punished for the same offence more than once'. The underlying idea of these provisions is that the accused ought to be protected against undue harassment through the criminal process.

(ii) Right to Legal Aid

Article 22(1) of the Constitution guarantees to every accused right to consult and be defended by a legal practitioner of his choice. This right has been given a special and elaborate treatment in sections 303 and 304 of the Code that not only recognise a right to be defended by a lawyer of choice but also a right to legal aid at state expense, where the accused is not a person with sufficient means. The right to legal aid was accorded additional support by the constitutional amendment in 1976 that introduced Article 39A, that makes it obligatory for the state to secure equal justice to all and provide free legal aid by suitable legislations or schemes. The Supreme Court has accorded constitutional recognition to free legal aid to poor to indigent accused and personal liberty under Article 21 of the Constitution.[13]

THE STAGE OF SENTENCING

After the commencement of the trial that leads to determination of guilt and conviction, the next vital stage is the sentencing stage. Sentencing, like trial is essentially a judicial function, which requires keeping in view the community views, the interest of the victim and the possibilities of socializing impact on the accused. The range of punishment is already provided in the substantive criminal law,[14] the actual sentencing involves the dishing-out of sentences in individual cases. The Code has express provisions that require the courts to follow reformative sentencing.[15] The following two issues in the sentencing stage deserve special mention.

(i) Right to pre-sentence hearing

The Code, under sections 235(2) and 248(2) has accorded statutory recognition to the right of the accused to be heard in matter of sentence. The courts have recognised this right as an attribute of the right to life and personal liberty under Article 21. A provision like this that gives to accused a say in the matter of sentence and bring out personal facts is very necessary for individualization of punishment. In recent times, the Courts have laid down guidelines to make the right meaningful.[16]

(ii) Pardon, Commutation and Remission of Sentences

Though the power of pardon is known as a prerogative power, it is in vogue even in the democratic societies like India. Such powers are enjoyed by the chief executive of the states (governors) and the Centre (the President), and also the states in their political capacity. The President and the governors exercise the power to pardon or commute in terms of articles 72 and 161 of the Constitution respectively. Though such power is based on subjective satisfaction, as the head of the states are supposed to be acting on the advice of the Cabinet, the power becomes subject to judicial review. In addition, the respective state governments also enjoy powers to remit and

---

[13] *Khatri (11)* v. *State* (1981) 1 SCC 627; *Suk Das* v. *State* (1986) 2 SCC 401.

[14] Indian Penal Code, 1860, ch III.

[15] Ibid., sections 360-61, and 354(3).

[16] *Malkiat Singh* v. *State* 1991 SCC (Cri) 976; *Shobhit Chamar* v. *State* (1998) 3 SCC 455.

suspend sentence,[17] and power to commute sentence.[18] But these powers are subject to the limitations introduced in section 433A, which fixes the minimum term of 14 years in the prisons in cases where life imprisonment is an alternative to death penalty. Such limitation has been held constitutionally valid by the Supreme Court of India.[19]

THE POST-SENTENCE OR PRISONIZATION STAGE

The post-sentence of prisonization stage brings into play the wide range of non-custodial and custodial measures. The most commonly deployed non custodial measure is probation release in terms of section 4 of the Probation of Offenders Act, 1958. Custodial sentences are executed in prisons constituted in terms of the national prison laws and state prison Acts and manuals. Prisons are used for safe and reformative custody not only of convict prisoners, but also of under trial prisoners who are remanded to judicial custody. Programmes for prisoners are underway in several prisons throughout the country.

V. EVIDENCE LAWS IN CRIMINAL TRIALS (A-LEVEL)

Past incidents are the concern not only of people connected with the law–lawyers, judges and police–but also of others like authors, historians, journalists and political commentators.

Authors, historians and journalists gather facts informally and exercise a fair amount of freedom in using them. The author's endeavour is circumscribed only by the requirements of logic and literary appeal. The

historian has to present the facts in the ruling or subaltern perspectives. The journalist focuses on sporadic incidents, usually of the immediate past.

The law person's source of facts as well as his ability to use them is considerably hedged by the legal framework that determines what kind of facts can be brought in, and for what objective.

The Indian Evidence Act, 1872, regulates the law persons' freedom to re-create events. These rules are based on common sense, logic and public policy. The courts– particularly the High Courts and the Supreme Court–have, in the course of applying and interpreting these rules, evolved a whole body of evidence laws.

EVIDENCE LAW RULES IN AN ADVERSARIAL SYSTEM

The Indian legal system is adversarial in nature. Unlike the inquisitorial system that is prevalent in countries like Germany, France, Sweden and Italy, the adversarial system is technical and rule oriented. It lays down, through clear statutory guidelines, the factors that are required to prove a fact in issue, the burden of the adversary party and the powers of the judge in drawing inferences. The key role assigned to a judge is reflected in provisions like section 3 of the Indian Evidence Act, 1872, (hereinafter 'Evidence Act') which defines the terms 'evidence', and 'proved'.

Evidence:
a) All statements that the court permits or requires... are called oral evidence.
b) All documents produced for inspection of the court...are called documentary evidence.

Criticality of Documentary Evidence

Though oral evidence (which comprises depositions made by witnesses before the judges,

---

[17] Indian Penal Code, 1860, section 434.
[18] Ibid., section 433.
[19] *Maru Ram* v. *State* AIR 1980 SC 217.

under oath and subject to cross-examination) has to be accorded primacy under the adversarial system, documentary evidence also plays a unique role in criminal trials.

Documentary evidence constitutes the first information report, *panchnama*, post-mortem report, case diary etc., and other material evidence such as the weapon of offence, blood stains, skin or hair samples, pieces of clothing or other objects connected with the crime. Such documentary evidence becomes a vital basis for re-constructing the incident and helps to substantiate the prosecution or defence's version.

However, since documentary evidence is mainly collected at the investigation stage, it is often influenced by the subjective bias or incompetence of the Investigating Officer (IO). It is, therefore, necessary for the media to check whether the correct documentary evidence is collected at the right time. For instance a prompt and comprehensive FIR not only mentions facts relating to the crime, but also includes strong clues relating to the offenders.

Proved

'A fact is said to be proved when, after considering the matters before it the court either believes it to exist…'.

Section 136 of the Evidence Act gives the judge the last say in matters of relevancy, and admissibility, the freedom of parties to adduce evidence or cross-examine and ask incriminating questions to the witness.

Yet another feature of the Indian adversarial system is that it maintains a clear demarcation between the fact or evidence required at the initial or the investigation stage from the facts or evidence at the trial or judicial stage. Immediately after the incident is reported to the police or it comes to the knowledge of the police, there is a process of gathering information about the incident and collecting all possible material evidence like the weapon, body, garments, shoes, etc. The police makes inquiries from parties who know about the incident. The day-to-day collection of information about the incident is compiled in the case diary. This *prima facie* (on first impression) evidence enables the police to determine whether or not the reported crime has been committed.

Once the investing agency is convinced that there is prima facie evidence about the commission of the crime, it will file a charge sheet. However, the facts or evidence contained in the police diary would not constitute evidence in court. It is excluded by virtue of section 162 of the Code of Criminal Procedure, 1973 (hereinafter 'Cr.P.C') that requires that for trial purposes the judge would require oral and documentary evidence afresh. However, certain evidence like a confession recorded by a Magistrate under section 164 of the Cr.P.C (that lays down elaborate procedure for recording of confession or a statement) and other material and documentary evidence can be used by the court.

Thus, the evidence law rules primarily relate to the trial stage. Before recording evidence at the trial stage, the judge frames charges and identifies the facts in issue.

Facts Must be Relevant

The facts of a case are determined in terms of the elements of the substantive laws. For instance, for the offence of culpable homicide (unlawful killing of a human being) the law requires: (a) death of a human being, (b) caused by the accused, (c) through an act or illegal omission, (d) with a guilty mind, in terms of the law.

The facts in issue would be: Did the death

occur in the course of the alleged incident? Did the accused cause the death? Did the accused cause the death with a guilty mind? Did the accused have any justification?

Since a variety of facts can be related to these facts in issue, the court cannot permit unlimited facts to be brought in. Evidence law resolves this dilemma by a simple common sense principle, which states that only such facts that are relevant to the facts in issue are to be permitted. Section 5 of the Evidence Act states: 'Evidence may be given in any suit or proceedings of the existence or non-existence of any fact in issue and of such other facts as are hereinafter declared to be relevant, and of no others'.

Sections 6 to 55 of the Evidence Act relate to different types of relevant facts:

(a) Fact logically near the issues in question (sections 6–16).
(b) Facts in statement form (sections 17–33).
(c) Facts that are part of formal or informal records (sections 34–44).
(d) Facts in the form of a third party or expert opinion (sections 45–51).
(e) Facts relating to character of parties (sections 52–55).

Of these 50 sections devoted to the issue of relevancy, certain categories of facts have special evidentiary significance.

The first category of relevant facts are those that occurred at the same time, place and can be described as an integral part of the transaction that is sought to be re-created. Such facts are described as *res gestae* (part of the same transaction facts) facts under section 6.

The immediate outer circle facts are made relevant under sections 7, 8 and 9. They constitute either the occasion, cause or effect of the fact in issue or which relate to preparation, motive or effect of the fact in issue or which

introduce, explain the fact in issue or establish time, place of the incident or the identity of the parties. Circumstantial evidence falls under these sections. Take the example of a murder in a train. Even if there is no direct evidence of crime, the fact relating to occasion (under section 7) that on the night of the murder the accused and the victim were travelling together, assumes importance.

Section 10 is a special relevancy provision relating to conspiracies. This provision creates an exception to the common sense rule that holds a person accountable for anything said, done and written by him alone and not by anyone else. Section 10 is based on the principle of agency, which treats every conspirator as an agent of another and makes fact coming in statement, action or written form from anyone between whom there is a prima facie conspiracy, as relevant. The general rule of relevancy gets extended only in cases of conspiracies. The only limitation imposed in this extended rule of relevancy is:

(a) The fact in stated, written and action form must come from any of the persons between whom there is a *prima facie* conspiracy.
(b) The fact must be in reference to common intention of the conspiracy.
(c) It must relate to a period when the alleged conspiracy subsisted.

In *Mirza Akbar* v. *King Emperor*,[20] the wife had confessed that Mirza Akbar had misled her into being unfaithful to her husband, the deceased, and that the accused had played a key role in getting him murdered. The Privy Council held that such a confessional fact would not be relevant in terms of section 10, because it was given after the conspiracy was

[20] (1949, Privy Council)

executed. The court laid down that only such statements are relevant under section 10, which are made during the period when the conspiracy is 'afoot'.

Admissions and confessions are another category of very important relevant facts. Rules relating to this category of facts are contained in sections 17 to 31. The distinctive feature here is that unlike the earlier category—which mainly relates to facts that centre around the acts or behaviour of parties and others or which relate to occasion, preparation or consequence of the event—this category focuses on spoken or stated category of facts, whose relevance lies not in the fact that a statement was made, but in the facts that relate to the contents or what was actually stated by the concerned parties.

For example, the fact that the accused made a statement or cried on being confronted after the crime may be a relevant fact under section 8. But if fact is adduced as to the contents of a statement or what is spoken, it may be relevant under section 17 either as an admission or a confession. Since by their very nature, an admission or confession implies a direct or indirect accepting of the fact in issue, the main evidentiary issue in such cases remains admissibility.

The three important rules relating to admissibility of confessions are contained in section 24 (inadmissibility of an involuntary confession), section 25 (inadmissibility of a confession to the police) and section 26 (inadmissibility of a confession in police custody). Section 27 lifts the ban on inadmissibility in such cases where the confessional statement is corroborated by the fact of discovery of independent material evidence.

Apart from admissions and confessions, yet another set of relevant facts are contained in sections 32 and 33. Section 32 (I) provides the rule of relevancy of a dying declaration. A dying declaration is an exception to hearsay rules, as it permits a third person to bring before the court a statement of a person who is dead. The statement must either give the cause of death or the circumstance in which the death occurred. The Supreme Court in *Kushalrao* v. *State of Maharashtra*,[21] has laid down that the dying declaration does not require corroboration and that, if otherwise found reliable, it has a high evidentiary value.

In the chapter of relevant facts the rules relating to opinion evidence or forensic evidence (sections 45 to 51) are unique, as they permit even third party or strangers to the incident to express their opinion. The sole aim of making opinion evidence relevant is to create space for scientific knowledge or expert opinion relating to incidents available to the judge. However, the expert evidence, be it that of a medical, fingerprint or fire arm expert, is never binding on the judge. But in view of the investigation agencies' growing dependence on scientific methods of detection through genetics and computers, there is a need to examine opinion or expert evidence.

The relevancy rules relating to character of parties, contained in sections 52 to 55, separate legal judgements from moral judgments. The underlying idea is that the past formal or informal assessments about a person should not influence the current trial, which must be based on facts that are found relevant and, admissible by the present court.

However, the character evidence provisions do create some serious anomalies: In rape cases, according to section 54, the previous bad character of the accused cannot be brought in. But, in terms of section 155 (4) the facts

[21] AIR 1958 SC.

relating to the previous immoral character of the prosecutrix can be brought in.

Facts Must be Admissible

All evidence that is admissible has to be relevant, but all relevant evidence is not admissible. The most notable and controversial admissibility rules relate to confessions to a police officer and confessions in police custody.[22] The rationale behind the inadmissibility of these is a blanket distrust of the police, which often leads to the exclusion of the best evidence. That is the reason why in certain special legislations like the Terrorist and Disruptive Activities Act, 1987 and the Prevention of Terrorism Act, 2001 (both now repealed), there is a reversal of such inadmissibility rules. Furthermore, the Supreme Court has also, by interpreting 'confession to police' as strictly those confessions where they are made in the physical presence of the police or at least to their hearing, limited the ambit of exclusion by virtue of section 25,[23] held that a confessional letter addressed to the S.H.O. and left by the side of the murdered person was not hit by section 25.

Inadmissibility based on public policy is reflected in the rules relating to privileged evidence—sections 121 to 129—coming from diverse sources. Three important categories of privileged evidence are those related to matrimonial communications, affairs of state, and professional communications.

Matrimonial communications are privileged and neither spouse can either be compelled or permitted to bring such communications before the court through their oral testimony. However, the Supreme Court has held[24] that there is no violation of the rule of privilege if the spouse hands over the evidence to a third party, who brings the alleged communications before the court.

Matters of privilege based on affairs of state are meant to protect unpublished state records from being disclosed. However, the courts have made considerable inroads into state privilege, and require all evidence to be produced at least for the examination of the court. In a famous case, *State of Uttar Pradesh* v. *Raj Narian*,[25] that challenged former Prime Minister Indira Gandhi's elections on grounds of abuse of state machinery—had involved adducing evidence from state records which were claimed as being privileged. The Supreme Court refused to grant absolute privilege, and ordered the government to let the court have access to the documents.

BEST EVIDENCE RULE

The idea of best evidence relates to a wide variety of rules that aim at securing the best possible evidence for constituting a standard form of proceedings in any legal trial. The rule is understood as:

i. *Direct, and not hearsay evidence must be given*

This rule implies that in the case of oral evidence only, the person who had actually observed the event should come forward to testify. He should testify to what he had personally heard, seen or felt.

ii. *Primary evidence is to be preferred over secondary evidence*

In case of documentary evidence, the original or primary evidence is to be preferred over secondary evidence, which might contain omissions and mistakes (Sections 60 and 64). Similarly, in certain cases documentary evidence must be preferred over oral evidence (Sections 91 and 92).

---

[22] Indian Evidence Act, 1872, sections 25 and 46.
[23] *Sita Ram* v. *State* 1966 SC.
[24] (*M.C Verghese* v. *T.J. Ponnan* AIR 1970 SC 1876.
[25] (1975) 4 SCC 428.

iii. *Generally evidence of statements, conducts and writings must be proved only against its maker*

This rule creates a prohibition against the use of evidence relating to one against the other, unless he or she is part of a conspiracy.

iv. *At times, circumstantial evidence may prove to be more reliable than the testimony of a witness*

This is based on an assumption that the circumstances do not lie, while the witness may act and testify according to his interest. However, even circumstantial facts come before the court through human testimony, which is subject to the same fallibility.

RULES REGARDING TAKING OF EVIDENCE

Once the quality of evidence is ensured, by passing it through the gates of relevancy, admissibility and best evidence pre-conditions, the next set of rules relates to the procedure for bringing the evidence before the court.

(i) Burden of Proof

The two opposing parties, in an adversarial system of trial, would obviously be interested in establishing their view point. For such substantiating and negating, the parties are required to undertake the burden of proving their case or disproving the other's case through relevant facts or evidence. The general rule for burden of proof is that the party making an allegation or presenting a plaint bears the primary responsibility of proving it. For instance, in a criminal case the state or the prosecution has the obligation or the primary burden to prove the allegation. The defense would assume the burden of proof only in respect to the plea raised by it. In criminal cases, the burden of proof for the prosecution is heavier because criminal jurisprudence is based on a presumption of innocence of the accused. However, in special legislation, the legislature can shift the burden from the prosecution to the accused.

(ii) Competence of Witnesses

All oral evidence comes before the court through witnesses. Any person who can understand events and communicate with the court, either through statements, signs or actions, is a competent witness. Even a child, who is mature enough to appreciate the nature of events, can appear as a witness. According to the Evidence Act, the sex of the witness does not affect his or her competence as a witness. This is an improvement over religious evidence laws, particularly the Islamic Evidence Law, which treated female evidence as having half of the value of male evidence. Also, there is no fixed number of witnesses required for proving any crime. The judge enjoys sole discretion of being satisfied by the witnesses. The witnesses can bring any facts before the court, subject to rules discussed earlier, and the opposite party is free to impeach the credit of the witness. Even in matters of impeaching the credit of the witness, the judge retains the last say and can either permit or prohibit the counsel from doing so.

Accomplice or Approver

In criminal trials, an accomplice or approver is a person who has earlier been a party to the crime but later turns a state witness to give testimony on the facts of the crime. Approver witness or approver evidence is vital in organised crimes, in which either no witnesses are available or they are too terrified to testify for fear of reprisals. Section 308 of the Cr.P.C allows the prosecution to select one or two approvers, on a promise of pardon and withdrawal from joint prosecution.

The evidentiary rules relating to accomplice or approver evidence are laid down in sections

133 and 114(b) of the Evidence Act. Section 133 lays down a rule of law that treats an accomplice as a compete witness and regards a conviction based on the accomplice's testimony as legal. However, section 114(b) incorporates a rule of caution that approver evidence is not creditworthy unless it is corroborated by independent evidence. Section 114(b) has, through judicial interpretations, almost become an independent rule of law, which in some sense claims superiority over the rule of law contained in section 133.

There was a time when the evidence of the prosecutrix in a rape case was treated as accomplice evidence, and was not considered credible. However, after realizing the fallacy of such a treatment, the law has undergone a substantial change in the area of prosecutrix evidence. The judiciary has done away with the rule of corroboration in the cases of prosecutrix evidence. More importantly, the legislature has introduced a strong presumption under section 114(A), according to which if the prosecutrix testifies that the intercourse was without consent, the court shall presume absence of consent.

(iii) Sequence and Examination of Witnesses

The process of the initial leading of evidence is known as the examination-in-chief, which has to be performed by the prosecution or the plaintiff side. The examination in chief involves presentation of the witnesses by the party that has made the allegation. After the examination-in-chief, the defense gets a chance to cross-examine each witness and lead its own witnesses. Then, the prosecution gets a second chance of re-examination. Since the presentation of witnesses and cross-examination has to be conducted in an open court and in the presence of the accused, often, in cases of

serious and organized crime, some witnesses are reluctant to give truthful deposition. In cases of serious crimes there is a need to undertake effective witness protection programmes.

RULES REGARDING DRAWING OF INFERENCE FROM EVIDENCE

The court enjoys a fair degree of freedom in matters of drawing inference from the evidence produced before it. However, the Evidence Act provides certain rules that guide the court in matters of drawing inference and entertaining evidence through the rules of presumption and estoppel.

(i) The Rules of Presumption

Presumptions are certain inferences based on common sense and natural course of events and ordinary human responses to them. For example, it can be presumed that a person who remains silent in the face of serious allegations against him, has something to hide. Since all the presumptions are not codified we can divide the presumptions into those of fact and law.

Presumptions of law or the statutory presumptions are those that are recognised under the Evidence Act and other laws. The Evidence Act recognises two categories of presumptions: rebuttable and irrebuttable presumptions. The former presumptions are further classified into 'may presume' and 'shall presume' types.

In the case of irrebuttable presumptions, the court 'must presume' or the matter is conclusively presumed. The parties are precluded from adducing evidence to rebut the presumption, and the court is bound to draw an inference that is indicated by the statutory presumption.

Apart from common sense, presumptions are sometimes based on public policy. The notable example of an irrebuttable presumption based on public policy is contained in Section 112 of the Evidence Act, which lays down that the court must presume that a child born during wedlock and within 280 days of dissolution of marriage, the wife remaining unmarried, is legitimate. The policy underlying this provision is that the law must presume every child to be legitimate and not permit parties to adduce evidence to dispute legitimacy.

(ii) The Rules of Estoppel

The rules of estoppel limit the freedom of the court and the parties in the matter of adducing evidence. The rule of estoppel can come into operation only where one party has represented a particular set of facts, which have inspired the other party to rely upon the represented facts and alter his position to his detriment. Under such a situation, the party that made the earlier representation is precluded from giving evidence against his earlier position.

The rules of drawing inference help the judge to arrive at a conclusion about the fact in issue and give finding regarding the proof or the disproof or the allegations. Often, the conclusion stage comes after the lapse of a considerable period of time, during which witnesses may fall ill, die or become unsure about their testimony due to loss of memory or confusion. Loss of such genuine witnesses not only limits the range of facts available to the court for arriving at a conclusion also impairs the quality of the judicial finding itself.

VI. CONCLUSION

Law is impersonal and distanced from reality, in terms of time and place. It looks for facts that have potential of technically recreating the event. Thus for the facts to be identified as the one's that will be used for recreating the past events depends upon the following.

First, they must appeal to the police that has to file a charge sheet after investigation. Second, they must be found to be adequate by the prosecution to initiate legal action. Third, the court must accept the facts as sufficient for determining the guilt and arriving at a conclusion of liability.

It is only after this that the raw facts become capable of technically recreating legal events. The gap between the real event and the legal event is bound to remain because the legal event is not a consequence of, but the cause for, subsequent legal action. In law, the successful enactment of the past events is the beginning of the story, not its end.

Offences Against Women

VED KUMARI

I. INTRODUCTION

Crime is a normal phenomenon and is found in all societies; what constitutes an offence varies, however, in time and space. Usually the crime is an act which is perceived harmful to society as a whole, and is declared to be an offence punishable by law. Offences can be classified in many ways depending on the purpose of classification. From the moral perspective offences are classified as *mala in se* (inherently wrong) and *mala prohibitia* (prohibited pursuant to some policy decision). In order to provide a stern punishment for a more severe crime they may be categorised by the nature of offence—serious or petty. They may be grouped together for laying down similar criteria for offences in that group like offences against human body, property, marriage, nation, currency, weights and measure and so on. Sometimes the special characteristics of the victims as a group, e.g., women, children, schedule caste and schedule tribe, etc., require differential treatment. Offences may also be divided by reference to their territorial application, being local or general. They are also categorized as general or special by reference to their impact on the general moral, social and economic fabric of the society. This chapter focuses on 'offences against women'.

While women can be and are victims of all offences that can be committed against men like murder, extortion, grievous hurt, etc., the term 'offences against women' is used to focus on those offences in which only women are the victims, e.g., rape, dowry harassment and dowry death, cruelty to married women, sati, child marriage, female infanticide, female foeticide, sex-pre-selection, sexual harassment at workplace, domestic violence, trafficking of women and girls, etc. Women victims of these offences are placed in a very peculiar situation compared to other victims. The shame and social stigma attached to rape victims is unparalleled by any other victim of any other offence. Even within the legal system a rape victim was treated with suspicion and almost at par with an accomplice and the burden of proof was on her to prove that indeed she had been raped. In case of other offences listed above, in case of those which take place within the four walls of their own homes, all the evidence is under the control of the accused. By applying the same principles and procedure, women victims were grossly victimised again by the legal system. Trafficking of women and girls is an organized crime across national borders and needs concerted efforts of all the countries involved to bring the offenders to book and to ensure the reintegration of victims back in society. Keeping in view these special circumstances, many changes have been introduced in the existent criminal laws (Indian Penal Code, 1860 [IPC], Code of Criminal Procedure, 1973 [CrPC] and the Indian Evidence Act, 1872 [IEA]), and additionally, some special legislations have been enacted to deal with these offences.

While the practices of sati and female infanticide were recognized during the colonial period and made into offences, the practice of dowry came to be recognised as an offence from 1961. Despite the legislations, these social malpractices continue and have found new dimensions. Scientific developments in the area of sex-determination and sex-selection techniques are being used now

Mathura Rape Case

Mathura was about 17 year old dalit girl who had eloped with her lover. Her brother lodged a complaint of kidnapping. Mathura, her lover, her employer and her brother were about to leave the police station after recording statements when one of the two constables present there stopped Mathura from leaving. She emerged from the Police Station only after the others waiting for her outside became impatient and started making a noise resulting in gathering of people. She told them that she has been raped by one of the constable and while the other who was too drunk to have sexual intercourse leered at her private parts.

The District Judge acquitted the appellants holding that Mathura had sexual intercourse while at the police station but rape had not been proved and that she was habituated to sexual inter-course, but finding that her employer and her lover would get angry with her, she had to sound virtuous before them. The High Court reversed the order saying that "we have to see in what situation Mathura was at the material time. Both the accused were strangers to her…. It is, therefore, indeed, highly improbable that Mathura on her part would make any overtures or invite the accused to satisfy her sexual desire…. she could not have resisted … on account of the situation in which she had found herself especially on account of a complaint filed by her brother against her which was pending enquiry at the very police station…. Mere passive or helpless surrender of the body and its resignation to the other's lust induced by threats or fear cannot be equated with the desire or will."

The Supreme Court restored the order of acquittal and said that no marks of injury were found on the person of the girl after the incident and their absence goes a long way to indicate that the alleged intercourse was a peaceful affair. Consent to sexual intercourse by a woman due to fear of death or hurt is vitiated under the relevant legal provision but the High Court did not give a finding that her fear was shown to be that of death or hurt, and in the absence of such a finding. the alleged fear would not vitiate the consent.

to abort the female foetus or to ensure that female foetus does not get implanted in the uterus in the first place. The 2001 census figures show a national ratio of 945 girls to every 1000 boys in the 0-6 year age group. In Gurgaon in 2005, the child sex ratio, that is sex ratio in the 0-6 age group, was 824 girls to every 1000 boys. It is a telling figure, indicating the need to take all measures necessary to save the girl child. The law makes it an offence to determine the foetus of the child as also the pre-selection of foetus. However, it needs much more than merely the law to change the perception and discriminatory treatment meted out to women by state and social systems.

Women became the prime focus of criminal justice administration in India when the insensitivity of the Supreme Court to rape victims, especially in custodial situations was highlighted in the popularly known *Mathura* case[1] (see box) by the 'Open Letter Written to the Chief Justice of India'.[2] Many women's organizations joined hands and created a national demand for change in laws relating to women. Even though significant changes had been suggested by the Law Commission in its 42nd Report on the Indian Penal Code submitted in 1971, no heed was paid to those suggestions till the uproar raised by the decision in the *Mathura* case. The Law Commission of India in its 84th Report (1980) on Rape and Allied Offences suggested several amendments to the existing provisions in the IPC, CrPC and the IEA in line with the suggestions in the earlier Report and the laws relating to rape underwent significant amendments in 1983.

Certain common features are found in offences against women. Ordinarily women find it difficult to report a crime, especially in case of rape or when it is committed by their family members. Even when they do so, police try to dissuade them to register such offences to 'protect them' from shame attached with being a victim of rape or to maintain family ties. When registered, many times the investigation is done in a tardy manner. The vital evidence in most cases is under the control of the accused—the offence having been committed within the four walls of a house—and often results in acquittal. Many a times women victims themselves give in to family pressure and either withdraw the complaint, or change their statements during trial. Even when it results in conviction, the punishment imposed is not commensurate with the nature of crime and the harm caused by it.

Keeping these aspects in view, the IPC, CrPC and the IEA have since been amended many times and some new laws have been enacted. These seek to provide equal protection to women victims of rape and other offences by creating different principles of criminal liability in such cases by facilitating reporting, investigation, trial and punishment. Usually the offence has been made cognizable, which means that the police can start investigation of such offences on its own motion—nobody is required to file a report or complaint. In grave offences against women, the burden of proof has been shifted to the accused. If certain conditions prescribed by law are proved to exist beyond reasonable doubt by the prosecution in such cases, the law lays down a presumption that the accused is guilty. It means that the burden to prove that he is innocent is on the accused. This burden, however is not as great as that on the prosecution because he has to merely create a doubt in the mind of the judge that he perhaps did not commit the offence. The accused need not prove his innocence beyond reasonable doubt. The law has also prescribed mandatory minimum sentences to be imposed if the accused is proved guilty in such cases though less than mandatory minimum sentence may be given for special reasons which need to be specified.

In this chapter, the legal provision relating to various offences against women have been

---

[1] *Tukaram* v. *State of Maharashtra* (1979) 2 SCC 143.
[2] Baxi, *et al.*, 'Open Letter to the Chief Justice of India', (1979) 4 SCC (J) 17.

described in simple language along with the special issues and aspects relating to that offence for better understanding of the problems faced by women in seeking relief in each case as well as the changes made in those cases to provide better access to justice to women. The first part of the chapter deals with the offence of rape, second with offences relating to marriage, third with offences against girl child, fourth with sexual harassment at work place, fifth with domestic violence and sixth with trafficking of women and girls.

II. RAPE AND ALLIED OFFENCES

The Law Commission of India in its 84th Report referred to rape as the 'ultimate violation of self ...a humiliating event in a woman's life which leads to fear for existence and a sense of powerlessness'. It is defined in section 375 of the IPC as sexual intercourse by a man with a woman:

First – Against her will;
Secondly – Without her consent;
Thirdly – With her consent, when her consent has been obtained by putting her or any person in whom she is interested in fear of death or of hurt;
Fourthly – With her consent, when the man knows that he is not her husband, and that her consent is given because she believes that he is another man to whom she is or believes herself to be lawfully married;
Fifthly – With her consent, when, at the time of giving such consent, by reason of unsoundness of mind or intoxication or the administration by him personally or through another of any stupefying or unwholesome substance, she is unable to understand the nature and consequences of that to which she gives consent;

Sixthly – With or without her consent, when she is under sixteen years of age.

Sexual intercourse with his wife above the age of 15 years is not rape. Rape of a wife between the age of 12–15 and a wife living separately under a decree of judicial separation is punishable with maximum of two years of imprisonment as compared to minimum of seven years of imprisonment extending to imprisonment for life or for ten years for rape. Rape of a minor under the age of 12, including a wife, is at par with gang rape, custodial rape and rape of a pregnant woman punishable with more serious punishment, that is, minimum of ten years imprisonment extendable to life.[3]

---

[3] Section 376. Punishment for rape.—(1) Whoever, except in the cases provided for by sub-section (2), commits rape shall be punished with imprisonment of either description for a term which shall not be less than seven years but which may be for life or for a term which may extend to ten years and shall also be liable to fine unless the woman raped is his own wife and is not under twelve years of age, in which case, he shall be punished with imprisonment of either description for a term which may extend to two years or with fine or with both:

Provided that the court may, for adequate and special reasons to be mentioned in the judgment, impose a sentence of imprisonment for a term of less than seven years.
(2) Whoever,
(a) being a police officer commits rape-
(i) within the limits of the police station to which he is appointed; or
(ii) in the premises of any station house whether or not situated in the police station to which he is appointed; or
(iii) on a woman in his custody or in the custody of a police officer subordinate to him; or
(b) being a public servant, takes advantage of his official position and commits rape on a woman in his custody as such public servant or in the custody of a public servant subordinate to him; or
(c) being on the management or on the staff of a jail, remand home or other place of custody established by or under any law for the time being in force or of a women's or children's institution takes advantage of his

Section 114A of the IEA was also added in 1983, providing that in case of gang rape, custodial rape and rape of a pregnant woman, if sexual intercourse is proved and the woman says that she did not consent, the court shall presume that she did not consent. It means that thereafter, the burden to prove his innocence shifts on the accused. However, evidence of the past moral character of the victim woman remained admissible under section 155(4) of the IEA while no such evidence could be adduced about the accused. This sub-section got deleted only in 2002 and

official position and commits rape on any inmate of such jail, remand home, place or institution; or

(d) being on the management or on the staff of a hospital, takes advantage of his official position and commits rape on a woman in that hospital; or

(e) commits rape on a woman knowing her to be pregnant; or

(f) commits rape on a woman when she is under twelve years of age; or

(g) commits gang rape,

shall be punished with rigorous imprisonment for a term which shall not be less than ten years but which may be for life and shall also be liable to fine:

Provided that the court may, for adequate and special reasons to be mentioned in the judgment, impose a sentence of imprisonment of either description for a term of less than ten years.

Explanation 1.-Where a women's is raped by one or more in a group of persons acting in furtherance of their common intention, each of the persons shall be deemed to have committed gang rape within the meaning of this sub-section.

Explanation 2.-"women's or children's institution" means an institution, whether called and orphanage or a home for neglected women or children or a widows' home or by any other name, which is established and maintained for the reception and care of women or children.

Explanation 3.-"hospital" means the precincts of the hospital and includes the precincts of any institution for the reception and treatment of persons during convalescence or of persons requiring medical attention or rehabilitation.

a proviso added to section 146(3) stating that 'in a prosecution for rape or attempt to commit rape, it shall not be permissible to put questions in the cross-examination of the victim as to her general immoral character'. This section continues to refer to the victim of rape as 'prosecutrix' even though the state is the prosecutor in all offences including rape and all other victims are referred to either as victims or complainants and is a discriminatory reference to rape victims.

Since its amendment in 1983, the IPC also makes seduction for sexual intercourse punishable when it is done by a man in authority in a police station, hospital or other women's institutions over a woman in his custody or under his charge.

Other related offences to rape are assault or use of criminal force to outrage a woman's modesty (section 354), word, gestures or acts intended to outrage the modesty of a woman (section 509) and attempt to rape (section 375 or section 376 read with section 511). All of these are distinct offences though sometimes it becomes difficult to distinguish them. If there is even the slightest of penetration of the penis in the vagina, it is rape as the penetration need not be complete. If the man was trying to penetrate but did not succeed for whatever reason, it is attempt to rape. If there was exposure of private parts or gestures suggesting sex, the offence is outraging modesty. If there was any apprehension of use of force involving touching the woman or her clothing or actual use of force aimed at outraging her modesty, it is the offence of sexual assault under section 354. Hence, if a woman is travelling in a bus and a man makes lewd remarks to her, or exposes his private parts to her, he commits the offence of outraging her modesty. While doing so, if he does something which creates an apprehension in the mind of the victim that force is going to be used against her—even if no such force is actually used—it is sexual assault.

The question of nature of offence came in for sharp focus in the *Sakshi* case,[4] in which the father used to finger his six-year old daughter and expose her to his friends. The offence was held to be that of sexual assault and not that of rape. Indian courts have applied the offence of rape to the limited situation of penile penetration of vagina. All other kinds of penetration—anal and oral by penis or anal, oral or vaginal by any other object have been treated either as assault or unnatural offence. A suggestion was made that all these acts should be covered within the definition of rape in the *Sakshi* case but the Supreme Court refused to do so by judicial interpretation, as that will lead to lot of confusion in the minds of police which are not highly educated, and lawyers and judges who all are trained in the traditional meaning of the definition. However, the Supreme Court gave the following directions laying down special rules of procedure to protect child victims while giving evidence:

(i) A screen or some arrangement may be made in the court so that the child does not see the body or face of the accused and is traumatised again.

(ii) Cross-examination may be done by supplying the questions to the judge who will put them to the victim in a language understood by her and which does not embarrass her.

(iii) The child witness should be allowed sufficient breaks as and when required.

It may be of interest to have a quick look at the differential age chosen for giving valid consent for sexual intercourse and leaving one's parents' home. A girl above the age of 16 can give a valid consent for sexual intercourse and no man is liable for rape if the girl has given the consent freely. However, she cannot be allowed to be taken out of the keeping of her lawful guardian and anyone doing so will be liable for kidnapping if the girl is below is the age of 18 years. Many times girls in the age group of 16-18 after eloping with their boyfriends end up in women's institutions, or police stations or brought back to their parents home after a complaint of kidnapping is lodged against their boyfriends who are charged with the offence of kidnapping from the lawful guardianship under section 361 of the IPC.

III. OFFENCES RELATING TO MARRIAGE

This part dealing with 'offences relating to marriage' covers many more offences than those covered in the chapter in the IPC with the same heading and includes discussion of offences of child marriage, dowry, dowry death, cruelty to married woman, and sati.

Law prescribes the age of 18 in case of girls and 21 in case of boys as the age at which they can lawfully marry, but child marriages abound in India. So far such marriages have been held to be valid, though punishable with imprisonment. A new legislation, namely, the Prohibition of Child Marriage Act, 2006, has made a child marriage voidable at the option of the underage party to the marriage within two years of attaining majority. A voidable marriage means that it is valid till the aggrieved party approaches the court requesting it to annul the marriage. The court, while annulling the marriage, is required to order return of all money, valuables, ornaments, or

[4] (2004) 5 SCC 518.

other gifts (or an equal amount thereof) exchanged on the occasion of marriage by both sides. Suitable arrangements for maintenance of the female contracting party may also be directed to be made till her remarriage on her request, keeping in view the standard of living enjoyed by her and the capacity of the paying party. Children conceived or born out of such marriages before their annulment are deemed to be legitimate children for all purposes. Right to their custody, maintenance and access to them is to be determined by reference to the best interest of the child.

The chapter in the IPC on offences relating to marriage is limited to bigamy, adultery, procuring consent to sexual intercourse or cohabitation by pretending to be lawfully married, or going through the ceremony of marriage without there being a lawful marriage, etc. The offences under this chapter of IPC can be committed by either men or women and they can be punished in the same manner except in case of adultery. In case of adultery on the complaint of the husband, the lover of his wife can be prosecuted but the wife is not liable for the offence. On the other hand, neither an adulterous husband nor his lover is liable to be prosecuted. The law assumes proprietary rights of the husband over his wife's sexuality and denies to the wife any agency in the decision-making of committing adultery. There is move to change adultery from a criminal offence to a social wrong meaning thereby that adultery will become a ground for divorce for the aggrieved party but not a penal offence only at the instance of the husband.

Offences relating to dowry are found at three places: (i) cruelty to married women (section 498A IPC); (ii) dowry death (section 304B IPC) and the Dowry Prohibition Act,

1961. Giving, taking or demanding dowry was declared to be an offence by the Dowry Prohibition Act, 1961. In 1983, changes were made in the Dowry Prohibition Act, the IPC, the IEA and the CrPC for more effective investigation and prosecution in case of dowry harassment. The definition of dowry was expanded in the Dowry Prohibition Act with provisions for keeping a list of articles given in relation to marriage; two new offences of cruelty to married women (section 498A) and dowry death (section 304B) were added to the IPC; provision for inquest was made in the CrPC in case a woman died in unnatural circumstances within seven years of marriage (section 174(3)) and presumption of causing death was laid down in the IEA against the husband and his relatives if a woman committed suicide within seven years of marriage (section 113A) or died and there was demand for dowry soon before her death (section 113B).

The practice of sati is yet another social malady connected with marriage, where widows are burnt alive on the pyre of their dead husbands. This practice was most prevalent in West Bengal, where the Dayabhaga system of Hindu law was in operation, recognizing women's right to property. In Rajasthan, in its earlier form, Rajput women jumped into a pyre without their husbands in a practice called *jauhar*, to save themselves from being kidnapped by Muslim invaders after their husbands were believed to have been defeated and killed in war. The practice was abolished by law and made an offence in 1829. Its continued practice found national focus in 1987 with the 'sati' of Roop Kanwar, an 18-year old childless widow who was forced to die on her husband's pyre. The Commission of Sati (Prevention) Act was passed in 1987, prohibiting the commission and glorification of sati. It is believed in

	Cruelty to married woman (IPC)	Suicide (IPC)	Dowry Death (IPC)	Domestic Violence Act
Victim	Married woman	Married woman	Married woman	Any woman in domestic relationship
Action by victim	Complaint by victim	Commits suicide	Dies in unnatural circumstances	Complaint of abuse
Time limit	No period prescribed	Within 7 years	Within 7 years	No period
Prescribed wrongful actions	- Mental or physical cruelty of such nature as to drive the woman to commit suicide - Harassment to coerce her or any other person to meet unlawful demand for property or due to failure to meet such demand	Abetment	Demand of dowry soon before her death	Physical, Sexual, Verbal, Emotional, Economic Abuse Harm or injury to a person related to her
Presumption	None	Presumption of guilt if above conditions exist	Presumption of guilt if above conditions exist	N A
Nature of Remedy	Criminal	Criminal	Criminal	Civil
Consequential orders if found guilty	Imprisonment up to 10 years and fine	Imprisonment up to 3 years	Imprisonment for minimum 7 years – up to life	Right of residence to woman, restraint order, ejection of abuser, compensation, Counselling Criminal sanction against offender if restrained order breached

Rajasthan that if a woman commits sati, seven generation of her family go to heaven. While this cannot be proved either way, sati *mandirs* generate enough income for her seven generations to live comfortably on it.

Offences relating to marriage cannot be curbed by law alone. For such laws to effectively curb these practices, women need to recognize the worth of their being in their own right and not only by reference to their status as a wife. They need to explore and create more options to make their lives liveable in the absence of a husband.

IV. OFFENCES RELATING TO GIRLS

'Son preference' in India has resulted in elimination of girls by various means. In earlier times, female infanticide was more common.

In today's technologically advanced world, girls are being prevented from being born by resorting to abortion of the female foetus after sex-determination, or by using the sex-pre-selection method to get implant of only those eggs that are fertilized with the male chromosome.

Large scale female foeticide led the government to enact the Pre-natal Diagnostic

Chart 1: Sex Ratio in India Over the Years

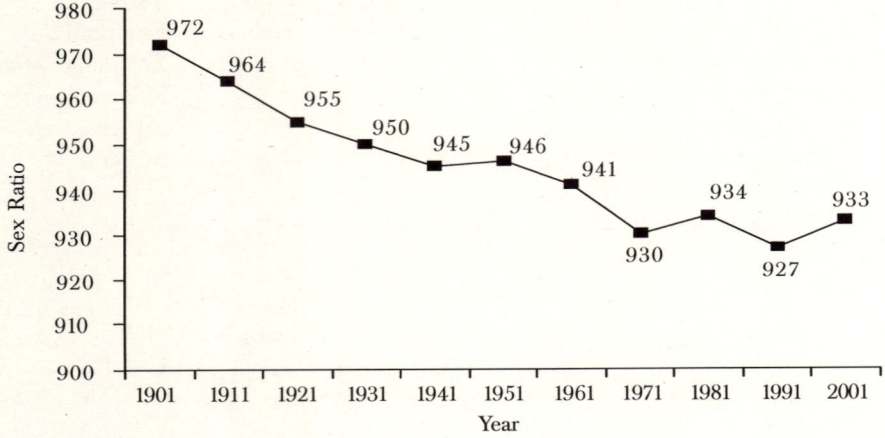

Chart 3: Child Sex Ratio during 1991 and 2001

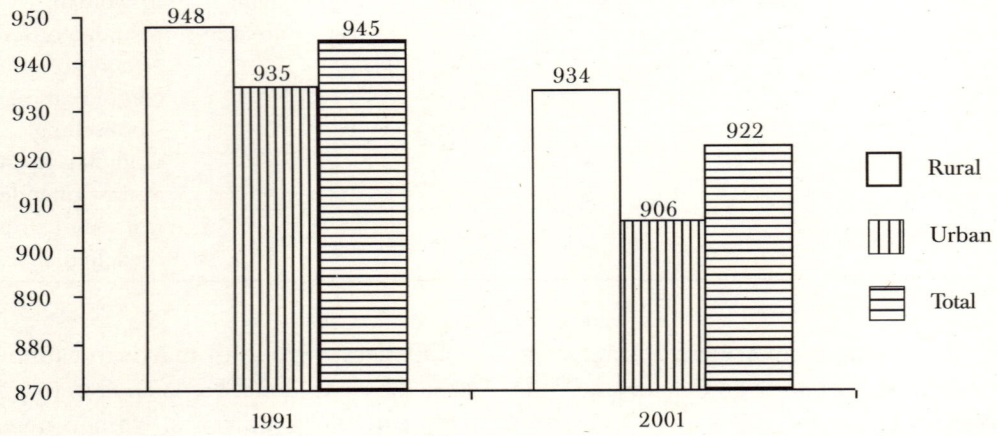

Source: Annual Report on the Implementation of the Pre-conception and Pre-Natal Diagnostic Techniques (Prohibition of Sex-selection) Act, 2005, PNDT Division, Ministry of Health and Family Welfare, Government of India.

Techniques (Regulation and Prevention of Misuse) Act, 1994. This Act made specific provisions for the use, regulation and monitoring of ultrasound machines to curb their misuse for detection of the sex of the foetus. The Act was amended in 2002 and renamed the Pre-conception and Pre-natal Diagnostic Techniques (Prohibition of Sex Selection) Act (PNDT Act) to meet the challenge of pre-conception sex selection of the foetus. It brought within its ambit, the techniques of pre-conception sex selection. The PNDT Act prohibits determination and disclosure of the sex of foetus, as well as any form of advertising about facilities of pre-natal determination of sex. It prescribes imprisonment up to five years and a fine up to Rs. 1,00,000 for contravention of its provisions.

Despite the law the number of girls to boys in the 0-6 age group is continuing to decline (see Charts 1 and 3 above).

Map 1 clearly shows that the problem has acquired alarming proportions in rich and developed states and is not limited to certain states. Even the state of Kerala, with the highest literacy rate for women and having more females (16,360,955) than males (15,468,664), according to the 2001 Census, has fewer girls than boys in the 0-6 years age group.

Prosecution in criminal cases usually requires a victim who will complain and put pressure on the police and prosecution to pursue the matter. In case of offences under the NDPT Act, the female foetus is the only victim and does not have anybody who will fight on its behalf. Success in prosecution is dependent on availability of evidence. In these cases the evidence is with the perpetrators of crime. The seekers and providers of illegal services both join hands and defeat or circumvent the provisions of law. Also, equally important is the fact that sex selective abortion seems so much less horrendous compared to female infanticide. Educated people in cities will be horrified on learning that their neighbour has killed a new-born baby girl.

Map 1

There is however no social reaction if a female foetus is aborted even though the reason for such abortion is that it was a female foetus.

The legislation has proved to be ineffective in view of various myths and perceptions surrounding female foeticide and sex-pre-selection. It is said sometimes that fewer number of girls in society will enhance their status. It undermines the fact that in places where sex-selection is rampant, there can be increase in violence against women, rape, abduction, trafficking and onset of practices such as polyandry. It is also believed, albeit wrongly, that only couples with two or more daughters opt for sex selection. Therefore, it does not affect the overall child sex ration. In fact, data indicates that even for the first-born, there is preference for a male child. This trend is even more noticeable where the first-born is a daughter. It surely is not an effective tool for controlling population. Population control is essential for improving quality of life and not for its annihilation. It is vehemently argued that it is more humane to eliminate a female foetus than subjugate her to a life of discrimination. By this logic, it would be justifiable to eliminate poor people than let them suffer a life of poverty and deprivation. It is not the girl child that is the problem but the practice of sex selection. The problem of dowry cannot be solved by resorting to sex selective abortions. Its solution lies in recognizing the root cause of the subordinate status of women in society. It is also erroneously believed that banning sex selection amounts to denying a mother her inalienable right to choose the sex of her child. In real life, the choice of aborting a female foetus is not free. It is exercised due to fear of violence, neglect, rejection or desertion and also from the desire to establish one's value in the family.

V. SEXUAL HARASSMENT AT WORK PLACE

The well celebrated *Vishaka* case[5] was brought by social activists and NGOs by filing a writ petition in the Supreme Court for enforcement of the fundamental rights of working women under Article 14 (right to equality before law and equal protection of law), Article 19 (freedom to move freely and practice any profession or to carry on any occupation, trade or business) and Article 21 (right to life). The Supreme Court reiterated that gender equality is a universality recognized human right and it includes protection from sexual harassment and right to work with dignity. It referred to the UN Convention on Elimination of All Forms of Discrimination against Women (CEDAW) which has been ratified by the Government of India in 1993. Article 11 of this CEDAW provides:

'1. States Parties shall take all appropriate measures to eliminate discrimination against women in the field of employment in order to ensure, on basis of equality of men and women, the same rights, in particular: (a) The right to work as an inalienable right of all human beings;...'.

The general recommendations of CEDAW in this context specifically mention that, 'Equality in employment can be seriously impaired when women are subjected to gender specific violence, such as sexual harassment in the work place'. The Supreme Court recognized that while a violation of these rights was not uncommon, there was a vacuum and no law in existence dealt with sexual harassment of women at work place. The cause for filing this writ petition was the case of Bhanwari Devi, a *sathin* (village social worker) in Rajasthan who was allegedly gang raped by four men of

[5] *Vishaka* v. *State of Rajasthan* (1997) 6 SCC 241.

the upper caste family when she thwarted a child marriage in their family as part of her official responsibility. The Supreme Court laid down certain guidelines to be followed till a law was passed by Parliament on the subject. As of now, the Protection of Women against Sexual Harassment at Workplace Bill, 2007 is pending before Parliament and the Vishaka guidelines continue to regulate this offence.

According to the Vishaka guidelines sexual harassment includes such unwelcome sexually determined behaviour (whether directly or by implication) as:

(a) physical contact and advances;
(b) a demand or request for sexual favours;
(c) sexually coloured remarks;
(d) showing pornography;
(e) any other unwelcome physical verbal or non-verbal conduct of sexual nature.

All employers, private and public, have been put under an obligation to take active steps to prevent sexual harassment by formulating policy against sexual harassment and by advertising it in an appropriate manner at the work place. If such sexual harassment constitutes a criminal offence, the employer is required to file a complaint with appropriate authority. If it amounts to misconduct, appropriate departmental disciplinary action should be taken. The employer should also ensure that the victim and witnesses are not victimized or discriminated against. The victim may seek the transfer of the perpetrator or her own transfer.

Sexual harassment leads to physical, emotional and economic consequences for the victim. The physical manifestation is in the form of headaches, upset stomach, nausea, vomiting, insomnia, loss of appetite; emotional in the form of fear, confusion, hurt, anger, shame, helplessness, depression, loss of

---

Myths about Sexual Harassment

Myth: Some women ask to be sexually harassed by the way they act or dress.

Fact: When a businessman gets robbed, we don not blame him for being well dressed. We blame the robber. Yet, when a woman is sexually harassed, we blame her for the way she looks. There are no excuses for harassment, regardless of how a woman looks. In any case, even women who do *not* dress or behave in a 'sexy' way get harassed.

Myth: If you ignore harassment, it will go away.

Fact: It will not. Research shows that simply ignoring the behaviour is ineffective; harassers generally will not stop of their own accord. Ignoring such conduct may even be perceived as condoning or encouraging it.

Myth: Sexual harassment is inevitable when men and women work together.

Fact: While attraction between the sexes might be inevitable, uninvited sexual overtures are not.

Myth: Many women make up and report incidents of sexual harassment to get back at employers or colleagues who have angered them.

Fact: Unless a woman feels harassed, she does not complain unnecessarily.

Myth: Sexual harassment is really just a form of flirting and women enjoy it, even if they pretend not to.

Fact: Sexual harassment is disrespectful and offensive. If a person is interested in another person, they show it in a respectful way, not by sexually harassing the other person.

http://www.fwld.org.np/sexhar.html

---

job motivation or self-confidence; and economic with loss of job, wages or promotion. It also affects the organisation resulting in low productivity and profitability, and tarnished image.

VI. DOMESTIC VIOLENCE

While the family is celebrated as an institution offering love and affection, care, nourishment and support, the experience of many women is that it is a place for violence. This experience has been well recognised with the passing of the Protection of Women from Domestic Violence Act, 2005 (PWDV Act). This Act provides civil remedies to protect a woman subjected to domestic violence in addition to the criminal offences mentioned in Part II of this chapter. Criminal sanctions arise under this Act in case of breach of the court orders passed to protect the woman victim. Only women can make a complaint under this legislation and only an adult male relative with whom the woman has lived in domestic relationship or his relatives are recognized as perpetrators. Relief may be sought by any woman in domestic relationship with the male perpetrator of violence, unlike penal offences which are limited only to married women. The PWDV Act includes sister, daughter, mother, wife, wife of fraudulent or bigamous marriages, including women living in relationships like marriage, amongst the victims of domestic violence.

This Act recognises the right of women to reside in shared residence free from violence whether that residence is owned or tenanted singly or jointly.

Domestic violence includes:

- Physical abuse: bodily pain, harm, or danger to life, limb, or health, Impairment of the health or development of the aggrieved person and includes assault, criminal intimidation and criminal force.

- Sexual abuse: any conduct of a sexual nature that abuses, humiliates, degrades or otherwise violates the dignity of woman.
- Verbal and emotional abuse: insults, ridicule, humiliation, name calling and insults or ridicule specially for not having a child or a male child; repeated threats to cause physical pain to any person in whom the aggrieved person is interested.
- Economic abuse: Depriving woman of any economic or financial resources, disposal of household effects to her detriment and without her consent, prohibition or restriction to continued access to resources or facilities.

Various orders that may be passed on a complaint of domestic violence include:

- compensation or damages
- counselling
- residence in a shared household
- Restraint order
  - no violence against children, others
  - not to sell or give up property
- Removal of respondent from the household

A complaint of domestic violence may be filed before a protection officer, a service provider, the police or directly before the magistrate.

Protection officers and service providers are to advise and help aggrieved person to file complaint. The first date of hearing should be fixed not beyond three days. The notice must be served within two days and the complaint should be disposed of within 60 days of the first hearing. In case an order of counselling is made, the next hearing to review the progress should be held within two months. The matter is to be dealt with by judicial magistrate first class or metropolitan

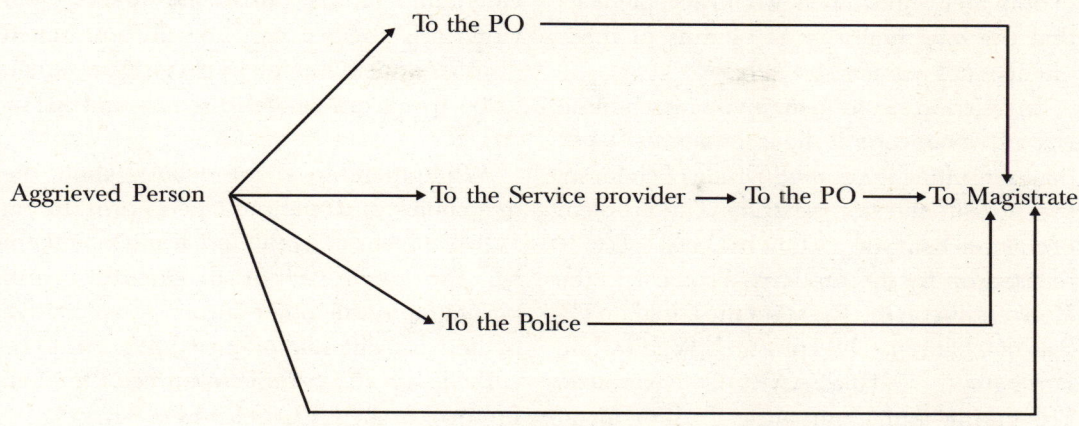

Complaint Procedure

Source: PPP by Lawyers' Collective: Women's Rights Initiative (2007)

magistrate. Violation of protection order is a cognisable and non-bailable offence which means that breach of the order need not be reported and arrest may be made by the police without a complaint by the victim. The punishment for breach includes imprisonment up to one year and / or fine up to Rs. 20,000.

VII. TRAFFICKING IN WOMEN AND GIRLS

According to US Trafficking in Persons (TIP) Report (2006), 600,000 to 800,000 persons are trafficked each year. Of these approximately 80 per cent are women and girls, and 50 per cent of them are minors. The problem of trafficking of persons for prostitution had found recognition in the Convention for the Suppression of the Traffic in Persons and of the Exploitation of the Prostitution of Others in 1949. In India, the IPC had inserted the offences of procuring and importing of girls for immoral intercourse since 1923. A special legislation to deal with the problem of prostitution, namely, the Suppression of Immoral Traffic in Women and Children Act (SITA),

was passed in 1956. It was amended and renamed as Immoral Traffic (Prevention) Act (ITPA) in 1986 to include in its ambit trafficking of men also though it is well recognized that most of the victims of trafficking for prostitution are women.

The IPC punishes procuring or importing of girls for immoral sexual intercourse punishable with ten years of imprisonment with fine. The Immoral Traffic (Prevention) Act, 1956 as amended in 1986, applies to procuring a 'person', in contrast with woman used in the IPC, for prostitution punishable with minimum imprisonment for three years but not more than seven years. If such offence is committed against the will of the person, then the maximum imprisonment may go up to 14 years. In case the offence is committed against a child under 16 years of age, the minimum imprisonment is seven years and maximum may be life imprisonment. It also includes provisions for rescue of children and persons forced into prostitution who are to be kept in corrective homes or protective homes till suitable arrangements for their rehabilitation are made. Even though ITPA applies to both men and women, it is an accepted fact that the vast majority of victims of these offences are women and girls.

Increase in sex tourism involving children is a grave concern at the international level, that is resulting in promoting sale of children, prostitution and pornography. The problem of children being the victims has been specially focused on by the Optional Protocol to the Convention on the Rights of the Child on the Sale of Children, Child prostitution and Child Pornography, and the SAARC Convention on Preventing and Combating Trafficking in Women and Children for Prostitution. Creation of special laws at the local, regional and international level is an indication of the wide spread nature of the problem and the need to take action at all levels. Recognising the transnational character of these offences, the Optional Protocol provides that the offences under it are extraditable and obligates the states to make arrangements for prosecution of offenders on their territories as well even when the offences is committed elsewhere. The SAARC Convention emphasises on the need for increasing mutual legal assistance for preventing and combating trafficking for prostitution. It also incorporates the principle of extradition or prosecution of offender for offences under the SAARC Convention. Trafficking of women and children happens not only for prostitution and pornography but also for domestic servitude, camel jockey, forced marriage, organ trade, bonded labour, etc. The reasons for these offences are wide spread—poverty, loss of family income suddenly, illiteracy and lack of awareness, civil and military conflicts, lucrative nature of the activity for trafficker, weak law enforcement mechanisms, marital problems, rape, incest, domestic violence, globalisation promoting mobility, demand for cheap labour and

entertainment, sex tourism and myths about virgin girls' ability to cure sexually transmitted diseases or demand for virgin girls presumed to be free from sexual diseases and HIV/AIDS.

While there are many debates about the free choice of women to take to prostitution as their means of livelihood, trafficking them for the purposes of prostitution and pornography and other purposes exploitative of them is a different offence that needs to be curbed with all available resources. Optional Protocol to the CRC believes

…that the elimination of the sale of children, child prostitution and child pornography will be facilitated by adopting a holistic approach, addressing the contributing factors, including underdevelopment, poverty, economic disparities, inequitable socio-economic structure, dysfunctioning families, lack of education, urban-rural migration, gender discrimination, irresponsible adult sexual behaviour, harmful traditional practices, armed conflicts and trafficking of children

VIII. CONCLUSION

Many laws have been made to deal with the problem of offences against women. The problem, however, cannot be effectively tackled by criminal law without support from other quarters. Offences against women have roots in the power relationship between a woman and a man and conceptualisation of women as inferior, weak, incapable of having an agency of their own and as property of men. Her (in)ability to deal with the violence arising there from is directly proportionate to the (dis)empowering mechanisms and opportunities (un)available to her to live her life on her own terms. Education, equal job and promotional opportunities recognising the caring responsibilities of women, reconstruction of woman as being normal human being without comparison with men, will go a long way in changing the perception about woman among men and women alike. Criminal law deals with the offender but has little role in prevention of commission of offences against women. Such limited role apparently cannot protect women against being subjected to violence in the first place.

Even after an offence has been committed, criminal justice administration with all its favourable provisions for women still is dependent on the observation of the rules of procedure and evidence by the implementing agencies. Unless they are sensitised and empathise with the need for such special provisions and procedure, such provisions are followed more often in their breach. A comprehensive approach is needed to change perceptions about women by creating more opportunities so that women can test out their strengths and use their abilities to the full realising their true worth and capacities. No nation can progress if half of its population lags behind with less education, poorer health, higher mortality ratio and discrimination in all spheres of life. Eulogising women as goddesses in their role as mothers but leaving them powerless as women and specially as wives, without any rights and equal status is a hypocritical response to discrimination not wanting to face the reality and bring about much needed change.

Criminal law has taken long strides in facilitating access to justice for women by making various provisions. Women can make use of those provisions only if they have the ability to deal with the social consequences of their legal actions. For example, if a woman reports rape, the special provisions, if observed in their true spirit will facilitate conviction if the offence has been committed. The criminal law, however, has no mechanism to deal with the mental trauma of the victim or psychological rehabilitation of the victim or the social fall out of such reporting resulting in social stigma, no marriage and few opportunities to be self reliant. A comprehensive approach empowering women to decide for themselves what they want and to be able to take decisions in their best interest is needed. It is necessary that the divide between public and private sphere be broken and similar legal principles and standard of equality, liberty and freedom applicable in the public sphere are applied in the domestic sphere as well.

Preventing Atrocities against the Scheduled Castes and Scheduled Tribes

Anupama Roy

The Bhotmanges were a Dalit family of Khairlanji in Maharashtra, owning a small plot of land. They had resisted attempts by the dominant sections of the village to construct a road through this land. On 29 September 2006, a mob of villagers attacked them while Bhaiyyalal, the father, was away. Bhaiyyalal's sons were killed and so were his wife Surekhi and daughter Priyanka, after being raped. Khairlanji was not a stray incident, nor are acts of violence against Dalits and the erosion of their rights confined to any single state. More recently, in March 2007, in Salwan in Karnal district of Haryana, Rajputs burnt down the houses of Dalits. Less than two years back in August 2005, Jat mobs had looted and burnt the Balmiki *basti* in Gohana, in Sonepat district of Haryana, almost three years after five Dalits were lynched in a police *chowki* in Duleena in Jhajjhar district, Haryana, by forward caste men. While the examples cited in this paragraph are from Maharashtra and Haryana, they manifest the way in which violence against Dalits is embedded in the social and political fabric of the entire country. It is not surprising, therefore, that the report on the Kahirlanji killings brought out under the Scheduled Castes/ Scheduled Tribes (Prevention of Atrocities) Act, 1989, by the Centre for Equity and Social Justice of the government's Yashwantrao Chavan Academy of Development Administration (YASHDA) and the Dr Babasaheb Ambedkar Research and Training Institute, Department of Social Justice, Government of India, found a 'deep rooted social conspiracy' toward facilitating the crime and subsequent suppressing of evidence on the part of certain communal forces as well as various elements from politics and administration' (emphasis added).

The above illustrations of what the Khairlanji report called a 'social conspiracy' where social groups, the local civil administration and political forces were complicit, show how existing constitutional safeguards and legal protections may be rendered ineffective by deeply entrenched social hierarchies sanctioned by ritual practices, resulting in routine and structural violence against Dalits and the erosion with impunity of their right to a life with dignity. In the sections that follow, this chapter will outline the constitutional, legal and statutory frameworks for the protection of the rights of scheduled castes and scheduled tribes. It will also examine the extent to which successive laws have been able to fulfil the promises made in the Constitution and achieve the objectives laid down in successive laws, primarily the Civil Rights Act, 1955, and the Scheduled Castes and Scheduled Tribes (Prevention of Atrocities) Act, 1989.

I. CONSTITUTIONAL FRAMEWORKS AND PROVISION OF EQUAL RIGHTS

The emergence of a sovereign Indian nation was premised on notions of equality. The idea of the nation as a politico-civil society of equal rights and obligations and constitutive of a sovereign and self-determined people, emerged as a consequence of multi-layered struggles against domination. While the struggle against colonial rule formed the overarching framework of the national liberation movement, the struggle against feudal and *brahmanic* dominance, sought to create a political community of equal citizens, by dismantling inequalities. The Indian Constitution presents a framework of equality which is premised on effacing ascriptive inequalities deriving from conditions of birth (e.g., caste hierarchies) in two ways: (1) by providing the right to equality as a fundamental right to all individuals irrespective of his or her conditions of birth, extending to all citizens equal protection against discrimination, and; (2) by committing the state to making special provisions for the socially excluded and disadvantaged groups by taking into account the specific kinds of discrimination that these groups face in society.

The Constitution of India prohibits discrimination on the basis of caste in all forms and entrusts the state with the responsibility of removing impediments to access and enjoyment of public places and in public employment. Articles 14 and 15 which constitute the fundamental right to equality lay down what may be called the anti-discrimination provisions. Article 14 provides that the state shall not deny any person equality before the law and equal protection of laws within the territory of India. Article 15(1) lays down that 'the State shall not discriminate against any citizen on grounds only of religion, race, caste, sex, place of birth or any of them'. It further provides that 'no citizen shall on grounds only of religion, race, caste, sex, place of birth or any of them be subjected to any disability, liability, restriction or condition with regard to—(a) access to shops, public restaurants, hotels and places of public entertainment; or (b) the use of wells, tanks, bathing *ghats*, roads and places of public resort maintained wholly or partly out of state funds or dedicated for the use of general public.

Yet, the equality provisions in the Constitution are not merely anti-discriminatory, based on the assumption of neutrality of the state towards all citizens, nor are they confined to individuals as bearers of rights. If, for example, one looks at articles 14 and 15, one sees that they assure equality before the law for every citizen and also seek to substantiate this equality by removing discrimination based on caste, religion, race, etc., thus mitigating differences provided by social contexts. They thereby reserve for the state, a commitment to community-ship, by allowing certain special provisions in favour of scheduled castes scheduled tribes and other backward classes. Article 15, for example, while laying down the provision of anti-discrimination, in clauses (3) and (4) reserves in the state the right to make exceptions to the anti-discrimination clauses by laying down that 'Nothing in this article shall prevent the State form making any special provisions for women and children' and 'for the advancement of any socially and educationally backward classes of citizens or for the Scheduled Castes and Scheduled Tribes', respectively.

Similarly Article 16, which guarantees equality of opportunity for all citizens in matters of public employment, also provides for compensatory discrimination in favour of certain communities. Thus, Article 16 (2) lays down that 'no citizen shall, on grounds only of religion, race, caste, sex, descent, place of birth, residence or any of them, be ineligible for, or discriminated against in respect of, any employment or office under the State'. Article 16(4) provides the exception saying that 'Nothing in this article shall prevent the State from making any provision for the reservation of appointment or posts in favour of any backward class of citizens which, in the opinion of the State, is not adequately represented in the services under the State'. Article 17 abolishes untouchability, a debilitating and humiliating condition of segregation imposed on the scheduled castes, forbidding its practice in any form. Article 23 prohibits traffic in human beings and *begar* and forced labour in any form.

Over and above these specific rights to equality which offer freedom from discrimination and social exclusion, and invest the state with a constitutional obligation to provide such conditions, the various rights to life enunciated and elaborated under Article 21 of the Indian Constitution perhaps provide an overarching framework within both which security against physical violence, equal protection under the principles of rule of law and a substantive right to life with dignity may be assured.

Part IV of the Constitution, titled Directive Principles of State Policy, contains certain non-justiciable rights. These rights, unlike fundamental rights, are not enforceable by courts, but are in the nature of reminders or directives for lawmaking, to usher in conditions in which the rights enumerated in the previous section become more meaningful. Like the previous section, the rights in this section also show a commitment to both the rights of the individuals and the special needs that emerge as a consequence of his or her membership of socially disadvantaged groups. Article 38, for example, directs the state to commit itself to 'promote the welfare of the people' by ushering in a 'social order' in which 'justice, social, economic and political, shall inform all the institutions of national life'. To achieve this, the state is asked to 'strive to minimise inequalities of income' and also 'eliminate inequalities in status, facilities and opportunities'. The significant reminder, however, is that this justice and equality is to be achieved 'not only amongst individuals but also amongst groups of people residing in different areas or engaged in different vocations'. Article 46 likewise instructs the state to 'promote with special care the educational and economic interests of the weaker sections of the people and in particular, of the Scheduled Castes and Tribes' and 'protect them from social injustice and all forms of exploitation'. By and large, the Directive Principles envisage an active role of the state in providing a range of socially ameliorative or welfare rights ranging from access to an adequate means of livelihood, equal pay for equal work, health and strength of workers, living wage for workers, provision of just and humane conditions of work, right to work, education, public assistance, equal justice and free legal aid, adequate nutrition and health, etc.

II. LEGAL FRAMEWORKS: TOWARDS PROTECTION AND DETERRENCE

Constitutional provisions assuring life and security to the scheduled castes and tribes have been made legally effective through specific laws. While the Protection of Civil Rights Act, 1955, provides penalties against the practice of untouchability, the Scheduled Caste and the Scheduled Tribes (Prevention of Atrocities) Act, 1989 (henceforth SC/ST PoA Act), prescribes severe penalties against a series of crimes listed as atrocities against SCs and STs. Both the laws provide exceptional provisions pertaining to presumption of innocence and bail. All offences under the Acts are cognizable so that the police can arrest the offender without warrant and start investigating the case without taking any order from the court. Both Acts require periodic presentation of reports by state governments, in Parliament, of the measures taken by them for implementing them. The SC/ST PoA in particular provides for the setting up of special courts with enhanced and overriding powers to try cases under the Act. While the Civil Rights Act approaches the issue in terms of socially enforced disabilities, the SC/ST PoA, by identifying a range of crimes against the SCs and STs as 'atrocities' acknowledges the violent and systemic nature of the repression faced by Dalits in a range of situations. Both laws, moreover, emphasize the fact that disabilities and repressions are deeply embedded in society, which, even when they make themselves manifest through specific incidents, are imposed by a dominant group and experienced collectively by the other. The provisions of the SC/ST PoA Act, come into play therefore, only when an offence is committed by a person/persons other than member of SC or ST community and against a person/persons of the SC or ST community.

PROTECTION OF CIVIL RIGHTS ACT, 1955

The Untouchability (Offences) Act, 1955 was enacted by the Parliament to give legal effect to Article 17 of the Constitution, which provided for the abolition of untouchability. The Act provided that where any of the forbidden practices under the Act 'is committed in relation to a member of a Scheduled Caste', the court shall presume, unless the contrary is proved that such act was committed on the ground of 'untouchability'.[1] Thus to facilitate a just trial, a special rule of evidence was introduced whereby the normal legal presumption was reversed to assume that the accused had committed the offence of untouchability until the contrary was proved. With this the burden of proof shifted from the prosecution to the accused, who had to prove his or her innocence. A further element of deterrence was introduced by providing enhanced penalty on subsequent conviction.[2]

The failure of the Act to check untouchability, led the government to appoint a Committee in April 1965 under the Chairmanship of Ilaya Perumal to suggest appropriate changes in the Act. Based on the Committee's recommendations the Act was comprehensively amended in 1976 and renamed the Protection of Civil Rights Act, 1955 (henceforth Civil Rights Act). The Civil Rights Act, 1955 was enacted with the objective of providing punishment for preaching and practicing untouchability. Under the amended Act the preaching and practice of untouchability or the enforcement of any disability arising therefrom and for matters connected

---

[1] The Untouchability (Offences) Act 1955, section 12.
[2] Ibid., section 11.

therewith, was made a cognizable and non-compoundable offence and the terms of imprisonment were enhanced.

The Act distinguished between different conditions of 'disability' that were 'enforced' owing to specific practices of untouchability such as,

(a)   religious (arising out of the prevention of any person from entering any place of public worship, from worshipping or offering prayers or performing any religious service in any place of public worship, or bathing in, or using the waters of, any sacred tank, well, spring or water-course);

(b)   social (arising out of preventing a person from access to any shop, public restaurant, hotel or place of public entertainment, or the use of utensils, and other articles kept in any public restaurant, hotel, *dharmshala*, *sarai* or *musafirkhana* for the use of the general public the practice of any profession or carrying on of any occupation, trade or business, trade or business, the use of or access to any river, stream, well, tank, taps or watering place, or bathing ghat, burial, or cremation ground, access to public conveyance, construction or acquisition or occupation of any residential premises, observance of any social or religious ceremony, or taking part in religious, cultural or social processions etc.).

Apart from these, punishments have been prescribed among other things, for refusing to admit persons to hospitals, dispensaries, educational institutions, hostels etc., for refusing to sell goods or render services, molesting or insulting persons on the ground of 'untouchability' or for an offence committed against the person or property of any individual as a reprisal or revenge for his having exercised any right accruing to him by reason of the abolition of 'untouchability' under Article 17 of the Constitution.

Although the punishments prescribed by the Civil Rights Act were not severe, ranging between imprisonment of one to six months and a fine between Rs. 100 and Rs. 500, it delineated the wide range of contexts within which the practice of untouchability makes itself manifest. The precise identification of the modes and conditions of enforcement of disability theoretically gave very wide powers to the government agencies to curb the practice of untouchability. Moreover, by empowering the government to impose collective fines on villagers, the Act recognised that untouchability manifested a condition of shared experiences of disability by entire communities, imposed by the dominant social group. It affirmed thereby that while in specific contexts untouchability may be experienced individually, more often than not it manifests a continuing pattern of oppression, which has shaped the hierarchically organized relationship among social groups. Thus section 10A(1) of the Act prescribes that the state government, if satisfied after an inquiry 'that the inhabitants of an area are concerned in, or abetting the commission of any offence punishable under this Act, or harbouring persons concerned in the commission of such offence or failing to render all the assistance in their power to discover or apprehend the offender or offenders or suppressing material evidence of the commission of such offence, the State Government may, by notification in the official Gazzette, impose a collective fine on such inhabitants and apportion such fine amongst the inhabitants who are liable collectively to pay it…'.

THE SCHEDULED CASTES AND SCHEDULED TRIBES (PREVENTION OF ATROCITIES) ACT, 1989

The ineffectiveness of the Civil Rights Act, 1955 to check continued and rampant physical violence against the SCs and STs, and in particular, a spurt in brutalities such as rape, mass murder, arson, grievous injuries, etc., led to the enactment of the Scheduled Caste and Scheduled Tribe (Prevention of Atrocities) Act in 1989. The law created special offences which were made triable by special courts. It categorized the various indignities and violence to which the SCs and STs were continuously subjected to as 'atrocities', marking a departure from the manner in which Dalits had always been dealt with as 'a matter of charity or compassion'.[3] The Preamble of the Act lay down that it intended to '*prevent the commission* of offences of atrocities against the members of the Scheduled Castes and the Scheduled Tribes, to *provide for Special Courts for the trial* of such offences and for the *relief and rehabilitation* of the victims of such offences and for matters connected therewith or incidental thereon' (emphasis added). If one looks at the portions that are emphasized, and reads the provisions of the Act it is amply clear that the Act intended to prevent atrocities by prescribing strong punitive measures which could deter recurrence of atrocities against SCs and STs.

The Rules under the Act were framed in 1995 (henceforth Rules) to provide specific, coordinated institutional mechanisms for the enforcement and implementation of the provisions of Act. The Rules provided, in particular, for special courts for the trial of offences listed as atrocities under the Act and for the relief and rehabilitation of the victims of such offences.

IDENTIFYING ATROCITIES

The Act broke new ground by laying down for the first time the multiple contexts and contours of atrocities suffered by scheduled castes and scheduled tribes.

Section 3 (1) of the Act while prescribing the punishment for offences of atrocities laid down:

Whoever, *not being a member* (emphasis added) of a Scheduled Caste or a Scheduled Tribe, -

(i)   forces a member of a scheduled Caste to a Scheduled Tribe to drink or eat any inedible or obnoxious substance;

(ii)   acts with intent to cause injury, insult or annoyance to any member of a Scheduled Caste or a Scheduled Tribe by dumping excreta, waste matter, carcass or any other obnoxious substance in his premises or neighbourhood;

(iii)   forcibly removes clothes from the person of a member of a Scheduled Caste or a Scheduled Tribe or parades him naked or with painted face or body or commits any similar act which is derogatory to human dignity;

(iv)   wrongfully occupies or cultivates any land owned by, or allotted to, or notified by any competent authority to be allotted to, a member of a Scheduled Caste or a Scheduled Tribe gets the land allotted to him transferred;

(v)   wrongfully dispossesses a member of a Scheduled Caste or a Scheduled Tribe from his land or premises or interferes with the enjoyment of his rights over any land, premises or water;

(vi)   compels or entices a member of a Scheduled Caste or a Scheduled Tribe to do 'begar' or other similar forms of forced or bonded labour other than any compulsory service for public purposes imposed by Government;

---

[3] See the discussion in K.G. Kannabiran, *Wages of Impunity*, Hyderabad, Orient Longman, ch 'We, the Other People', 2004, pp. 195-203.

(vii)   forces or intimidates a member of a Scheduled Caste or a Scheduled Tribe not to vote or to vote for a particular candidate or to vote in a manner other that provided by law;

(viii)   institutes false, malicious or vexatious suit or criminal or legal proceedings against a member of a Scheduled Caste or a Scheduled Tribe;

(ix)   gives any false or frivolous information to any public servant, and thereby causes such public servant to use his lawful power to the injury or annoyance of a member of a Scheduled Caste or Scheduled Tribe;

(x)   intentionally insults or intimidates with intent to humiliate a member of a Scheduled Caste or a Scheduled Tribe in any place within public view;

(xi)   assaults or uses force to any woman belonging to a Scheduled Caste or a Scheduled Tribe with intent to dishonour or outrage her modesty;

(xii)   being in a position to dominate the will of a woman belonging to a Scheduled Caste or a Scheduled Tribe and uses that position to exploit her sexually to which she would not have otherwise agreed;

(xiii)   corrupts or fouls the water of any spring, reservoir or any other source ordinarily used by members of the Scheduled Castes or the Scheduled Tribes so as to render it less fit for the purpose for which it is ordinarily used;

(xiv)   denies a member of a Scheduled Caste or a Scheduled Tribe any customary right of passage to a place of public resort or obstructs such member so as to prevent him from using or having access to a place of public resort to which other members of public or any section thereof have a right to use or access to;

(xv)   forces or causes a member of a Scheduled Caste or a Scheduled Tribe to leave his house, village to other place of residence,

shall be punishable with imprisonment for a term which shall not be less than six months but which may extend to five years and with fine.

SETTING UP OF SPECIAL COURTS

The Act provided for special courts[4] for speedy trial of cases. Accordingly, the state government, with the concurrence of the Chief Justice of the High Court, was to identify by notification in the Official Gazette, a Court of Session to be a special court to try offences under the Act.[5] Like the Civil Rights Act of 1955, the SC/ST PoA Act too provided the state government with the power to impose collective fine.[6]

PREVENTIVE ACTION

In addition the Act also empowered the District Magistrate or a Sub-divisional Magistrate or any other Executive Magistrate or police officer not below the rank of a Deputy Superintendent of Police to take preventive action under section 17 of the Act and declare an area prone to such atrocities, if they believed that a 'person or a group of persons not belonging to the Scheduled Caste or the Scheduled Tribes, residing in or frequenting any place within the local limits of his jurisdiction is likely to commit an offence or has threatened to commit any offence under this Act and is of the opinion that there is sufficient ground for proceeding, declare such an area to be an area prone to atrocities and take necessary action for keeping the peace and good behaviour and maintenance of public order and tranquillity and may take preventive action'.

OFFENCES RELATING TO ABETMENT AND FURTHERANCE OF COMMON INTENTION

The scope and magnitude of punishment for an offence under the Act was widened by

---

[4] Scheduled Caste and Scheduled Tribe (Prevention of Atrocities) Act, 1989, ch IV, sections 14 and 15.

[5] Ibid., section 14.

[6] Ibid., section 16.

extending the 'presumption as to offences' to cover 'abetment'[7] and 'furtherance of common intention'.[8] Thus section 8(a) lays down that a person (the accused) will be considered as having abetted the offence 'if it is proved that the accused rendered any financial assistance to a person accused of, or reasonably suspected of, committing, an offence…'. Section 8(b) lays down that 'if it is proved that the offence committed [by a group of persons] was a sequel to any existing dispute regarding land or any other matter, it shall be presumed that the offence was committed in furtherance of the common intention or in prosecution of the common object'.

ACCOUNTABILITY, PUNISHMENT FOR NEGLECT OF DUTIES, AND RESPONSIBILITIES OF PUBLIC OFFICERS

The Act made a public servant who 'wilfully neglected' the duties he was 'required to perform under the Act' punishable with imprisonment for a term not less than six months and extendable to one year. The Scheduled Castes and Scheduled Tribes (Prevention of Atrocities) Rules, 1995 (henceforth Rules) lay down some stringent norms that should be observed for effective investigation of case, speedy and fair dispensation of justice, and a supervisory mechanism to ensure that they were being observed. Thus an offence committed under the Act may be investigated only by an officer not below the rank of a Deputy Superintendent of Police and appointed by the state government/ Director General of Police/ Superintendent of Police after considering his past experience, competence, ability and sense of justice.[9] The investigation is to be completed

within 30 days and the report submitted to the Superintendent of Police, who in turn should forward it immediately to the Director General of Police of the state government.[10] All investigations done by the investigating officer are subject to review by the Home Secretary and the Social Welfare Secretary to the state government at the end of every quarter.[11] In addition, a Scheduled Castes and Scheduled Tribes Protection Cell is required to be set up by the state government under the charge of the Director or Inspector General of Police who is responsible for conducting surveys in identified areas and making inquiries.[12]

A nodal officer, preferably belonging to the scheduled castes or the scheduled tribes, is to be nominated by the state government for co-ordinating the functioning of the District Magistrates and Superintendents of Police, Investigating Officers and other officers responsible for implementing the provisions of the Act.[13] Similarly, a special officer not below the rank of Additional District Magistrate, Superintendent of Police or other officers responsible for implementing the provisions of the Act is to be appointed in the identified area to provide immediate relief and facilities to victims of atrocities, set up awareness centre and organise workshops in the identified area and co-ordinate with non-governmental organizations for providing necessary facilities and financial and other help.[14]

The Rules further provide for immediate relief, daily allowance, maintenance of

---

[7] Ibid., section 8(a).

[8] Ibid., section 8(b).

[9] The Scheduled Castes and Scheduled Tribes (Prevention of Atrocities) Rules, 1995, section 7(1)].

[10] Ibid., section 7(2).

[11] Ibid., section 7(3)].

[12] Ibid., section 8.

[13] Ibid., section 9.

[14] Ibid., section 10.

expenses and transport facilities to victims of atrocities, their dependents, and witnesses.[15] Moreover, they make the state government responsible not only for ensuring that the officer posted in an area prone to atrocity has 'the right aptitude and understanding of the problems of SCs and STs',[16] but also to ensure that 'persons from the Scheduled Castes and Scheduled Tribes are adequately represented in the administration and in the police force at all levels, particularly at the level of police posts and police station'.[17]

III. HOW HAS THE SCHEDULED CASTES AND SCHEDULED TRIBES ACT UNFOLDED IN PRACTICE?

While the SC/ST PoA Act and Rules are impressive both in their scope and the ways in which they attempt to identify, punish and prevent atrocities, it is significant that the last several years have seen a spate in acts of atrocities against SCs and STs. The findings listed in the report, mentioned at the beginning of this chapter, by the Centre for Equity and Social Justice, YASHDA and Dr Babasaheb Ambedkar Research and Training Institute, Department of Social Justice, Government of India, under the SC/ST (PoA) Act, which investigated into the Khairalanji killings are revealing in this context. It is significant that the report is titled 'Organised Killings of Dalits in Khairlanji' indicating the manner in which dominant sections of society as well as those responsible for maintaining law and order and implement the provisions of the SC/ST PoA Act are implicated in it.

Some of the findings of the report which came out in November 2006, within a couple of months of the episode (29 September 2006), are as follows:[18]

1. Throughout September 2006, certain communal elements visited Khairlanji and contributed to creating communal tensions in the village.

2. The police ignored the frantic call for help from Bhotmange and the Gajbiye brothers even while the killing was in progress on 29 September, hence allowing the heinous crime to happen.

3. Even after this shocking murder, the police did not file the FIR promptly and the Deputy Superintendent of Police as well as the Police Inspector in charge of Andhalgaon Police Station did not take any action promptly, even though they knew that this was a clear case of atrocity against dalits.

4. Extremely serious neglect was committed, perhaps deliberately, during the *post mortem* of the two women's bodies, which led to destruction of crucial evidence of rape. Blood samples, nail clippings, rectal swab, vaginal swab, and pubic hair samples were not taken which are must in the likelihood of rape. It is no surprise then that the local MLA who belongs to the BJP was reportedly present at the time of the *post mortem* on Priyanka's body.

---

[18] 'Organised killings of Dalits in Khairlanji Village, Tal. Mohadi District Bhandara'. A report under the SC/ST Prevention of Atrocities Act, 1989 cited in 'Suppressing the Voice of the Oppressed: State terror on protests against the Khairlanji massacre', report prepared by an all India team comprising of civil rights groups from Delhi, Mumbai and Nagpur, including, PUCL, Chhattisgarh, Lokshahi Hakk Sangathan, CPDR, Ramai Pratishthan, Mumbai, PUDR, Samajik Nyaya Samiti, Jaatiya Shoshan Virudh Sangahrsh Samiti, Sangharshrat Naujawan Sabha, Committee Against Violence on Women, 11 January 2007, p. 2.

---

[15] Ibid., section 11.
[16] Ibid., section 13(1).
[17] Ibid., section 11 (2).

5. The Special Inspector General of Police, Nagpur, Mr Pankaj Gupta, made a premature and irresponsible statement that no rape had taken place on the women victims and locals interviewed by the team stated that Mr Gupta had been paid a bribe to make such a statement.

6. The district authorities such as the District Magistrate, the Superintendent of Police and the Civil Surgeon remained aloof and indifferent to the Khairlanji atrocity, hence indirectly allowing the crime and the subsequent manipulation of evidence to happen.

7. The rank insensitivity displayed by the top echelons of the police department towards the Khairlanji atrocity sent totally wrong signals to the rest of the police force in the state.

FINDINGS OF THE ALL INDIAN TEAM: 'STATE TERROR' AND 'SOCIAL CONSPIRACY'

An all Indian fact finding team consisting of 14 civil rights and citizen's groups from Delhi, Mumbai and Nagpur along with PUCL Chhattisgarh, brought out a report titled 'Suppressing the Voice of the Oppressed: State Terror on Protests Against the Khairlanji Massacre', which investigated the atrocity at Khairlanji village, as well as the 'lengths to which the State went to suppress the facts of Khairlanji, and then to suppress the protests against it'. Going in particular into the various offences that were committed in Khairlanji under the SC/ST PoA Act under section 3 and section 8, it emphasized

...Although this Act is a powerful and precise weapon on paper, in practice it has suffered from a near-complete failure in implementation – upper caste policemen are reluctant to file cases against fellow caste members because of the severity of the penalties imposed by the Act (most

offences are non-bailable and the minimum punishment is five years) and the rate of conviction is abysmal. These two Acts [The Protection of Civil Rights Act 1955 and the SC/ST PoA Act 1989] have proved to be no more than paper tigers and so, in any given year, the number of dalits attacked in caste conflict is greater that the number of people of attacked in communal conflicts.[19]

ASSESSMENT BY THE NATIONAL HUMAN RIGHTS COMMISSION

The National Human Rights Commission's Report on Prevention of Atrocities Against SCs and STs (2007) has inquired into the manner in which the provisions of the SC/ST PoA Act have been implemented, whether the administrative structures required under the Act are in place and operational, and the extent to which it has been able to achieve its goal of preventing the commission of atrocities against SCs and STs. Citing from the National Crime Records Bureau (henceforth NCRB), the NHRC Report notes that from 1995, the figures of reported criminal cases of atrocities against the SCs and STs under the SC/ST PoA Act and other laws such as the IPC and Protection of Civil Rights Act, have shown a gradual decline. The NHRC report emphasises, however, that the decline in figures does not 'provide the true picture of the incidence of atrocities'. The Report cites a study conducted by Navsarajan, an NGO in Gujarat, which covered 11 atrocities-prone districts for four years. The findings of this study showed that 36 per cent of atrocities cases were not registered under the Atrocities Act and in 84.4 per cent of the cases where the Act was applied, the cases were registered under wrong

[19] See Report to the Nation by an All Indian Team, 'Suppressing the Voice of the Oppressed: State Terror on Protests against the Khairlanji Massacre', 2007, p. 10.

provisions with a view to concealing actual and violent nature of the incidents. The Navsarjan study also documented that 121.2 hours lapsed between registration of murder cases and initiation of police action. For rape cases the gap between the incident and the reported action was 532.9 hours. The non-registration of cases, apart from reflecting caste bias and corruption, was also due to the pressure on the police to keep reported crime rated low in their jurisdiction.[20]

As far as the nature of crimes is concerned, citing again the NCRB, the NHRC shows that among the reported crimes against the SCs/STs under the various Acts, from 1995-1999, there is a marginal decline under all heads of crime except rape which shows a marginal increase. As far as the geographical distribution of atrocities is concerned, the largest number of cases have been reported from Uttar Pradesh each year, primarily because Uttar Pradesh has the largest population of the scheduled castes as compared to other States. Besides Uttar Pradesh, Rajasthan, Madhya Pradesh, Gujarat, Andhra Pradesh, Tamil Nadu and Bihar are other states which show substantial incidence of crime against SCs and STs.[21] The Fifth Report of the National Commission on Scheduled Castes and Scheduled Tribes (1998-1999) uses 'volume of crime', i.e., the number of cases reported per unit of population, e.g., one lakh population of scheduled castes, as a measure for assessing incidence of such crime. The figures for the year 1998-99 indicate that the highest volume of crime against scheduled castes was in

Rajasthan (73 cases per one lakh population), followed by Gujarat (42 cases). The Seventh Report of the Ministry of Social Justice and Empowerment provides information on the number of cases per lakh of population of both SCs and STs for the year 2000. Rajasthan, with 51.05 number of cases per one lakh of SC and ST population, tops the list.[22]

The NHRC's assessment of the implementation and effectiveness of SC/ST PoA Act, 1989 examines it under several heads including the role of political leaders, the police, the civil administration, the judiciary and watch-dog institutions like the National Commission on Scheduled Castes and Scheduled Tribes. The conclusions of the NHRC are very significant; some of them may be summarized as follows:

(a) Political leaders: There has been by and large a vilification campaign against the use of the SC ST PoA Act. Nowhere in the country has the Act been vigorously enforced, and given the biases at various levels the Act has had little impact. In Maharashtra, for example, the Shiv Sena, made its repeal an election issue in 1995. After coming to power it began withdrawing over 1100 cases registered under the Act, alleging that these cases were false and registered out of personal bias. Similarly, Mulayam Singh Yadav, the leader of the Samajwadi Party accused the then SC Chief Minister of Uttar Pradesh, Mayawati, of a caste bias in enforcing the Act.

(b) Police Machinery: The problem, the report points out, starts with registration of the case itself. The police resort to various machinations to discourage SCs/STs from registering a case, to dilute the seriousness of the violence, to shield the

---

[20] The study by the NGO has been cited in the Report on Prevention of Atrocities Against Scheduled Castes published by the NHRC. See National Human Rights Commission, 'Report on Prevention of Atrocities Against Scheduled Castes', New Delhi, 2004, p. 33.

[21] Ibid., pp. 33-34.

[22] Ibid., pp. 34-37.

accused persons from arrest and prosecution and, in some cases the police themselves inflict violence in the form of custodial torture and death, encounter killings, criminalization of social activism and communities, raids of scheduled caste colonies when inter-community clashes take place, and collective penalization of individual transgression.

Citing from a report by Sakshi (Dalit Human Rights Monitor), and the Chennai Hearing of the National Campaign on Dalit Human Rights, the NHRC report identified the following methods used by police to deflect the objectives of the law:[23]

1. Not registering the case.
2. Pressurising the victim complainant to seek compromise to help perpetrators.
3. Foisting false cases against victims at the behest of perpetrators to pressure them to compromise.
4. Refusing to register cases under SC/ST PoA Act so as to avoid strong punitive measures against the accused.
5. Not citing proper sections of the SC/ST PoA Act so as to dilute the seriousness of the offence and help the perpetrators get a minor punishment, if convicted.
6. Registering FIR but not arresting the accused; shielding public

servants/local political leaders from arrest.

7. Against the specific stipulation of rule 7(1), an officer of a lower rank conducts the investigation and the Deputy Superintendent of Police simply puts his signature on it.
8. Delay in investigation and filing charge-sheet.
9. Granting of bail despite stringent provisions in the Act.

(c) The Judiciary: Apart from the police, the response of the judiciary, at both the trial and High Courts level, according to NHRC, has been equally responsible for blunting the impact of the SC/ST PoA Act.[24] The trends identified in the case of the judiciary are as follows:

1. Scrupulous observation of technicalities often takes priority over the intent of the Act and the merits of the case.
2. The prosecution is often quashed on the ground that the offence was not committed on account of caste, but lust and illicit intimacy in cases of rape, and political rivalry, enmity in case of murder, grievous hurt, etc.
3. There is a tendency to accept evidence from non-scheduled castes/tribes people only.
4. Personal beliefs and deep seated prejudices of the judges relating to both caste and gender play a role. In rape cases, for example, prejudices such as 'Rape is usually committed by teenagers and since the accused are middle class men

[23] Sakshi, *Dalit Human Rights Monitor*, Andhra Pradesh, 2000, pp. 100-104, cited in NHRC Report, ibid., pp. 114-117, 281-285 and the National Campaign on Dalit Human Rights, Chennai Hearing 18-19 April 2000 (2000: 314) cited in the NHRC Report, ibid., pp. 117, 279-280.

[24] NHRC Report, supra note 4, p 122.

and therefore respectable, they could not have committed the crime' and 'An upper caste man could not have defiled himself by raping a lower caste woman', are rampant.

IV. CONCLUSIONS

Apart from the Civil Right Act, 1955 and the SC/ST PoA Act, 1989 discussed above, there are other laws that aim at the elimination of specific social disabilities experienced by the SC/ST community directly or at removing conditions which are likely to affect them most. Among such laws are the Employment of Manual Scavengers and Construction of Dry Latrines (Prohibition) Act, 1993, Bonded Labour System (Abolition) Act, 1976, the Minimum Wages Act, 1948, etc. Despite such laws, as the opening paragraph of this chapter has emphasised, the violation of the dignity of SCs and STs and acts of violence and repression against them has continued. These violations reflect both a lack of adequate social consciousness and as the NHRC report suggested, the unwillingness of the political class and the law and order machinery, to address these issues in a way that deters future recurrences. The rising political consciousness among the SC and ST communities, augmented by changes in political structures at the local level have opened up possibilities of social change. But it has also unleashed repression against members of SC and ST communities. It is important, therefore, that a political will to implement the provisions of the SC/ST (PoA) Act be exhibited, the state governments take it upon themselves to see that that the norms and rules under the various acts are enforced, and the central government takes annual monitoring of reports by state government as provided under the SC/ST PoA Act with due seriousness.

Law of Contract

Raman Mittal

I. INTRODUCTION

The law of contract is one of the basic and fundamental branches of the discipline called 'law'. It is of utmost relevance to companies, governments, businessmen and to every one of us as we, in the course of our life, enter into innumerable contracts with a variety of persons.

Contract is an aspect of law that affects our day-to-day lives. It is hard to go through a day without entering into a contract. At the same time, contract law must explain and regulate complex transactions involving huge sums of money. Hence, the study of contract law is important not only for a lawyer but it is of relevance to people in general.

Contract law is said to be a part of 'private law' because it does not involve or bind the state or persons that are not parties to the contract. Some legal commentators have described contract law as a miniature legal system which persons establish between themselves; the contract becoming binding upon them as a sort of private and self-imposed law. Thus, contracts are voluntary and require an 'exercise of the will of the parties'.

The basic legal material for the study of contract law is the statute called the Indian Contract Act, 1872. As we belong to the common law tradition, the provisions of the statute should be supplemented with the cases decided by various courts of law. For the study of contract law it is also important to understand various Latin legal maxims which relate to the subject.

II. MEANING OF CONTRACT

Promises are what contracts are all about. A contract is made up of a promise of one person to do a certain thing in exchange for a promise from another person to do another thing. Contract law exists to make sure that people keep their promises and that if they do not, the law will enforce it upon them. Thus, a contract requires an agreement between the parties.

An agreement enforceable by law is a contract.[1] Not all agreements are contracts in the sense that law shall not enforce all the agreements that we make. So, the touchstone of a contract is its enforceability at law. Non-business, religious, or charitable agreements are not always contracts. In order to be a valid contract it has to conform to the provisions of the Indian Contract Act, 1872 (henceforth the Contract Act).

---

[1] Indian Contract Act, 1872, section 2(h).

INTENTION TO CONTRACT

To create a contract there must be a common intention of parties to enter into legal obligations. It is not every lose conversation that is to be turned into a contract, although the parties may seem to agree. The case of *Balfour* v. *Balfour*[2] has become a well-known illustration of this principle. Upon failure by a husband to pay a promised allowance, the wife sued. The court held:

There are agreements between parties which do not result in contracts within the meaning of that term in our law. The ordinary example is where two parties agree to take a walk together (or) arrangements which are made between husband and wife. They are not contracts because the parties did not intend that they should be attended by legal consequences. Each house is a domain into which the King's writ does not seek to run.

VOID AND VOIDABLE CONTRACTS

In general, there are two classifications of contracts that are not binding—void and voidable. A contract which ceases to be enforceable by law becomes void when it ceases to be enforceable.[3] If a contract is held to be void, the contract has never come into existence. For example, a contract is void if it is based on an illegal purpose or contrary to public policy; an example could be a contract with a hitman for contract killing. Such a contract will not be recognized by a court, and cannot be enforced by either party.

A contract is voidable if one of the parties has the option either to terminate the contract or to treat it as valid. For example, A forces B to sign a sale deed. This is an instance of voidable contract and B may choose to be bound by it or may avoid it.

SHOULD CONTRACTS BE IN WRITING IN ORDER TO BE BINDING?

There is no requirement under the Contract Act that offer and acceptance should necessarily be expressed in writing. The only requirement of law is that offer and acceptance should be communicated which may be by spoken or written words or by gestures or by conduct. However, any other law may specifically require that a contract be made in writing.[4] For example, all contracts relating to copyright have necessarily to be made in writing as per the provisions of Copyright Act, 1957. Furthermore, the existence of a written contract does not necessarily ensure its enforceability or validity. A contract can be deemed unenforceable if it requires a party to undertake an illegal act, if it was signed under coercion.

EXPRESS AND IMPLIED CONTRACTS

A contract can be either an express contract or an implied contract. An express contract is one in which the terms are expressed verbally, either orally or in writing. An implied contract is one in which some of the terms are not expressed in words. For example, by going to a doctor for a check-up, a patient agrees that he will pay a fair price for the service. If he refuses to pay after being examined, he has breached a contract implied in fact.

III. FORMATION OF CONTRACT

PROPOSAL

The first step in the formation of a contract is making of a proposal. To constitute a contract, there must be a proposal by one person to another and an acceptance of that proposal by the person to whom it is made. When one person signifies to another his willingness to

---

[2] *Balfour* v. *Balfour* [1919] 2 KB 571.
[3] Indian Contract Act, 1872, section 2(j).

[4] Ibid., section 10.

do or abstain from doing anything, with a view to obtaining the assent of that other to such act or abstinence, he is said to make a proposal.[5] A mere statement of a person's intention, or a declaration of his willingness to enter into negotiations is not a proposal and cannot be accepted so as to form a valid contract. A proposal must be a clear, unequivocal and direct approach to another party to contract. For this reason, advertisements, catalogues or store flyers are not proposals. Nor is a 'for sale' sign on a used car. The law calls these 'invitations to treat'; essentially invitations to the general public to come forward and make a proposal on a particular item.

A proposal, once made, can be revoked before acceptance. A proposal can also expire if a deadline for acceptance passes. If there is no specified deadline, then the proposal expires in a 'reasonable time', depending on the subject-matter of the contract. For perishable goods such as food, a 'reasonable time' would likely be a matter of days.

ACCEPTANCE

When the person to whom the proposal is made, signifies his assent thereto, the proposal is said to be accepted. The proposal, when accepted, becomes a promise.[6] Acceptance validates the contract; it gives it life. In the words of Anson, 'acceptance to an offer is what a lighted matchstick is to a train of gunpowder'. Acceptance produces something which cannot be undone. It results in a binding contract. Acceptance, to be valid, must be clear, unequivocal, unconditional and made by the person to whom the proposal is intended. The person making the proposal is called the 'promisor', and the person accepting the proposal is called 'promisee'.

Conduct can amount to acceptance in the proper circumstances such as the delivery of the goods mentioned in the proposal. The courts have laid down two conditions for conduct to be equated with acceptance: (1) that the conduct was an expression of acceptance and not done for some other reason or motive, and (2) that the action or conduct was intended as acceptance. If a judge were called upon to assess conduct for this reason, the judge would not weigh the acceptor's conduct subjectively, but would decide if a 'reasonable person' would infer acceptance from that conduct.

A proposal can also be made to the public at-large, such as the Carbolic Smoke Ball Co.[7] did in 1893. The company put a sum of money on deposit with a bank and said they would pay this money to anybody who got influenza while using their product. A consumer caught influenza, while using the product. The courts held that a special 'unilateral contract' could be created in these circumstances and the Smoke Ball Co. had to pay up. One trick proposers sometimes attempt is to say that the proposed acceptor's silence will amount to acceptance. This is invalid and cannot have the effect of forcing a person to a contract without the requisite of positive acceptance, delivered to the proposer, either in words or conduct.

CONSIDERATION

The Latin maxim *ex nudo pacto non oriture actio* means that out of a bare agreement no action arises. Consideration is a seminal requirement for the existence of a contract. The general rule is that there is no contract if there is no consideration. Consideration must be reciprocal, each party offering consideration.

[5] Ibid., section 2(a).
[6] Ibid., section 2(b).

[7] *Carlill* v. *Carbolic Smoke Ball Co* [1893] 1 QB 256.

Consideration cannot be something or some act which is illegal, immoral or contrary to public policy. If a certain act is punishable by some law, then it is 'illegal'. One 1875 English case, *Currie* v. *Misa,*[8] offered a definition of 'consideration': '…some right, interest, profit or benefit accruing to the one party or some forbearance, detriment, loss or responsibility given, suffered or undertaken by the other'.

The Contract Act defines consideration as:[9]

When at the desire of the promisor, the promisee or any other person has done or abstained from doing or does or abstains from doing, or promises to do or abstain from doing, something, such act or abstinence or promise is called a consideration for the promise.

This definition can be analysed by studying the following ingredients of consideration:

The act or abstinence which is to be a consideration for the contract must be done or promised to be done in accordance with the desire of the promisor. In *Durga Prasad* v. *Baldeo,*[10] the plaintiff, on the order of a collector of town, built at his own expense certain shops which came to be occupied by defendants. The defendants contracted to share a part of profit with the plaintiff in consideration of the plaintiff having expended money in the construction. But later on the defendants refused to pay the promised share. The plaintiff's action to recover the share was rejected by the court as the expenses incurred by the plaintiff towards building of shops were not at the desire of the defendants.

The doctrine of privity of consideration, which is followed under English law, means that consideration must move from the parties to a contract and not from any third party

who is stranger to contract. But this doctrine has no application under Indian law as section 2(d) clearly says that consideration may move from promisee or any other person. It means that as long as there is consideration for a contract, it is immaterial who has furnished it.

The expression appearing in section 2(d) 'has done or abstained from doing or does or abstains from doing, or promises to do or abstain from doing' means that consideration is an act or abstinence which has already been done at the desire of the promisor, or is in progress or is promised to be done in future. In other words consideration may be past, present or future. So, consideration need not be contemporaneous with contract. If A saves B from drowning and B later on promises to pay A for his unilateral act, then it would constitute a valid contract.

Consideration has to be something done at the desire of the promisor. Does it mean that even a worthless act will suffice to make a good consideration if done at promisor's desire? No, consideration must be of some value in the eyes of law as opposed to having value in the eyes of the parties. But courts are liberal in finding value in something to which parties have attached value. Consideration does not necessarily have to be quantified or quantifiable in monetary terms. Any discernible detriment to one of the parties could be that party's consideration.

It is not necessary that consideration is equal or adequate to the promise. Courts can hardly be expected to assume the job of settling what should be appropriate consideration for a promise. This is the business of the parties and not a matter for judicial interference. As such, a contract differs from a gift. This explains why we sometimes hear of very expensive objects sold for Re. 1 or $ 1; this is done to ensure that what is otherwise

[8] *Currie* v. *Misa* 1875 LR 10 Ex 153.

[9] Indian Contract Act, 1872, section 2(d).

[10] *Durga Prasad* v. *Baldeo* (1880) 3 All 221.

essentially a gift, comes with the legal protection of contract law.

The legislature has carved certain exceptions against the general rule discussed above. If a contract is expressed in writing and is registered under the law for the time being in force for the registration of documents, and is made on account of natural love and affection between parties standing in a near relation to each other, then even in the absence of considerations the contract is a valid one.[11]

CAPACITY

Law gives vast freedom to individuals to enter into contractual relationships. But this freedom is available to only those who have the capacity to enter into contracts. Section 11 of the Contract Act defines who are capable of contracting. It states: 'Every person is competent to contract who is of the age of majority according to the law to which he is subject, and who is sound mind and is not disqualified from contracting by any law to which he is subject'. That means minors, persons of unsound mind and disqualified persons are incapable of contracting.

Every person who has not attained the age of majority (generally 18 years) is a minor. In an important decision *Mohoribibi* v. *Dharmodas Ghosh*,[12] the Privy Council had a chance to interpret the nature of minor's contract. In this case a minor mortgaged his houses in favour of Brahmo Dutt–a money lender to secure Rs. 20,000. The money lender was aware of his minority but still he lent money to the minor. Upon failure on part of the minor to recover the money lent, the money lender sued him. The Privy Council held that the minor could not be compelled to pay back the mortgaged

amount. The reason was that since it was a contract by a minor who is incompetent to contract in the first place, any consequences that could emerge from contractual relations could not be imposed on him. While interpreting the Contract Act the highest court of that time laid down that the contracts by minors are void *ab initio*, i.e., they are void from the stage of inception and hence bereft of all legal consequences.

The reason for such an approach by the legislature is to protect the minor from fraudulent manipulations of others as well as from his own ignorance, inexperience and immaturity. But in the modern world a minor has necessarily to step out of house for travel, study and entertainment. So, it becomes imperative for him to enter into contractual relations with others. A strict application of this principle would make the life of a minor miserable. Courts and legislature have, therefore, carved out certain exceptions to this principle. One important exception is regarding necessities supplied to a minor. If a person, incapable of entering into a contract, or anyone whom he is legally bound to support, is supplied by another person with necessaries suited to his condition in life, the person who has furnished such supplies is entitled to be reimbursed from the property of such incapable person.[13]

A person is said to be of sound mind for the propose of making a contract, if, at the time when he makes it, he is capable of understanding it and of forming a rational judgment as to its effect upon his interest. A person, who is usually of unsound mind, but occasionally of sound mind, may make a contract when he is of sound mind. A person who is usually of sound mind, but occasionally of

[11] Indian Contract Act, 1872, section 25(1).
[12] *Mohoribibi* v. *Dharmodas Ghosh* (1903) 30 IA 114.

[13] Indian Contract Act, 1872, section 68.

unsound mind, may not make a contract when he is of unsound mind.[14] Contracts by persons of unsound mind are also void. Again, an exception is made for contracts for the delivery of necessaries of life for which even a mentally incompetent person would be liable. A sane man who is delirious from fever, or who is so drunk that he cannot understand the terms of contract, or form a rational judgement as to the effect on his interests, cannot contract whilst such delirium or drunkenness lasts.

Free Consent

A contract requires a meeting of the minds, which Roman law called *consensus ad idem*. This principle is contained in section 13 of the Contract Act which says, 'two or more person are said to consent when they agree upon the same thing in the same sense'. This requirement of a valid contract is fulfilled when there is free consent. Consent is said to be free when it is not caused by coercion, undue influence, fraud, misrepresentation, or mistake.[15] So, it becomes necessary to understand what is meant of all these elements which vitiate free consent.

Consent is said to be vitiated by coercion when it is obtained by committing any offence. Section 15 of the Act defines coercion as committing, or threatening to commit, any act forbidden by the Indian Penal Code, 1860 or the unlawful detaining, or threatening to detain, any property, to the prejudice of any person whatever, with the intention of causing any person to enter into an agreement. If the consent to a contract is obtained by implying coercion then it results in a voidable contract. For example, A holds out a pistol on B's skull

and threatens to shoot him in case he does not enter into a contract to sell his property at a certain price. B, under the impending threat, signs the contract. This is an instance of voidable contract because here the consent is caused by coercion.

Undue influence involves the unconscientious use by one person of power possessed by him over another in order to induce the other to enter into a contract. A contract is said to be induced by under influence where the relations subsisting between the parties are such that one of the parties is in a position to dominate the will of the other and uses that position to obtain an unfair advantage over the other.[16] It is a situation where mastery/control is obtained over the mind of one of the parties to contract, by insidious approaches and seductive artifices. The relationships which may develop a dominating influence of one over another are infinitely various and cannot be confined to an exhaustive list. A material distinction here has to be made between one's own folly and the undue influence exercised by another. Particularly, a person is deemed to be in a position to dominate the will of another where he holds a real or apparent authority over the other, or where he stands in a fiduciary relation to the other; or where he makes a contract with a person whose mental capacity is temporarily or permanently affected by reason of age, illness, or mental or bodily distress. Instances of real and apparent authority could include an income tax officer in relation to an assessee or a police officer in relation to an accused. Every relationship of trust, faith and confidence is a fiduciary relationship. The category of fiduciary relationship is a very wide one as confidence and trust is the

---

[14] Ibid., section 12.
[15] Ibid., section 14.

[16] Ibid., section 16.

foundation of numerous human transactions. Such relationships would include those between a lawyer and his client; a spiritual guru and his devotee; a doctor and his patient; a trustee with his beneficiary; a parent with his child; or a creditor with his debtor. If consent to a contract is caused by undue influence, the contract is voidable in the hands of the party whose consent was so caused.

Misrepresentation is when one of the parties to a contract made a wrong statement about some material element of the contract and, because of this statement, the other party entered into the contract. The Contract Act treats fraudulent misrepresentation differently from innocent misrepresentation. Section 18 of the Act deals with innocent misrepresentation. Here misrepresentation means and includes the following situations:[17]

1. The positive assertion of a material fact which the person making it believes to be true but which actually is false;
2. An innocent breach of duty of disclosure of a material fact which if disclosed could have had a bearing on the consent of the other party;
3. Innocently causing a party to agreement to make a mistake as to a material fact.

A contract that is affected by misrepresentation is voidable at the option of the person whose consent was so caused. But once the option of avoiding the contract is exercised, the contract becomes void as against both incapable of being revived again.

Fraud means and includes the following acts committed by a party to a contract with intent to deceive another party thereto, or to induce him to enter into the contract.[18]

1. Suggestion by one party that a material fact is true when he believes that it is false;
2. Active concealment of a fact by one having knowledge or belief of the fact;
3. A promise made without any intention of performing it;
4. Any such act or omission as the law specially declares to be fraudulent.

Mere silence as to facts likely to affect the willingness of a person to enter into a contract is not fraud, unless the circumstances of the case are such that require the party to speak up. For example, A sells, by auction, to B, a horse which A knows to be unsound. A says nothing to B about the horse's unsoundness. Here A has no duty to speak up so he does not commit any fraud. But if B says to A 'if you do not deny, I shall assume this horse to be sound'—here, if A says nothing then he commits fraud. When the consent in a contract is caused by fraud, the contract is voidable in the hands of the person whose consent was so caused. A party to contract, whose consent was caused by fraud or misrepresentation, may, if he thinks fit, insist that the contract shall be performed, and that he shall be put on the position in which he would have been if the representations made had been true. If such consent was caused by misrepresentation or by silence amounting to fraud, the contract is not voidable, if the party whose consent was so caused had the means of discovering the truth with ordinary diligence.

If one or both parties have been mistaken about an element of the contract, then there is no *consensus ad idem*. Where both the parties to a contract are under a mistake as to a matter of fact essential to the contract, the contract is void.[19] A contract caused by a mistake as defined under section 20 is void. Here a

---

[17] Indian Contract Act, 1872, section 18.
[18] Ibid., section 17.
[19] Ibid., section 20.

distinction is to be made between mistake of fact and mistake of law. If a contract is entered into between two parties where both were under a mistake of certain legal position then it is not void. The reason is that everybody is expected to know the law and ignorance of law is no excuse. Therefore, section 20 only talks about mistake of fact. But an erroneous opinion as to the value of the things which forms the subject-matter of the contract, is not be deemed a mistake as to a matter of fact.

In *Ram Chandra* v. *Bisra Ganesh Chandra*,[20] the vendor sold all rights in land including the right to mine. The purchaser bought the land only for mining. In fact vendor had no rights to mine himself and he was totally unaware of this fact. The contract was held to be void because of mistake.

IV. DISCHARGE OF CONTRACT

Contractual relationship springs out of acceptance of a proposal and this relationship comes to an end by discharge of contract. A contract may be discharged by performance, agreement, breach, or frustration.

DISCHARGE BY PERFORMANCE OF CONTRACT

Performance occurs when parties to the contract fulfil their obligations precisely and completely in accordance to the terms of the contract. If it appears from the nature of the case that it was the intention of the parties to a contract that any promise contained in it should be performed by the promisor himself, such promise must be performed by the promisor. In other cases, the promisor or his representative may employ a competent person to perform it.[21] For instance, A promises to pay B a sum of money. A may

perform this promise, either by personally paying the money to B, or by causing it to be paid to B by another; and if A dies before the time appointed for payment, his representative must perform the promise, or employ some proper person to do so. On the other hand, A promises to paint a picture for B. A must perform this promise personally because the nature of contract is such that it has to be performed by the promisor himself otherwise it loses relevance.

When a contract consists of reciprocal promises to be simultaneously performed, no promisor need perform his promise unless the promisee is ready and willing to perform his reciprocal promise.[22] A and B contract that A shall deliver goods to B at a price to be paid by instalments, the first instalment to be paid on delivery. A need not deliver, unless B is ready and willing to pay the first instalment on delivery. B need not pay the first instalment, unless A is ready and willing to deliver the goods on payment of the first instalment.

When a party to a contract promises to do a certain thing at or before a specified time and fails to do such thing at or before a specified time, the contract or so much of it as has not been performed, becomes voidable at the option of the promisee, if the intention of the parties was that time should be of essence of the contract.

DISCHARGE BY FRUSTRATION

Section 56 lays down the simple principle that 'an agreement to do an act impossible in itself is void'. For example, A agrees with B to discover treasure by magic. The contract is void. This is an instance of something which was impossible from the very beginning. But performance of a contract may become

---

[20] *Ram Chandra* v. *Bisra Ganesh Chandra* 39 IC 78.

[21] Indian Contract Act, 1872, section 40.

[22] Ibid., section 51.

impossible subsequent to the formation of contract. A contract to do an act which, after the contract is made, becomes impossible or unlawful, becomes void when the act becomes impossible or unlawful.[23] This is what we mean by frustration of contract. In *Taylor* v. *Caldwell*,[24] the defendant agreed to let music hall to the plaintiff for a concert to be held there. Before that concert could be held, the hall was destroyed by fire without the fault of any of the parties. The plaintiffs sued defendants for loss and compensation. This was held to be a case of physical impossibility and accordingly the defendants were not liable.

Frustration means the occurrence of an intervening event or change of circumstances so fundamental as to be regarded by law both as striking at the root of the contract and as entirely beyond what was contemplated by the parties when they entered into the contract. The common basis on which the mutual understanding was based has failed. Frustration has to be distinguished from commercial hardship. The alteration in circumstances must be to such an extent as to upset altogether the purpose of contract. A minor change here and there will not frustrate a contract. Frustration cannot be invoked just because the contract has suddenly become more difficult or expensive for one of the parties, if the party was partly responsible for the intervening event which destroyed the object of the contract, or if the event was foreseeable. By way of a term of the contract, the parties may specifically bar a defence of frustration and make their contract absolute.

Mutual rights of parties in case of frustration are adjusted. When a contract becomes void, any person who has received any advantage under such contract is bound to restore it, or to make compensation for it, to the person from whom he received it.[25] A contracts to sing for B at a concert for Rs. 1000, which is paid in advance. A is too ill to sing. A is not bound to make compensation to B for the loss of the profits which B would have made if A had been able to sing, but must refund to B the 1000 rupees paid in advance.

DISCHARGE BY AGREEMENT—NOVATION

If the parties to a contract agree to substitute a new contract for it, or to rescind or alter it, the original contract need not be performed.[26] When parties to a contract agree to substitute the existing contract with a new contract that is called novation. A owes money to B under a contract. It is agreed between A, B and C that B shall thenceforth accept C as his debtor, instead of A. The old debt of A to B ends, and a new debt from C to B has been contracted. In *Nagendra Kumar* v. *Hindustan Salts Ltd.*,[27] the petitioner was appointed in response to an advertisement. He was placed in a lower scale than that mentioned in advertisement. The petitioner accepted the placement, worked for some time and then claimed the advertised pay scales. It was held that the principle of novation applies to such a situation and petitioner's claim was rejected.

The party who has the right to demand the performance of a contract may remit or dispense with it, wholly or in part; or extend the time for performance; or accept any other satisfaction instead of performance.[28] A promises to paint a picture for B. B afterwards

---

[23] Ibid., section 56.

[24] *Taylor* v. *Caldwell* QB (1963) 122 ER 309.

[25] Indian Contract Act, 1872, section 65.

[26] Indian Contract Act, 1872, section 62.

[27] *Nagendra Kumar* v. *Hindustan Salts Ltd.* (2001) 1 Guj CD 532.

[28] Indian Contract Act, 1872, section 63.

forbids him to do so. A is no longer bound to perform the promise.

DISCHARGE BY BREACH

Breach of contract is a legal concept in which a contract is not honoured by one or more of the parties by non-performance or interference with the other party's performance. When a party to contract renounces his liability arising under the contract or by his own act makes it impossible for the contract to be performed or fails to perform such obligation the contract stands discharged by breach.

V. REMEDIES FOR BREACH OF CONTRACT

There are several options available to the court in cases of breach of contract. The preferred remedy is damages. Specific performance and injunction could be other remedies which are ordered usually when an award of damages would be 'inadequate'.

DAMAGES

Damages are an attempt by the court to compensate the innocent party to the contract, the party that suffers the breach. The most cited case of all time when it comes to damages is *Hadley* v. *Baxendale,*[29] where a broken shaft was given to a carrier to bring to a repair shop. The carrier was not told that the absence of the shaft meant complete work stoppage for the owner. The carrier was in breach of contract by being several days late in delivery. The plaintiff claimed damages for loss of profits. Admitting to damages, the defendant nevertheless argued that the loss of profit damages were too remote. The court said that damages should be restricted to what:

…may fairly and reasonably be considered either arising naturally, i.e., according to the usual course of things, from such breach of contract itself, or such as may reasonably be supposed to have been in the contemplation of both parties, at the time they made the contract, as the probable result of the breach of it. Now, if the special circumstances under which the contract was actually made were communicated by the plaintiffs to the defendants, and thus known to both parties, the damages resulting from the breach of such a contract would be the amount of injury which would ordinarily occur from a breach of contract under these special circumstances so known and communicated.

The principle of *Hadley* v. *Baxendale* finds expression in section 73 of the Contract Act which says that the party who suffers breach is entitled to receive compensation form the party who has broken the contract for any loss or damage caused to him which naturally arose in the usual course of things from such breach, or which the parties knew, when they made the contract, to be likely to result from the breach of it. Such compensation is not to be given for any remote and indirect loss of damage sustained by reason of the breach.

Damages in case of breach may be envisioned as a part of the very contract which has been breached. If a contract contains any stipulation by way of penalty, the party complaining of the breach is entitled, whether or not actual damage or loss is proved to have been caused thereby, to receive from the party who has broken the contract reasonable compensation not exceeding the penalty stipulated for.[30] A gives B a bond for the repayment of Rs. 1,000 with interest at 12 per cent at the end of six months, with a stipulation that, in case of default, interest shall be payable at the rate of 75 per cent from the date of default. This is a stipulation by way of penalty,

---

[29] *Hadley* v. *Baxendale* (1854) 156 ER 145.

[30] Indian Contract Act, 1872, section 74.

and B is only entitled to recover from A such compensation as the court considers reasonable.

SPECIFIC PERFORMANCE AND INJUNCTION

There may be circumstances in which it would be unjust to permit the defaulting party simply to buy out the injured party with damages. The court may make an order of what is called 'specific performance', requiring that the contract be performed. An order for specific performance is discretionary remedy, which has been provided for under the Specific Relief Act, 1963. This type of remedy has been called 'coercive' and is obviously directed at getting the faulty party to fulfil their obligation.

An injunction is another coercive legal remedy which can be used in some breach of contract cases where an order is made to a party by the court to refrain from doing something that would breach the contract, to stop from continuing an ongoing breach, such as misuse of leased premises.

VI. QUASI CONTRACT

A quasi contract is a situation similar to contract. It is not in fact a contract; rather, it is a means for the courts to remedy situations in which one party would be unjustly enriched were he or she not required to compensate the other. It is a legal substitute of a contract. For example, an unconscious patient treated by a doctor at the scene of an accident has not agreed (either expressly or by implication) to pay the doctor for emergency services, but the patient would be unjustly enriched by the doctor's services were the patient not required to compensate the doctor. The Contract Act states various situations where it has wished to create an obligation on a non-contracting party.

NECESSITIES SUPPLIED TO A PERSON INCAPABLE OF CONTRACTING

If a person who is incapable of entering into a contract (like minor or a person of unsound mind) is supplied by another person with necessaries, the person who has furnished such supplies is entitled to be reimbursed from the property of such incapable person.[31] The rationale for such a provision is that the supplier of necessities cannot claim under a contract as the other party is simply incapable to enter into contract.

PAYMENT OF MONEY DUE BY ANOTHER

A person who is interested in the payment of money which another is bound by law to pay, and who therefore pays it, is entitled to be reimbursed by the other.[32] For example, B holds land under lease from A. The revenue payable by A to the government being in arrears, his land is advertised for sale by the government. Under the revenue law, the consequence of sale will be annulment of B's lease. B, to prevent sale and consequent annulment, pays to the government the sum due from A. A is bound to make good to B the amount so paid.

PERSON ENJOYING BENEFIT OF NON-GRATUITOUS ACT

Where a person does anything for another person, or delivers anything to him, not intending to do so gratuitously, and such another person enjoys the benefit thereof, the letter is bound to make compensation to the former in respect of, or to restore, the thing so done or delivered.[33] In *Shyam Bihari* v. *State of Bihar*,[34] a lecturer was appointed by university

---

[31] Ibid., section 68.

[32] Ibid., section 69.

[33] Ibid., section 70.

[34] *Shyam Bihari* v. *State of Bihar* (1991) 2 BLJR 1222.

and he worked for some time after such appointment. Later on it was discovered that the contract was void as the post was not sanctioned by the state. It was held that the university is liable to pay him the salary for the period during which he worked.

RESPONSIBILITY OF FINDER OF GOODS

A person who finds goods belonging to another, and takes them into his custody, is subject to the same responsibility as a bailee.[35] Once he takes charge of the goods found, he is bound to take as much care of the goods as a man of ordinary prudence would, under similar circumstances, take of his own goods.[36]

THING DELIVERED UNDER MISTAKE OR COERCION

A person to whom money has been paid, or anything delivered, by mistake or under coercion, must repay or return it.[37] For example, a railway company refuses to deliver up certain goods to the consignee, except upon the payment of an illegal charge for carriage. The consignee pays the sum charged in order to obtain the goods. He is entitled to recover so much of the charge as was illegally excessive.

VI. CONCLUSION

Man as a social animal performs various activities and one of the important amongst them is promising. Yes, we make innumerable promises in our day to day life—children promise to behave better, lovers promise to marry, the producer promises to supply goods in time, the land owner promises to let out his land and so on and so forth. Though, contract law is based on the Latin maxim *pacta sunt servanda* (pacts must be kept), yet law is not concerned with many of the promises that we make. Only the promises that are made by competent parties for a valid consideration and that are done by the exercise of free consent are deemed to be valid and enforceable contracts at law.

No one knows when humans first started making promises. But a peep into various religions and cultures shows that down the ages we have placed great emphasis on keeping our promise. Consequently, much thought has gone into this aspect of our lives leading to finer developments and strict principles. In the journey of law, a day came when we codified these principles which are now available in enacted statutes the world over. Law of contract is called one of the basic laws because it further branches into various other subjects of law. Today no law course can do without a proper study of law of contract. Needless to say, it is of utmost importance to one and all.

---

[35] Indian Contract Act, 1872, section 71.

[36] Ibid., section 151.

[37] Ibid., section 72.

Labour Laws and the World of Work in India

Kamala Sankaran

In January 2000, the total number of persons in India in the work force was 396.7 million, of which 237.50 million were in agriculture and the remaining 107.25 million were in non-agriculture employments. Of these, more than 85 per cent of the workers were in the un-organized sector (often also termed the informal economy) that is largely not covered under the labour laws. These unorganized workers are to be found mainly in agriculture (roughly 68 per cent), and in the non-agricultural sector in small informal enterprises employing less than ten workers, and also consists of unpaid family workers and domestic workers. Another characteristic feature of the work force in India is that a large number of women workers are in the unorganized sector. Estimates indicate that over 93 per cent of working women are employed or engaged in the unorganized sector. Given the millions in the work force in India, the challenge before labour law is to ensure that the rights of working persons are protected and that exploitative or inhuman conditions of work do not exist.

There are numerous labour laws in India. In India's federal Constitution, labour related matters occur in the concurrent list.[1] As a result, both central and states legislatures have the power to enact legislation on these matters. There are presently over 60 central legislations dealing with labour matters and together with state level laws or state level amendments to central laws, their number runs into hundreds. It must be noted that in our constitutional scheme, with Presidential assent, state legislatures are permitted to amend central laws made under the concurrent list. Further, in several central labour statutes, the powers of enforcement and implementation have been given to state government, as also the power to make rules as conferred by the laws. The result is that there is considerable variation in the *content* of a centrally enacted law (because of state level amendments or state level rules) and also in their administration across different parts of the country, quite apart from independent state level labour legislation adding to the diversity.

The unequal bargaining position of workers vis-à-vis the employers resulting in unequal employment contracts has been one of the starting points of present-day labour law. Early trade union efforts at organizing workers, with

---

[1] Constitution of India, Concurrent List, Entry 22: Trade unions; industrial and labour disputes; Entry 23: Social security and social insurance; employment and unemployment.

the focus of protecting their interests and bettering their conditions of work met with the fierce and often brutal resistance by the employers, the police and the law which branded such organising efforts as 'conspiracies' to harm the employers' interest. Apart from trade union and political efforts aimed at legalizing such trade union organizations, struggles were also waged to improve their conditions of work, through ensuring an eight-hour working day, safe and hygienic conditions of work, an end to the employment of child labour, increase in wage rates, etc. The rights at the workplace were often written into the employment contracts or, as has more often been the case in India, incorporated into the law as essential aspects of an employment relationship (standing orders) and thus ameliorated working conditions. Yet, as noted above many of the existing labour laws apply to larger establishments employing ten or 20 workers or to certain sectors or kinds of establishments alone and thus apply to around 15 per cent of the work force.[2] Other reasons why the labour laws have a limited coverage is that they apply where there is a clear employer-employee relationship and as a result those engaged via intermediaries and self employed persons are excluded; definitions used in the labour laws apply only to 'workmen', or those working in specific sectors, and as a result, non-workmen (administrative or managerial staff) and those employed in sectors where the law does not apply, may get excluded.

One of the features of the labour laws is the protective provisions relating to women and children. Thus, preventing children from working long arduous hours and their total prohibition from certain forms of work, the ban on women performing night work (which is now subject to review by legislators and the courts), the prevention of sexual harassment at the workplace; such provisions have meant that the law does not strive only to prevent discrimination, it can takes measures to achieve substantive equality. Another aspect of labour law that is often criticised is that complying with its myriad and complicated standards are time consuming and costly. It must be borne in mind that these laws by and large deal with working conditions and thus benchmark standards that are needed to achieve what the International Labour Organisation now terms 'decent work'. However, there are several debates raging in India today on the need to introduce 'flexibility' in the labour laws so that there can be a better industrial climate. This is bitterly opposed by trade unions as they see it as an assault of globalisation on their hard-won rights. Given the poor working conditions and wage levels of bulk of the population, and the fact that they are mostly outside the protection of the labour laws, it would be vital to increase the number of persons coming under labour law protection at the present time to reduce vulnerability and poverty.[3]

Labour laws in India broadly fall into certain categories. Since most of the labour laws are

---

[2] Government employees, by and large, are not covered by labour legislation. Their service conditions are governed by rules made by the central and state governments under powers granted to them by the Constitution. This branch of law is often termed as 'service' law as distinct from labour law which governed industrial employees in the private and public sector.

[3] The Government of India set up a national commission to go into the question of providing protection to the workers in the unorganized sector. Its recommendations are under consideration of the government, and several draft bills providing for social security and minimum conditions of work are pending approval. See 'Report of the National Commission on Labour' 2002.

premised on an employer-employee relationship, regulating this employment contract has been an important focus of labour laws. The following table gives a broad categorisation of laws

Classification of Important Centrally Enacted Labour Laws

Category	Law	Important provisions
Employment Relations	Trade Unions Act, 1926	Formation and registration of trade unions.
	Industrial Disputes Act, 1947	Settlement of industrial disputes, strikes, lockouts, lay-off, retrenchment, closure.
	Industrial (Employment) Standing Orders Act, 1946	Certification of standing orders that regulate the terms of employment.
Conditions of Work	Factories Act, 1948\Mines Act, 1952; Plantations Act, 1951 Beedi and Cigar Workers (Conditions of Employment) Act, 1966; Building and Other Construction Workers (Regulation of Employment and Conditions of Service) Act, 1966; Cine Workers and Cinema Theatre Workers (Regulation of Employment) Act, 1981; Inter-State Migrant Workmen (Regulation of Employment and Conditions of Service) Act, 1979; Motor Transport Workers Act, 1961; Sales promotion Employees (Conditions of Service) Act, 1976; Weekly Holidays Act, 1942; Working Journalists and Other Newspaper Employees (Conditions of Service) and Miscellaneous Provisions Act, 1955; Contract Labour (Regulation and Abolition) Act, 1970; Child Labour (Prohibition and Regulation) Act, 1986	Safety, health, hygiene, hours of work, spread over, overtime, night work in these different sectors or for the specified categories of employees.

(Continued on next page)

(Continued from previous page)

Category	Law	Important provisions
Wages and Monetary Benefits	Minimum Wages Act, 1948	Fixes minimum wages for specific employments
	Payment of Wages Act, 1936	Specifies the wage-period, date of payment of wages and authorised deductions from wages
	Equal Remuneration Act, 1976	Mandates the payment of equal wages for men and women for same or similar work, prohibits discrimination on the grounds of sex at the time of recruitment and promotion
	Payment of Bonus Act, 1965	Regulates the payment of bonus
Social Security	Industrial Disputes Act, 1947	Provisions of retrenchment, lay-off, closure compensation
	Workmen's Compensation Act, 1923	Employers liability for injuries/disablements arising out of and in the course of employment
	Employees' State Insurance Act, 1948	Insurance for specific benefits such as sickness, maternity, disablement, death and old age
	Employees' Provident Funds and (Miscellaneous Provisions) Act, 1952	Contributory provident fund, pension scheme for workers
	Maternity Benefit Act, 1961	Paid maternity leave and cash benefit
	Payment of Gratuity Act, 1970	Gratuity payment
Miscellaneous	Contract Labour (Regulation and Abolition) Act, 1970	Abolition of contract labour
	Child Labour (Prohibition and Regulation) Act, 1986	Abolition of child labour
	Bonded Labour System (Abolition) Act 1976	Abolition of bonded labour

We now look more closely at some of these laws.

I. MINIMUM WAGES ACT, 1948

The International Labour Organisation adopted Convention No. 26 and Recommendation No. 30 relating to minimum wage-fixing machinery in trades or part of trades in 1928. This Convention provided that each member-state (and India had been a founding member since 1919) should create or maintain a machinery whereby minimum rates of wages could be fixed for workers employed in trades in which no arrangement existed for effective regulation of wages by collective bargaining and where wages were very low. This in turn had an impact in India and the Royal Commission on Labour (1931) recommended that an enquiry establish which were the unorganized industries where such minimum wages ought to be fixed. Labour enquiry committees were appointed in the provinces and subsequently in 1943, a Labour Investigation Committee was appointed to investigate the question of wages and earnings as also the social and living conditions of labour. Interestingly, the eighth meeting of the Standing Labour Committee (March 1946) recommended that a separate legislation be enacted for the unorganized industries covering issues such as hours of work, minimum wages, working conditions etc. Eventually however, the Minimum Wages Bill was introduced in the Central Legislative Assembly dealing with fixation of minimum wages in 'sweated' industries and the bill was passed and came into force on 15 March 1948.

The act extends to the whole of India and provides for the fixation of minimum wages for employments listed in the Schedule. The appropriate government (the state governments) have the discretion to add to the schedule those employments in which the workers require the protection of the act. It must be borne in mind that the minimum wages are fixed only for the scheduled employments, with the unfortunate result that a large number of persons working in industries or occupations not listed, can continue to be paid wages less than the notified minimum wage.

The courts have held that fixation of minimum wages is part of the constitutional goal of providing a living wage as provided in the Directive Principles of State Policy (Article 43) and are not unreasonable restriction on the employers to carry on their trade or business under article 19(1)(g) of the Constitution, and are in fact reasonable and in the interest of the general public and protected by Article 19(6) of the Constitution that permits reasonable restriction on the right to be imposed on these grounds.[4] Further, courts have categorically held that the inability of the employer or business to pay minimum wages can be no ground to challenge the fixation of minimum wages, because if 'an industry is unable to pay its workers at least a bare Minimum Wage then that industry has no right to exist'.[5] In other words, payment of minimum wage is the first charge upon industry.

The term 'minimum wage' has not been defined in the act. According to the Fair Wages Committee appointed in 1948, a minimum wage should provide not merely for the bare subsistence of life but for the preservation of the efficiency of the worker by providing for some measure of education, medical requirement and amenities. The criteria evolved by the Tripartite 15th Indian Labour Conference

[4] *Bijoy Cotton Mill* v. *State of Ajmer* 1955 I LLJ 129 (SC).

[5] *M/s. Crown Aluminum Works* v. *Their Workmen* 1958 I LLJ 1 (SC); also see *Edward Mills Co. Ltd* v. *State of Ajmer* AIR 1955 SC 25.

(1957) has now been endorsed by the courts,[6] which provide that wages should be need-based and cater to: (1) the standard working class family considered to comprise three consumption units for one earner; (2) the minimum of requirement calculated on the basis of net intake of calories as recommended for an average Indian adult of moderate activity; (3) the clothing requirement estimated per capita of 18 yards (as stated in 1957) which for a family of four would amount to 72 yards per annum; (4) the expenditure towards rent to be based on the rent corresponding to the minimum area provided for under the industrial housing scheme of the government, and; (5) fuel, lighting and other miscellaneous items of expenditure that would amount to 20 per cent of minimum wage.

The court, while endorsing this recommendation of the Indian Labour Conference, has now added that additional components to the minimum wages also need to be factored in: (1) children's education; (2) medical requirements; (3) minimum recreation including festivals and ceremonies, and; (4) provision for old age, marriage, which together should constitute 25 per cent of the total minimum wage.[7]

Sections 3 and 5 provide for the manner and the procedure by which fixation and revision of minimum wage should take place. Section 8 empowers the central government to create an Advisory Board which has to advise the central and state governments in the matter of fixation and revision of minimum wages. The state government can fix minimum wages for the employments specified in the schedule to the act.

The rate of wage could be a time-rated, piece-rated, a guaranteed time-rate (a minimum rate of remuneration to apply in the case of employees employed on piece-work in order to secure to such employees a minimum rate of wages had they worked on a time, rather than a piece–rate basis) and an overtime rate. The minimum rate of wages is also supposed to consist of a basic wage and a special allowance which is to be adjusted in accordance with the variation in the cost of living index. The wages of an employee working in an establishment in which less than 1000 person are employed is to be paid by the seventh of the month, and in other cases by the tenth of the month.[8]

The minimum wages payable under the act are to be paid in cash; however where there is a custom to pay a part or whole of the wages in kind, the government may authorise payment either wholly or partly in kind. The Supreme Court in the well-known case of *People's Union for Democratic Rights* v. *Union of India*, brought as public interest litigation, has observed that non-payment of minimum wages to the employees is a breach of the fundamental rights enshrined in article 23 of the Constitution and amounts to forced labour or *begar*. The court held that where a person provides labour or services to another for remuneration which is less than the minimum wage, the labour or service provided by him clearly falls within the scope and ambit of the term 'forced labour'. Thus, economic compulsion that makes a person to work for less than the minimum wage also amounts to forced labour. The court further noted that whenever any fundamental rights that are enforceable against private individuals such as the rights enacted in articles 17, 23 or 24

---

[6] *Standard Vacuum Refining Co.* v. *Its Workmen* (1961) 1 LLJ 108 (SC).

[7] *Workmen represented by the Secretary* v. *The Management of Raptakos Brett & Co Ltd* AIR 1992 SC 504.

[8] Minimum Wage (Central) Rules 1950 r 21 (1) (i).

are violated, it is the constitutional obligation of the state to take the necessary steps to prevent such violation and to ensure observance of the fundamental right of the individual by the persons who is transgressing it.[9]

Under section 19 of the act, inspectors can be appointed. The courts have, in some public interest litigations, directed the government to tighten up the inspection machinery and to ensure that close and detailed inspection be carried out by fairly senior inspection staff to ensure observance of labour laws.[10] Section 20 prescribes that a claim application for payments less than the minimum rate of wages should be made before the Authority within six months from the date from which the minimum wage became payable. The state government could appoint a Commissioner of Workmen's Compensation or an officer of the rank of a Labour Commissioner or an officer with the experience as a judge of a Civil Court or a stipendiary Magistrate as an authority to hear claims arising out of payment of less than the minimum wages, payment for days of rest and overtime. If the workman is covered under the Payment of Wages Act, 196(?), the recovery of shortfalls in payment of minimum wages under the Minimum Wages Act, 1948 can be made by filing claims As is the case is most labour laws, violation of the law can also attract penal provisions. There is punishment of up to six months or a fine of Rs. 500 or both which has been prescribed under the act.

Despite several provisions in the act for enforcement, the reality is that millions of persons still stand outside its protection, either because their employments are not covered (for example in several states domestic service is not an employment for which minimum wages are notified) or even where it is fixed, lack of knowledge, lack of organisation, capacity to access the remedies on the part of the workers leads to lack of compliance of the act. For instance, in 2004-05, a mere 4205 persons filed claims under the central sphere complaining of non-payment of minimum wages.[11] Non-payment of minimum wages is rampant and this is one of the basic labour laws that needs to be vigorously enforced.

II. TRADE UNIONS ACT, 1926

Alongside the industrialization of India that began in the nineteenth century arose the formation of trade unions. The textile mills in Nagpur and Bombay, the coal industry at Jamshedpur, and the railways, saw the beginnings of the trade union movement in the country. However, these attempts at organizing the workers were treated as illegal conspiracies under the law applicable at that time, and were viewed as combinations of workers who were conspiring to breach their contract of employment by demonstrations and strikes. The formation of the Indian Trade Unions Congress in 1920 acted as a catalyst for more unions to be formed across the country, and the result of this movement was the passing of the Trade Unions Act, 1926, that confers legality on the formation of trade unions, provides for registration of trade unions, defines the rights and obligations of such trade unions and their immunities. The Constitution has recognized the right to form associations and trade unions as a fundamental right under article 19(1)(a). All citizens of India, except those specifically excluded under the Constitution are entitled

[9] 1982 II LLJ 454(SC). Also see *Sanjit Roy* v. *State of Rajasthan* AIR 1983 SC 328.

[10] *Labourers Working in Salal Hydro Electric Project* v *State of Jammu & Kashmir* AIR 1984 SC 177.

[11] Ministry of Labour and Employment, Annual Report 2005–06, 2006, p. 30.

to exercise this right. Article 33 of the Constitution specifically allows the exclusion, by law, of members of the armed forces, the police and other security forces from the ambit of this right.

The Trade Unions Act, 1926 extends to the whole of India. The act defines a trade union as a combination, whether temporary or permanent, formed primarily for the purpose of regulating the relations between workmen and employers, or workmen and workmen, or between employers and employers, or for imposing restrictive conditions on the conduct of any trade or business and includes any federation of two or more trade unions. Thus, not only trade unions of workers, but also, around 189 trade unions of employers, are registered under the act;[12] The Employers' Federation of India is a well-known trade union of employers. Since the act allows a trade of workmen to be registered, it is not necessary that only those workmen employed by an employer can form a trade union; the Self Employed Women's Association (SEWA) formed initially in Ahmedabad is a large trade union registered under the act and which has presently hundreds of thousands of members who are self employed vegetable vendors, hawkers, home-based workers, *chikan* workers, etc. Of course, workers who are employed by an employer form the bulk of the trade unions in India. Of the 300 million strong work-force in the country, less than a tenth are organized into trade unions;[13] these are primarily concentrated in the large factories, mines, public sector units, banks and insurance companies.

Another aspect of the definition of trade unions that needs to be noted is that a trade union can be registered only if the workmen are employed in a trade or industry. (The expression 'employed' is understood in the broad sense of 'engaged' or 'employed', so that self-employed persons are also treated as workmen). Because of this stipulation of restricting trade unions under the act to trade or industry, trade unions have been registered in those establishments that are deemed to fall into these two expressions. Thus, workmen in educational institutions, hospitals, banks, shops, commercial establishments, plantations and agriculture have formed trade unions. However government employees (excluding those in the industrial establishments of the government such as railways or ordnance factories) may form associations, which are constitutionally permitted to form associations but cannot register these as trade unions under the act. There is no absolute right given to a person to be admitted as a member of a particular trade union. Unless there is an express provision in a law or the constitution of the trade union that a person possessing the requisite qualifications cannot be refused membership, such a right cannot be read as part of the Trade Unions Act, 1926.[14] Likewise, no workman can be compelled to become a member of a trade union.[15]

The act, though a central one, is implemented by the states which appoint Registrars of Trade Unions. Following an important amendment in 2001, any seven or more persons can form a trade union and apply for registration of the act, provided at least ten per cent or 100 of the workmen, whichever is less, are engaged or employed in the establishment or industry with which it is connected,

---

[12] See http://labourbureau.nic.in/TU%202k2%20Statement%204.1.htm, last accessed on 15 July 2007.

[13] 6,973,000 members of registered trade unions submitting returns.

[14] *Mohammed Ibrahim* v. *Asansol Iron and Steel Workmen's Union* (1954) 1 LLJ 1.

[15] Ibid.

and are the members of such trade union, on the date of making of application for registration. The application needs to be accompanied by the rules of the trade union and certain essential information such as the names and addresses of the members making the application, the details of the office bearers and their occupation, and if the trade union has been in existence for more than a year prior to the making of the application, a statement of the assets and the liabilities of the union. The rules must stipulate the method of electing the office bearers, the maintenance of a list of members, the minimum member-ship fees, and the heads on which the general funds of the trade union can be spent. The trade union is also permitted to have a political fund which it can use to intervene in the political process—field candidates, support elections, print periodicals and pamphlets. This is a hard won right, because many trade union struggles are aimed not only in wresting concessions from the employers, but also in making changes in the laws concerning working conditions for the working class as a whole. The link between the trade union movement and the political movement is recognized in the act which permits the setting up of such a political fund. The Registrar can call for further information and if satisfied that the requirement of the act has been complied with, can grant registration of the trade union. This registration is liable to be cancelled if obtained by fraud or mistake with prior two months' notice to the trade union.

Once registered, the trade union should ensure that only 50 per cent of its office bearers are 'outsiders', i.e., not connected with the trade or industry to which the trade union relates. The presence of 'outsiders' is a characteristic feature of Indian trade unions. Initially, educated persons of middle class background

or activists from outside were instrumental in creating consciousness among the workers for the need to organise, and were naturally also elected leaders of the trade unions. The rule that only 50 per cent of the office bearers could be such outsiders is there to ensure development of internal leadership, which has greatly increased. The act also stipulates that children below the age of 15 years should not be permitted to become members of the trade union. This is an unfair provision, given that child labour is not completely banned under the Child Labour (Prohibition and Regulation) Act, 1986, and yet, such children are deprived of trade union membership. Registered unions are also obliged to send regular returns to the Registrar. Upon registration, a member of a trade union can no longer be prosecuted for committing a conspiracy against the employer; this however does not preclude them from being prosecuted for any other offence during the course of their trade union activity. Further, the trade union, its office bearers and members also cannot be made financially liable in civil suits in certain cases such as causing losses to the employer in business for legitimate trade union activities done in furtherance of trade disputes.

This is an act dealing with the registration of trade unions and not their recognition. An amendment of 1947 dealing with recognition has not been brought into force. Certain states have introduced legislation to deal with the matter of recognition of trade unions, which are not covered in the present text.[16]

There are, at present, around 68,000 regi-stered trade unions in India.[17] The average

[16] See, for instance, the Bombay Industrial Relations Act, 1946 and the Maharashtra Recognition of Trade Unions and Prevention of Unfair Labour Practices Act, 1971.

[17] There were 68, 544 registered trade union in 2002

membership of a trade union is 893 persons, which is fairly small. Their average income is very low and is less than Rs. 85,000 a year. This is hardly sufficient for maintaining a trade union office or carrying out the activities in furtherance of workers' interests. The amendment to the Trade Unions Act, 2001 in raising the numbers required for registration seeks to reduce the multiplicity of unions. Yet given the vast numbers of workers in the unorganized sector who fall outside trade unions, unionising this huge work force remains a daunting task.

II. INDUSTRIAL DISPUTES ACT, 1947

The setting up of the railways, canals and public works led to several disputes between workers and the employer. The Employers and Workmen (Disputes) Act, 1860 incorporated principles for the criminal breach of contract, i.e., any worker leaving his job in breach of contract was liable to be arrested and sent back to work. This principle, which amounted to indentured labour was widespread and facilitated the large scale mobilisation of labour for the burgeoning industrial and plantation sector. The criminal breach of contract principles in the law were repealed in 1932. Subsequently, other laws were passed to deal with disputes, notably the Trade Disputes Act, 1929, which gave way eventually to the Industrial Disputes Act, 1947. The preamble states that it makes provision for the investigation and settlement of industrial disputes. The act applies to all industries as defined in the act. This expression has resulted in much litigation and in the celebrated *Bangalore Water Supply* case of 1978, the court

according to the Labour Bureau, Government of India. See http://labourbureau.nic.in/TU%202k2%20Statement%202.1.htm, last accessed on 15 July 2007.

applied a functional test, including any activity involving the systematic co-operation of employers and employees to produce goods and services for the public at large. Thus, organized activity such as factories, mines, educational institutions, hospitals, research institutions, municipalities and charitable activities which fell within the ambit of this test are now treated as falling within the scope of the act. Certain activities of a spiritual nature such as religious activities, domestic service, sovereign governmental activities and casual or voluntary activities alone were excluded. An amendment in 1982 sought to modify the definition of 'industry' to counteract the effect of this judgement and exclude educational institutions, hospitals, research institutions, *khadi* and village industries from the scope of the act. But this amendment is yet to be brought into force due to opposition from the trade unions and also the lack of an alternate dispute settlement law for such excluded activities/establishments.

When a dispute exists or is apprehended, the appropriate government can refer the dispute to one of the authorities specified in the act to prevent or to bring about a settlement of the dispute.

Works committees, consisting of equal numbers of employers and workmen representatives, are required to be constituted in every industrial establishment employing a hundred or more workmen. The function of these committees is to remove causes of friction between the employers and workmen, in the day-to-day working of the establishments and to promote measures for securing amity and good relations between them. However, despite some good progress in the fifties, the institution of works committees rarely fulfils these aims in practise.

There are a variety of institutions for

settlement of disputes under the act, such as conciliation, arbitration and adjudication. Each state government can appoint conciliation officers whose main function is to bring the parties together and foster an amicable settlement of the dispute. Conciliation Boards can also be appointed in some cases. Conciliation is compulsory in the case of disputes in public utility services and optional in the case of other establishments. Time limits have been prescribed for the settlement of disputes in conciliation—14 days in the case of a conciliation officer and two months in the case of the board of conciliation from the date of notice of strike. A settlement arrived at in the course of the conciliation proceeding will be binding for such period as may be agreed upon between the parties and where no period is agreed upon for a period of one year, and will continue to be binding, until revoked by two months notice by either party to the dispute. Parties are also free to mutually agree to appoint their dispute to an arbitrator whose award would be final.

Labour Court and industrial tribunals have been created for the adjudication of disputes.[18] The appropriate government has the power to compulsorily refer an industrial dispute for adjudication if it considers it expedient. In addition, both parties to a dispute can also jointly refer a dispute to the tribunal for adjudication. Strikes and lock-outs are prohibited during the pendency of conciliation and adjudication proceedings. The decision of the adjudicator, known as an award, is published by the approximate government in the Official Gazette and is binding on all the workmen in the establishment, whether or not they were members of the trade union that first raised the dispute.

The act has several other features to regulate the employer employee relationship. These are, briefly:

1. Workmen have the right to receive notice for any change in their working conditions or terms of employment;

2. Where workmen are to be laid-off on grounds of shortage of electricity, raw materials, breakdown of machinery or natural calamity, they are entitled to lay-off compensation at the rate of 50 per cent of their wages;

3. Where workmen are retrenched (i.e., permanently made redundant) retrenchment compensation is payable at the rate of 15 days wages for every year worked, that would help them cope with sudden unemployment;

4. Where an establishment is closed down permanently, workmen are entitled to closure compensation;

5. Where a strike is declared in an illegal manner, workmen are liable to be proceeded against by the employer for committing a misconduct and are not liable to be paid for the duration of the strike; where the employer has declared a lock-out illegally the employer is liable to pay wages to the workmen for the duration of such illegal lock-out. The employer has a right to punish workmen for a misconduct done while in employment. The list of acts which constitute misconduct is certified under the Industrial Employment (Standing Orders) Act, 1946. Upon a misconduct being committed the workman needs to be issued a charge sheet and a domestic enquiry needs to be

---

[18] There are at present 22 Central Government Industrial Tribunals in addition to the Industrial Tribunals and Labour Courts set up by the different state governments. See Ministry of Labour, 'Annual Report 2005–06.

conducted by the employer, where the workman should have a fair opportunity to present his case. If the charges stand established in the domestic enquiry, the employer may take disciplinary action against the workman, including dismissal of the workman for grave misconduct. In cases where a workman is sought to be dismissed where a dispute is already pending before a labour court or tribunal the prior permission of the adjudicator needs to be taken.

There are a large number of cases pending before the labour court in India. In 2000, there were 5,33,038 cases pending in the labour courts and of these 28, 864 had been pending for more than ten years. Similarly, in 2003, 12, 674 cases were registered in Central Government Industrial Tribunals and only 846 cases were disposed of that year.[19] Thus, while the law aims for a smooth settlement of disputes, adjudication is often a long-drawn out process. This has considerably weakened the position of workers as can be seen in the dwindling numbers of person-days lost due to strikes and the increase in the loss due to lock-outs which exceed lost person-days due to strikes.[20]

III. MATERNITY BENEFIT ACT, 1961

This important act providing maternity right to women amongst other related rights, applies to factories, mines, plantations and circuses. However, the act does not cover those factories or establishments to which the provisions of the Employees' State Insurance (ESI) Act, 1948, apply. This is because the social security benefits covered by the ESI Act provide for maternity benefits under their social insurance scheme. The act was amended in 1989 to extend its applicability to shops and establishments employing ten or more persons. The act benefits all categories of women workers whether employed directly or through any agency for wages. The women worker should have worked for at least 80 days in the preceding 12 months to claim maternity benefit and medical bonus.

The central government is responsible for administration of the provisions of the act in mines and the circus industry; the state governments are responsible for its administration in factories, plantations and other establishments.

The rights provided under the act are varied. Firstly, no employer may knowingly employ nor can a woman work in the six weeks immediately following the day of delivery. Further, if the woman so requests, an employer shall not give arduous work or work that involve long hours of standing or work that that may adversely affect her health in the period of six weeks preceding her delivery (in case the women does not wish to avail of maternity leave in this period) nor the period of one month immediately receding this period. The maximum period for which a woman can avail maternity benefits is a period of 12 weeks, of which at least six weeks should be availed of after the delivery. The act provides for the payment of maternity benefit. The rate of benefit shall be at the rate of the 'average daily wage' for the period of her actual absence preceding and including the day of delivery and for the six weeks immediately following that day. In the case of miscarriage,

[19] Anant, T.C.A., R. Hasan, P. Mohapatra and S.K. Sasikumar, 'Labour Markets in India: Issues and Perspectives', in *Labour Markets in Asia*, J. Felipe and R. Hasan (eds.), London, Palgrave Macmillan, 2006, p. 246.

[20] Ibid., p. 251.

the act allows leave with wages at the rate of maternity benefit for six weeks immediately following the date of miscarriage. Additional leave with wages at the maternity benefit rate for a maximum period of one month is also admissible in the case of illness arising out of pregnancy, delivery and premature birth of the child or miscarriage. The act also provides for payment of medical bonus at the rate of Rs. 250. This obligation to pay the bonus does not apply to employers who provide for pre-natal confinement and post natal care free of charge. Women are also eligible for six weeks leave of absence in case of medical termination of pregnancy and two weeks leave with wages to women workers who undergo tubectomy operation.

A woman worker claiming benefits under the act should have actually worked in an establishment for a period of not less than 80 days preceding the date of her expected delivery. For the purpose of calculating the days of qualifying period, the days on which she has been laid off or which were holidays during the period are to be included.

Women are protected against dismissal or discharge during or because of pregnancy. A woman is eligible for maternity benefit even after her dismissal, provided the dismissal is not on grounds of misconduct.

For contravention of the act or rules by any employer, minimum three months or imprisonment or a minimum fine of Rs 2000 or both have been provided for. Contra-vention of the act can also be treated as a criminal offence, however, so the court can take cognizance of a prosecution unless it is instituted with the sanction of the inspector.

IV. CONCLUSION

Many questions are currently being raised about the kind of labour laws we require in India today. There are many who feel that in order to make India an attractive destination for foreign direct investment, protection provided by labour laws should be considerably diluted so that there is 'labour flexibility' and growth. Labour laws have historically served as a countervailing force to provide basic rights to working persons. Given the large numbers of persons already outside the scope of such protective legislation, labour law reform, far from focusing on dilution of benefits, needs to concentrate on extending minimum benefits to the millions of person working in the unorganized sector, so that they are guaranteed their social security and decent conditions of work. The constitutional goal of achieving social justice can be realised by broadening the reach of the labour law. In addition, extending the scope of labour law would bring Indian legislation in conformity with its international obligations.[21]

[21] India has ratified several International Labour Organisations Conventions, which it is bound to comply with; in addition, India has also acceded to the International Covenant on Civil and Political Rights and the International Covenant on Economic, Social and Cultural Rights, which contain may provisions dealing with rights of working persons.

Environmental Law

M. ROOPA

I. INTRODUCTION

Concern over environmental degradation and pollution, a discernible trend after 1970, has motivated and inspired action, both at the local and global level, to conserve and protect the environment. In India, this concern has emphasized the need for attention of both the judiciary and the legislature. Degradation of forest cover, air and water pollution, carbon emissions, and protection of bio-diversity are a few illustrations of the range of environmental issues that are being addressed through policy, legislative, executive and judicial intervention.

The burgeoning environmental movement both within the country and outside has consistently drawn attention to these issues. The collective effort to promote 'sustainable development' has been described by the Brundtland Commission as 'development that meets the needs of the present without compromising the ability of future generations to meet their own needs'. Striking the right balance between economy, development, and ecology is the core of protecting and conserving the natural resources. The debate over what constitutes sustainable development in different contexts, has been raging for several years now.

This chapter examines the theoretical aspects of environmental law. The attempt here is to provide a broad understanding of the concepts and principles of environmental law in the country, while explaining how concerned citizens could use that knowledge in promoting the cause of environment. The chapter elaborates in-depth on certain issues that are topical, as well as some of those that are historical, having contributed to the development of environmental law in the country.

II. BRIEF HISTORY OF ENVIRONMENTAL LAW IN INDIA

Prior to 1970, legislation with regard to the environment dealt primarily with control of water pollution and protection of water-based resources. The Indian Penal Code, 1860, contained provisions on offences affecting public health and safety, which covered aspects like water, air and noise pollution. Judicial intervention was limited to claims made under the Indian Penal Code and tort law for nuisance and negligence. Even the Indian Constitution did not contain provisions with regard to the environment.

It was only in 1976, four years after the Stockholm Conference, that the 42nd amendment to the Constitution of India, introduced Article 48A and 51 A(g) to the Directive Principles of State Policy. Article 48A obligates the state to protect and improve the environment and Article 51A(g) requires the citizens to protect and improve the natural environment including forests, lakes, rivers and wild life, and to have compassion for living creatures.

The Constitutional amendment also made changes in the legislative powers of the Centre and the states, relating to the environment. 'Forest', 'wildlife', and 'population control' were subjects in the exclusive domain of the state legislatures, but the amendment transferred these to the concurrent list, enabling both the states and the centre to make laws on these subject matters.

In 1974, the central government passed the first major environmental law—The Water (Prevention and Control of Pollution) Act. This was followed up with other major enactments such as the Forest (Conservation) Act, 1980, The Air (Prevention and Control of Pollution) Act, 1981 and The Environment (Protection) Act, 1986. In the recent past, the National Environment Tribunal Act, 1995, was enacted to set up an exclusive tribunal to hear claims of compensation related to accidents concerning toxic substances. Further, the National Environment Appellate Authority Act, 1997 was enacted to establish an authority that would hear appeals against orders granting environmental clearance in designated areas where industrial activity is restricted under the Environment (Protection) Act, 1986.

The judiciary has also been proactive in protecting and conserving the environment. It has devised various innovative methods to provide redress and ensure practical solutions to several environmental issues. By setting up 'green Benches', both the Supreme Court and the High Courts have played a pivotal role in developing the environmental jurisprudence in the country.

III. ENVIRONMENTAL LAW IN INDIA

What comprises 'environmental law' in India? Apart from the black letter law contained in the Constitution of India and the various statutes, it must be emphasized that both the judiciary and the executive also make law. The judiciary, while deciding cases, interprets the law, thus clarifying and filling up the gaps; this is termed 'judge-made law'. The executive, in implementing the law, is empowered to issue orders, rules and regulations, termed broadly as 'delegated legislation'. Here we look only at the laws made by the legislature and the judiciary and discuss only some important aspects contained in them.[1]

PROVISIONS IN THE INDIAN CONSTITUTION

The Constitution of India contains specific provisions on environmental protection. These are articles 48A, 51(A)(g), 243-ZD (3) and 243-ZE(3). The right to environment has also been read into articles 14, 19 and 21 of the Constitution by the courts.

Article 21 of the Constitution states that 'No person shall be deprived of his life or personal liberty except according to procedure established by law'. Though no specific mention is made, the right to a wholesome environment, has been read into the right to life guaranteed by Article 21 of the Indian Constitution by the Supreme Court and the High Courts. Article 14 enshrines the fundamental right to equality, while Article 19(1)(g) enshrines the right to practise any profession, or carry on any occupation, trade or business,

---

[1] For a more detailed list of enactments that constitute 'environmental law' in India, see Box I.

which is subject to reasonable restrictions. These two fundamental rights also impinge on the right to a clean environment that is implied in this reading of Article 21.

The Constitution (Seventy-fourth Amendment) Act, 1992, provides in Article 243-ZD(3) that every district planning committee shall, in preparing the development plan have regard to 'environmental conservation'. Article 243-ZE(3) provides for a similar provision in cases of metropolitan planning committees.

Article 253 of the Constitution empowers the Parliament to make laws to implement India's international treaty obligations. International standards and norms are thus incorporated into the domestic/national legislation.

ENVIRONMENTAL LEGISLATIONS

A brief overview of the specific legislations relating to environment such as air, water, forests and wildlife are discussed in this section. One of the first enactments was the Water (Prevention and Control of Pollution) Act, 1974, which sought to introduce regulatory agencies for controlling water pollution. The Pollution Control Boards at the Centre and in the states were set up by this Act. A related legislation, the Water (Prevention and Control of Pollution) Cess Act, 1977, sought to augment the resources of these regulatory agencies. Subsequently, the Air (Prevention and Control of Pollution) Act was enacted in the year 1981 and the task of implementation of this legislation was also entrusted to the same regulatory agencies created under the Water (Prevention and Control of Pollution) Act, 1974. Since these two enactments sought to deal only with water and air pollution problems, the need was felt for a more comprehensive legislation to deal with the larger issue of environment, particularly in the light of the Bhopal Gas Disaster.

Thus, in 1986, the Environment (Protection) Act was enacted. While it entrusted certain functions to the regulatory agencies (Pollution Control Boards) the Act provided a broader mandate to the central and state governments to protect and conserve the environment.

Conceptually, the three enactments Air (Prevention and Control of Pollution) Act, 1981, the Water (Prevention and Control of Pollution), 1974 and the Environment (Protection) Act, 1986 are similar. The acts vest regulatory authority in state boards and empower these boards to establish and enforce standards for effluents being discharged by polluting factories into water or air. A Central Board performs the same function in union territories as the state boards and it also co-ordinates activities among states.

According to section 2 of the Environment (Protection) Act, 1986, 'environment' includes water, air and land and the inter-relationship which exists among and between water, air and land, and human beings, other living creatures, plants, micro-organisms and property. The same enactment defines 'environmental pollution' as the presence of any environmental pollutant in the environment. It goes on to define an 'environmental pollutant' as any solid, liquid or gaseous substance present in such concentration as may be, or tend to be, injurious to the environment. These definitions have been found wanting, as they do not capture within them other possible pollutants such as heat, energy, sound and nuclear radiation.

Under the Air (Prevention and Control of Pollution) Act, 1981 all industries operating within designated air pollution control areas must obtain a license or a 'consent', from the state boards. The state boards are required to prescribe emission standards for industry and automobiles after consulting the central board and noting its ambient air quality standards. Similarly, under the Water (Prevention and Control of Pollution) Act, 1974, the boards control sewage and industrial effluent discharges by approving, rejecting or conditioning applications for consent to discharge. The state boards also check water pollution by advising the state governments on location of industries. Under the (Environmental) Protection Act, 1986, the Central Government has the power to protect and improve the environment; plan and execute a nation-wide programme for the prevention, control and abatement of environmental pollution; set standards for the quality of the environment in its various aspects and for the emission or discharge of environmental pollutants from various sources; undertake preventive measures such as restricting areas in which any industry or operations shall not be carried out subject to certain safeguards; carry out inspections, and conduct research and awareness building exercises.

The Wild Life (Protection) Act was passed in 1972 to provide for state wildlife advisory boards, regulations for hunting wild animals and birds, establishment of sanctuaries and national parks, regulations for trade in wild animals, animal products and trophies. The Act bans the harming of certain endangered species and also regulates the hunting of certain other species listed in the schedules. The Act is administered by wildlife wardens and their staff. The much-publicised case of the shooting of a black buck by Salman Khan, the film star, is being tried under this Act.

After 1990, three new Acts have come into existence. The Public Liability Insurance Act enacted in 1991, imposes a 'no-fault' liability upon the owner of hazardous substances and in the event of an accident, provides for immediate relief to the victims. The owner of hazardous substances is mandated to take out an insurance policy covering potential liability from an accident. Simultaneously, the owner is also required to contribute to the Environmental Relief Fund established by the Central Government. The fund shall, in the event of an accident, after verification, provide compensation to the victims.

The National Environment Tribunal Act of 1995 empowers the Centre to set up a national tribunal at New Delhi with the power to entertain applications for compensation for death or injury caused by an accident during the handling of hazardous substance.

The National Environment Appellate Authority Act, 1997 requires the central government to constitute a national environment appellate authority for hearing appeals against the orders granting environmental clearance in areas where restrictions are imposed on setting up any industry or carrying on any operation or process.

COURTS AND THE DEVELOPMENT OF ENVIRONMENTAL JURISPRUDENCE

While mapping the path of development of environmental jurisprudence, it may be noted that a proactive judiciary has contributed vastly in protecting the environment in the country. Some important decisions are highlighted here. They are discussed thematically and not necessarily, chronologically.

Right to Life

As mentioned earlier, the right to wholesome environment has been read into the right to life guaranteed by Article 21 of the Indian Constitution by both the Supreme Court and the High Court. In *Subhash Kumar* v. *State of Bihar*,[2] the right to life under Article 21 of the

---

[2] AIR 1991 SC 420

Constitution has been held by the court to include the right of enjoyment of pollution-free water and air. The court has clarified that if anything endangers or impairs the quality of life in derogation of laws, a citizen has the right to have recourse to Article 32 for removing the pollution of water or air which may be detrimental to the quality of life.

In *Indian Council for Enviro-Legal Action* v. *Union of India*,[3] the Supreme Court has implemented right to wholesome environment as a part of the right to life enshrined in Article 21 of the Constitution. In this case, private companies manufacturing hazardous and inherently dangerous chemicals like oleum (concentrated form of sulphuric acid) had been allowing toxic, untreated waste waters to flow out freely. The toxic substances percolated deep into the bowels of the earth, polluting the aquifers and the subterranean supply of water. The water in the wells was rendered unfit for human consumption and for cattle, as well as for cultivation, resulting in disease, death and disaster in the village and surrounding areas. The Supreme Court held that:

If an industry is established without obtaining the requisite permission and clearances and if the industry is continued to be run in blatant disregard of law to the detriment of life and liberty of citizens living in the vicinity, this court has the power to intervene and protect the fundamental right to life and liberty of the citizens of the country.

In *M.C.Mehta* v. *Union of India*,[4] the petitioner stated that the foundries, chemical/hazardous industries and the refineries at Mathura were emitting sulphur dioxide which when combined with oxygen with the aid of moisture in the atmosphere, forms sulphuric acid. This caused 'acid rain' which had a corroding effect on the gleaming white marble of the Taj Mahal in adjoining Agra. The Supreme Court held that the emissions resulted in violation of the right to life of the people living in the Taj area as well as damaged the prestigious Taj monument. The Supreme Ccourt directed 292 industries to change over from coke/coal to natural gas as industrial fuel and ordered stoppage of functioning and relocation of those industries which were not in a position to obtain gas connections for any reason.

In *Obayya Pujari* v. *Member Secretary, KSPCB, Bangalore*,[5] the Karnataka High Court held that pollution caused by stone crushing has adverse effects on human health, animals and vegetation, and therefore, violates right to life guaranteed under article 21 of the Constitution. The court held that the fact that the units were licensed or held necessary permission would not prevent it from issuing necessary directions, in as much as the interests of the units have to give way to larger interests of the society.

In *Narmada Bachao Andolan* v. *Union of India*,[6] it was argued that the construction of a large dam like Sardar Sarovar Dam would result in ecological disaster and violation of Article 21. The court balanced the environmental effects of the Sardar Sarovar Project with national or public interest in view of the need of water and power for increasing population. The court held that mere change in environment does not per se violate rights under Article 21 especially in the present case where steps were taken to improve ecology, environment and rehabilitation in case of displacement.

In *MC Mehta* v. *Union of India*,[7] the Supreme

---

[3] AIR 1996 SC 446.
[4] AIR 1997 SC 734.
[5] AIR 1999 Kant 157.
[6] AIR 2000 SC 3751.
[7] AIR 2001 SC 1948.

Court held that air pollution in Delhi caused by the vehicular emissions was in violation of Article 21 and therefore, the court directed all commercial vehicles operating in Delhi to switch to CNG fuel mode to safeguard the health of the people.

In *Sayeed Maqsood Ali* v. *State of Madhya Pradesh*,[8] the Madhya Pradesh High Court held that noise pollution amounts to violation of Article 21 of the Constitution.

Right to Equality

In *Rural Litigation and Entitlement Kendra, Dehradun* v. *State of Uttar Pradesh*,[9] a large number of lessees of limestone quarries were involved. The mining activities resulted in pollution of the Mussoorie hills range that form a part of the Himalayas. The issue of development and environment was brought into sharp focus for the first time in this case and the court laid emphasis on the need for reconciling the two in larger interest of the country. The court pronounced against indiscriminate renewal of the mining leases and directed closure of the mines which caused pollution.

RIGHT TO PROFESSION, TRADE OR BUSINESS

The fundamental right to carry on any occupation, trade or business is subject to reasonable restrictions which may be imposed in the interest of the general public as provided under Article 19(6) of the Constitution. The right to carry on a business or trade ceases when it causes a threat to the environment or the health of the general public. In *Rural Litigation and Entitlement Kendra, Dehradun* v. *State of Uttar Pradesh*,[10] it was pointed that as a

result of the closure order, the workmen employed in the limestone quarries would be thrown out of employment thereby resulting in the contravention of their fundamental right to profession under Article 19(1)(g) of the Constitution. The Supreme Court stated that it would be a price to be paid for protecting and safeguarding the right of the people to live in a healthy environment. However, the court directed the government to start reclamation of the areas forming the limestone quarries and employing the workers for the afforestation and soil conservation programme to be taken up in that area. Similarly, in Obayya Pujari's case, discussed above, the court held that the interests of the society are to be balanced with the interests of the citizens to carry on business.

Public Interest Litigation

Indian courts have been one of the most progressive in the world. In a bid to protect the environment, the courts have relaxed the rule on *locus standi* and entertained several public interest litigations. The activism of the courts has also encouraged several individuals and groups to approach the courts for redress. Notable among these, is Mr M.C. Mehta, a Delhi based lawyer, who has raised several important issues such as the leak of oleum gas from a factory in Delhi, impact of pollutants from the Mathura refinery on the Taj Mahal and vehicular pollution in Delhi.

One of the first PILs on environment was the *Rural Litigation and Entitlement Kendra* case (discussed above). In *Vellore Citizens Welfare Forum* v. *Union of India*,[11] the Supreme Court was asked to address the issue of pollution caused by 900 tanneries in five districts of Tamil Nadu. The court observed that the

---

[8] AIR 2001 MP 220.
[9] AIR 1985 SC 652.
[10] AIR 1997 SC 734.

[11] AIR 1996 SC 2715.

leather industry has no right to destroy the ecology, degrade the environment and pose a health hazard. It cannot be permitted to expand or even continue with the present production unless it tackles by itself the problem of pollution created by the industry. Each polluting industry was asked to pay a 'pollution fine' of Rs. 10,000, which was to be kept under a separate 'Environment Protection Fund', to be utilised to compensate the affected persons as identified by the authorities and also for restoration of the damaged environment. The units that were shut down by the court would be permitted to reopen only after they had set up effluent treatment plants to the satisfaction of the Pollution Control Board, after obtaining its consent.

In another Public Interest Litigation, *Indian Council for Enviro-legal Action* v. *Union of India*, the Supreme Court implemented the right to wholesome environment as a part of the right to life. In this case, private companies manufacturing hazardous and inherently dangerous chemicals like oleum, discharged untreated toxic sludge in the open, polluting aquifers and rendering wells and water streams unfit for human consumption. The Supreme Court found that the chemical manufacturing companies were flouting the provisions of the law and held the polluters liable for ecological remediation measures. In doing so, the principle of 'polluter-pays' was applied in this public interest litigation case.[12]

In *M.C. Mehta* v. *Kamal Nath,*[13] the Supreme Court laid down the innovative principles of environmental jurisprudence. In this case, a private company in which the Union Minister Kamal Nath had direct links, had built a club

on the banks of the river Beas in Kullu-Manali, thus encroaching on forest land. It was reported in the press that the club had diverted the course of the river, in a bid to prevent it from flooding the club house. This news report was brought to the notice of the Supreme Court, which issued three judgements over the span of seven years. In its first judgement in 1997, it applied the 'public trust doctrine' which states that certain resources like air, seas, waters and forests are of public importance and can never be made the subject of private ownership. The doctrine imposes a duty on the state to protect the resources for the enjoyment of the general public, as it is the trustee of all natural resources. Hence, notice was issued to the Government of Himachal Pradesh and the club. In its second judgement in 2000, the court held that in the case of violation of Article 21, the court can award exemplary damages in a public interest litigation. In its third judgment in 2002, the court fixed the quantum of exemplary damages as ten lakhs.

There has been considerable criticism of the courts' ability to balance competing interests, in public interest litigation cases. It has been found that in enforcing pollution standards the courts have also adversely impacted rights of workers' working in the factories that are ordered to be shut down or relocated. Similarly, in protecting forest and wildlife, rights of tribal population have been discounted.

IV. SELECT ENVIRONMENTAL ISSUES AND THE LAW

FOREST AND WILDLIFE

Forest cover is a vital component of a healthy and sustainable environment. However, they are being continually eroded by development

---

[12] For a brief synopsis of the environmental law principles as laid down by the courts, see Box II.

[13] AIR 2000 SC 1997.

projects such as mining, roads, dams and the wood and pulp industry. During the colonial period, the British viewed the forests as a revenue generating resource and depleted vast tracts of forest cover. State control and monopoly over the forests was ensured by enacting the Indian Forest Act, 1865. This was subsequently replaced by a more comprehensive legislation titled the Indian Forest Act, 1927. This legislation continues to be in force in independent India. Besides these national enactments, the state governments have enacted laws to protect and conserve forests. To complete the picture on the forest laws, the Wildlife Protection Act, 1972, also needs a mention. This enactment lays down the procedures and guidelines for the creation and management of national parks, sanctuaries, and community managed protected areas.

The transfer of forests from the State List to the Concurrent List of the Constitution empowered the Central Government to enact the Forest (Conservation) Act, 1980, to conserve and manage the forests. The Forest (Conservation) Act, 1980 makes it obligatory for the state government to obtain permission of the Central Government for (a) dereservation of reserved land; (b) for the use of the forest land for non-forest purposes.

One of the cases challenging mining operations in the reserve forest area in the Doon Valley was the *Dehradun Valley* case.[14] The lime stone quarrying led to dust and debris clogging rivers and springs in the region and destroyed the valley's landscape with the blasting away of hills. This adversely affected the agricultural lands, drinking water and the forest cover in the region. The Supreme Court in this case ordered the closure of all mines in the area and set up a rehabilitation committee

to displace the miners. Similarly, the illegal mining activities in the Sariska National Park in Alwar, Rajasthan were challenged in *Tarun Bharat Sangh, Alwar* v. *Union of India*. The Central Government, under section 3 of the Environment (Protection) Act, 1986 expressly prohibited the carrying on of mining operations, except with the permission of the Central Government, in the areas covered by Project Tiger. However, no such permission had been obtained and the court held that the mining operations being carried out in the tiger reserve as violative of the law.

Two other cases that have impacted forest conservation in the country are: (a) *TN Godavarman Thirumulkpad* v. *Union of India*,[15] and; (b) *Samatha* v *State of Andhra Pradesh*.[16] In *Godavarman*, the Supreme Court directed the closure of saw mills and mining operation in Arunachal Pradesh which resulted in the felling of forests. The court (i) banned the felling of any trees in the tropical wet evergreen forests of Tirap and Changlang in Arunachal Pradesh; (ii) issued detailed directions for the protection and sustainable use of the forests; (iii) ordered the formation of regional committees for implementation and monitoring of the courts orders. This judgment has been criticised for the several contradictions that have emerged as a result of the court taking on the role of the adjudicator, administrator and legislator.

In the *Samatha* case, the Supreme Court held that the expression 'forest land' does not mean only reserved forest and extended its meaning to cover tracts of land covered by trees, shrubs, and other vegetation. The court ordered the state governments to examine the mining activities being carried out on forest land. On the issue of tribal rights, the Supreme Court

[14] AIR 1985 SC 652.

[15] AIR 1997 SC 1228.
[16] AIR 1997 SC 3297.

held that the lands in scheduled areas be preserved for the social-economic empowerment of the tribals.

Forests are home to the tribal populations too. The growing awareness to protect the environment has meant larger tracts of land being brought under the categories of national parks, sanctuaries and reserve forests. Such notifications have simultaneously sought to displace and exclude tribals from their homeland and their source of livelihood. Further, several litigations seeking to further the protection of the forests have not adequately represented the cause of the tribals. Reconciling the traditional rights of the tribals, with that of the environment, is a growing challenge for the state institutions.

INDUSTRIAL POLLUTION, HAZARDS AND LIABILITY

Increased industrial activity and the resultant pollution, needs to be monitored and regulated effectively. The Bhopal Gas tragedy (see Box III), one of the worst industrial disasters in the world, revealed the horrors of industrial pollution. Following the gas leak, the Central Government enacted the Environmental (Protection) Act in 1986. Section 2 (e) of the Act defines hazardous substance as 'any substance or preparation which, by reason of its chemical or physico-chemical properties or handling, is liable to cause harm to human beings, other living creatures, plants and micro-organism, property or the environment'. To regulate the possible hazards from industrial activity and, more recently from newer technologies (bio-technology) being introduced in the agricultural field, the Central Government has enacted several rules under the Environment (Protection) Act, 1986. These include: (a) Hazardous Wastes (Management and Handling) Rules, 1989; (b) Manufacture,

Storage and Import of Hazardous Chemical Rules 1989; and (c) Rules for the Manufacture, Use, Import, Export and Storage of Hazardous Micro-organisms/Genetically Engineered Organisms or Cells, 1989.

Remedies for harm caused due to negligence and accidents have been brought before the courts under both tort and criminal law. The Bhopal Gas Disaster however helped focus on several legal issues of liability of industries (see box). Following the Bhopal case, another case of leak of oleum gas from an industrial unit of the Shriram Foods and Fertilisers Industries situated in Delhi resulted in injuries to several persons. Advocate and environmental activist M.C. Mehta approached the court[17] and several expert committees were set up to look at the issues. Based on the recommendation of the committees, the court laid several conditions for the grant of permission to Shriram Foods to continue operating their industry. In doing so, the Supreme Court suggested that a high powered committee be set up by the Government of India to: (i) ensure that there are no defects or deficiencies in the design, structure or quality of their plant or machinery; (ii) there is no negligence in maintenance and operation of the plant and equipment and necessary safety devices and instruments are installed and are in operation and (iii) proper and adequate safety standards and procedures are strictly followed. Notably, the court laid down the principle of absolute liability in the case of industrial accidents involving hazardous substances. The court stated that a 'hazardous or inherently dangerous activity in which it [the industry] is engaged must be conducted with the highest standards of safety and if any harm results on account of such activity, the enterprise must

---

[17] *M.C. Mehta* v. *Union of India* AIR 1987 SC 965.

be absolutely liable to compensate for such harm without any harm without any regard to the fact that the enterprise had taken all reasonable care and that harm occurred without any negligence on its part'.

In order to ensure that adequate compensation is provided for without delay, to victims of industrial disasters, the Public Liability Insurance Act, 1991 was enacted. The owner of the industry involved in an accident is required under the Act to pay specified amounts to the victims as interim relief based on 'no-fault' liability. Section 4 of the Act, makes it mandatory for the owner of a hazardous unit to obtain an insurance policy to cover the liability. Many concerns on industrial pollution, more particularly of liability—both civil and criminal—of individual actors involved in accidents have not been adequately addressed. With growing trade and technological advancement, the technical knowledge and competence of the authorities in charge of preventing environmental pollution, needs to be enhanced and updated on a war footing.

V. RECENT INTERNATIONAL AND REGIONAL DEVELOPMENTS

What are some of the developments on the international platform? Developments on the international front, though not always binding, encourage debates within and amongst nations, while setting down the norms that countries can aspire towards. Many domestic laws are now being inspired and influenced by international conferences and conventions. In this section, we discuss the historical developments internationally and look at some of the current debates.

In 1972, the United Nations Conference on Human Environment was held in Stockholm,

marking the precursor to the development of international environmental law. The conference led to the Stockholm Declaration, providing for an international action plan for co-operation on environmental matters and the United Nations Environment Programme was established. The next major international conference was held in Rio de Janeiro, in 1992. In the meanwhile, in 1987, the Montreal Protocol was adopted to provide for broad guidelines that would restrict and regulate activities that would prevent the depletion of the ozone layer.

The Rio Conference of 1992, officially called the United Nations Conference on Environment and Development (UNCED) resulted in five declarations, *viz.*, Rio Declaration on Environment and Development, Convention on Climate Change, Convention on Biodiversity, Forest Principles and Agenda 21. The conference also led to the creation of the UN Commission on Sustainable Development, which is mandated with the task of promoting sustainable development through the integration of environmental and economic objectives. The Commission on Sustainable Development is a permanent forum, which reviews reports from governments, and international organizations efforts to implement Agenda 21, discuss financial and technical issues, and recommend further actions to promote sustainable development.

More recently, the World Summit on Sustainable Development was held in Johannesburg in 2002. Held a decade after the Rio conference, the world community reaffirmed their commitment to sustainable development through economic development and environmental protection, and introducing social development as another vital element. The Summit acknowledged that eradication of poverty was the key to achieving sustainable development and hence seeks to set up a World Solidarity Fund to promote social and human development.

The Johannesburg Plan of Implementation reiterates the need to implement the Rio principles and Agenda 21 and the need to promote the ratification and implementation of International Environmental Treaties, especially the Montreal Protocol, to prevent the depletion of ozone layer, the Climate Change Convention and its Kyoto Protocol, the Biodiversity Convention and its Bio Safety Protocol and the Convention to Combat Desertification.

A. Kyoto Protocol: This protocol, adopted in 1997, sets specific goals for countries to reduce the emission of greenhouse gases, which contribute to the global warming. The Kyoto Protocol is an agreement made under the United Nations Framework Convention on Climate Change and it seeks to reduce the emissions of carbon dioxide and five other greenhouse gases or permit for emissions trading among countries if they maintain or increase emissions of these gases. The objective of the protocol is the 'stabilization of greenhouse gas concentrations in the atmosphere at a level that would prevent dangerous anthropogenic interference with the climate system'. Countries are separated into two general categories: developed countries, who have accepted strict GHG emission reduction obligations; and developing countries, who have no GHG emission reduction obligations. Kyoto includes 'linking mechanisms' which allow for developed countries to meet their GHG targets by purchasing GHG emission reductions from elsewhere. In August 2002, India signed and ratified the Protocol. India, and other developing countries were exempt from the requirements of the framework of the Kyoto Protocol as historically they are not seen as the main contributors to the greenhouse gas emissions impacting climate change.

B. Convention on Biodiversity: This framework convention seeks to conserve biodiversity, promote sustainable use of bio resources, and share the benefits received from the genestock. In January 2000, the parties to the Convention on Biological diversity adopted the Cartagena Protocol on Biosafety. This Protocol establishes the 'Biosafety Clearing-House' which serves as a means through which information on biosafety is made available to the parties. The Protocol seeks to protect biological diversity from the potential risks posed by living modified organisms resulting from modern biotechnology.

VI. ROLE OF CONCERNED CITIZENS

How can one use the laws that are stated above, in protecting and conserving the environment? Judicial remedies for environmental issues and problems can be found in tort law, criminal law, statutory law (such as the specific environmental legislations discussed in the preceding sections) and constitutional law (writ jurisdiction). The direct recourse available to citizens and groups (under Article 226 to the High Court and under Article 32, to the Supreme Court), provides an effective remedy to environmental concerns. We have also discussed above the positive aspects of public interest litigation, in promoting the cause of the environment. It is therefore possible for an individual or a group of people concerned about an environmental problem to approach the courts to seek relief and remedy. Until the enactment of the Environmental (Protection)

Act, 1986 the power to prosecute for environmental pollution was vested in the government. Section 19 of the Act, provides for citizens or 'any person' the right to move the court, after giving a notice to the government of not less than 60 days, for an offence committed under the Act. After the notice period, citizens can file a complaint before the magistrate.

There are other forums that can also be used effectively to ensure protection and conservation of the environment. These may be created through a statute or through executive orders. Proactive citizens' participation, through the effective use of these means and procedures, can contribute immensely to the cause of protecting the environment. Active and informed participation wherever there are environmental impact assessments undertaken for large developmental projects, participation at public hearings, effective use of the Right to Information Act, 2005, and a vigilant citizenry can contribute to achieving the goals of sustainable development and protection of the environment.

VII. CONCLUSION

In the end, one might well ask, why is it important to protect the environment? Is it more important to ensure forest cover as opposed to iron ore mining, which provides employment and contributes to the development of the economy? Are tigers more important than the expansion of agriculture, which adds to the food security of the country? These and several such questions, do raise the contesting claims being made on our natural resources. The need to balance these competing claims is a challenge not only for the legislature and the judiciary, but also the society at large. In the choices we make in our everyday lives, we determine the future of the planet.

Box I
Laws and rules relevant to the environment in India

- The Water (Prevention and Control of Pollution) Act, 1974
- The Water (Prevention and Control of Pollution) Rules, 1975
- The Water (Prevention and Control of Pollution) Cess Act, 1977
- The Water (Prevention and Control of Pollution) Cess Rules, 1978
- The Air (Prevention and Control of Pollution) Act, 1981
- The Air (Prevention and Control of Pollution) Rules, 1982
- The Environment (Protection) Act, 1986
- The Environment (Protection) Rules, 1986
- Hazardous Wastes (Management and Handling) Rules, 1989
- Manufacture, Storage and Import of Hazardous Chemical Rules, 1989
- The Forest (Conservation) Act, 1980
- The Forest (Conservation) Rules, 1981
- The Wildlife Protection Act, 1972
- The Wild Life (Transactions and Taxidermy) Rules, 1973
- The Wild Life (Stock Declaration) Central Rules, 1973
- The Wild life (Protection) Licensing (Additional Matters for Consideration) Rules, 1983
- The Wild Life (Protection) Rules, 1995
- The Wild Life (Specified Plants – Conditions for Possession by Licensee) Rules, 1995
- The Public Liability Insurance Act, 1991
- The Public Liability Insurance Rules, 1981
- The National Environment Tribunal Act, 1995
- The National Environment Appellate Authority Act, 1997

Box II
Environmental Law Principles:

The Precautionary Principle: Beginning with *Vellore Citizens' Welfare Forum* v. *Union of India*,[18] the Supreme Court has explicitly recognized the 'precautionary principle' as a principle of Indian environmental law. The precautionary principle means that the environmental measures taken by the state authorities must anticipate, prevent and attack the cause of environmental degradation. In the *Narmada Bachao Andolan* v. *Union of India*,[19] case, the court stated: 'When there is a state of uncertainty due to the lack of data or material about the extent of damage or pollution likely to be caused, then, in order to maintain the ecology balance, the burden of proof that the said balance will be maintained must necessarily be on the industry or the unit which is likely to cause pollution'. Hence, where there are threats of serious and irreversible damage, lack of scientific certainty should not be used as a reason for postponing measures to prevent environmental degradation. The 'onus of proof' is on the industry or the developer to show that their action is environmentally benign.

The 'Polluter Pays' Principle: The Supreme Court calculates environmental damages not on the basis of a claim put forward by either party, but through an examination of the situation by the court, keeping in mind factors such as the deterrent nature of the award. However, it held recently that the power under Article 32 to award damages, or even exemplary damages to compensate environmental harm, would not extend to the levy of a pollution fine. The 'polluter pays' rule has also been recognized as a fundamental objective of government policy to prevent and control pollution.

Box III
BHOPAL

Union Carbide, an American company, set up a small plant in Bhopal in 1969. Called the Union Carbide India Ltd, the company manufactured pesticides. Until 1979, the Company manufactured methyl isocyanate (MIC), a dangerous chemical, from the parent company. After 1979, it started to manufacture the same at the Bhopal unit. On the night of 23 December 1984, a dangerous chemical reaction occurred in the Union Carbide factory when a large amount of water got into the MIC storage tank. In the next two hours, 40 tons of MIC leaked out of the storage tank and escaped into the air, spreading eight kilometres into the city. Nearly 4,000 people were killed and several more seriously injured. Exposure to MIC has resulted in damage to the eyes and lungs and has caused respiratory ailments such as chronic bronchitis, gastrointestinal problems like hyperacidity and chronic gastritis, ophthalmic problems, vision problems, neurological disorders such as memory and motor skills, psychiatric problems including varying grades of anxiety and depression, musculoskeletal problems and gynaecological problems among the victims. The survivors still suffer from the injuries caused and continue to live with disability and disease. The victims were largely poor families in settlements around the factory. The Bhopal disaster was the result of poor safety standards, poor maintenance and poor accountability to the community, at large.

[18] AIR 1996 SC 2715.
[19] AIR 2000 SC 3751.

After the disaster, the Government of India passed the Bhopal Gas Leak Disaster (Processing of Claims) Act, 1985. The Act gave the Central Government the power to represent all the claimants in appropriate forums. The government, under the act, also formulated the Bhopal Gas Leak Disaster Scheme, for the registration, processing and determination of compensation to each claim and appeals, if any. Pursuant to the Act, the Government of India sought to sue UCC in the United States for relief. However, the US courts dismissed the case stating that the site of the accident was in India and hence the forum for adjudication cannot be in the US. In the meanwhile, in a case filed in the district court in Bhopal, the judge ordered an interim compensation of US $ 270 million, to be disbursed to the victims. UCC appealed against this order and the Madhya Pradesh High Court reduced the amount to US $ 192 million. Both UCC and the government appealed against this order and the Supreme Court in 1989, awarded US $ 470 million (Rs. 715 crores) to the Government of India for and on behalf of all the Bhopal victims in full and final settlement of all claims. The Supreme Court also terminated all the civil, criminal and contempt proceedings against the corporate officials pending in the Indian courts. However, in 1991, the Supreme Court modified the order by setting aside its earlier order quashing the criminal proceedings against the corporate officials.

The Concept of Religious Personal Laws

ARCHANA PARASHAR

I. INTRODUCTION

India is a democratic polity that also contains a plurality of laws in the area of personal relations. Commonly these laws are referred to as Religious Personal Laws (RPLs) and generally, in the matters of marriage, divorce, children and succession, various religious communities are governed by their respective RPLs.[1] One of the more contentious outcomes of this state of affairs is that generally women in each community have lesser rights than men. The legislative reforms of various RPLs have been uneven and the government of the day has selectively accepted the claim of religious sanctity and thus inviolability of (some of) these laws. This selective deployment of the concept of RPLs shows that the governing authorities use it as a political tool, more often than not to the detriment of women. However, since the Constitution of India contains a guarantee of equality, including sex equality, the obvious question is how can the RPLs and the Constitution co-exist? In order to answer this question we need to go back to the origins of the concept of the RPLs. In the following discussion I will trace the origin of the idea of the RPLs, explain the role of English colonial administration in their development and argue that the contemporary Indian government can and should 'reform' all RPLs in order to guarantee gender equality.

II. PERSONAL AND TERRITORIAL LAWS

The laws in Europe made a distinction between personal and territorial laws. As a general rule, in personal matters a person carried his law with him wherever he went. In all other matters the law of the territory where he happened to be present, applied to him. This idea combined with another rule that ecclesiastical laws generally governed personal matters and

---

[1] For instance, Hindus are governed by the Hindu Marriage Act, 1955, Hindu Succession Act, 1956, Hindu Adoptions and Maintenance Act, 1956 and the Hindu Guardianship and Minority Act 1956; Muslims are governed by the *Shariat*, by virtue of the Muslim Personal Law (Shariat) Application Act, 1937, the Dissolution of Muslim Marriages Act, 1939, and the Muslim women (Protection of Rights on Divorce) Act, 1986; Christians are governed by the Indian Christian Marriage Act, 1872, the Divorce Act, 1869 and the Indian Succession Act, 1925; Parsees are governed by the Parsi Marriage and Divorce Act, 1936, and the Indian Succession Act, 1925. In addition, there is the Special Marriage Act, 1954, available to anyone, but designed more specifically for two persons wishing to marry who, however, belong to different religions.

thus the notion of religious personal laws came into being.

However, in the Indian sub-continent this division into personal and religious or territorial and non-religious laws was not known. Before the arrival of the British colonizers, their respective religious laws governed Hindus and Muslims, with very few exceptions. Islam was first introduced into the Indian sub-continent in the early eighth century. Even though by the thirteenth century Shariat had become established, there is academic debate about the extent of its application. The Mughal rulers were Hanafis, and the *qazis* administered this law. It is generally believed that the Hindus were left free to be governed by their laws, except in the case of criminal matters.[2] Initially the British administrators were not interested in the political governance of the sub-continent and were content to be able to conduct their trade in relatively settled conditions. However, gradually with the expansion of the British colonial power, it became imperative that the political and judicial institutions be moulded to suit the needs of the colonizers. The British administrators first acquired the judicial authority and then the legislative authority over the peoples of India. It is in this gradual acquisition of legal power that the concept of RPLs was introduced into the Indian legal lexicon.

The early settlements of the British in India were called factories. These were small territories granted by the local rulers to the British merchants of the East India Company, who lived in these 'factories', had their warehouses there, and conducted their trade activities. It was only gradually that the Company came to exercise administrative and then judicial authority in different parts of the country. The developments in the provincial or *moffusil* towns and in the Presidency towns took place under different circumstances. The Charter of Charles II in 1661 authorized the East India Company to exercise judicial authority inside the factories. Meanwhile, in the moffusil towns, Warren Hastings' plan of 1772 provided for the establishment of civil and criminal courts. Significantly, Article 23 of the Regulation II of 1772 'saved' for the Hindus and Muslims the right to apply their own religious laws in the matters of inheritance, marriage, caste and other religious usages or institutions. This provision became the foundation for the differentiation between personal and other civil matters.[3]

The Charter of George I in 1726 authorized the establishment of the King's courts in the towns of Bombay, Calcutta and Madras. Even though this charter was silent about the jurisdiction of these courts over the native inhabitants, they on their own resorted to these courts.[4] In the Presidency towns, it was only in the Act of 1781 that the Supreme Court was given civil jurisdiction over native inhabitants. Section 17 of the Act provided that with regard to Hindu and Muslim applicants, 'their inheritance and succession to land rent and goods and all matters of contract and dealing between party and party should be determined in the case of Mahomeddans and Hindus by

---

[2] See for example, Pearl, David, *A Text Book on Muslim Law*, London, Croom Helm, 1979, p. 21; Sarkar, J., *Mughal Administration*, fourth edn, Calcutta, M.C. Sarkar, 1959.

[3] Ilbert, C., *The Government of India: A Brief Historical Survey of Parliamentary Legislation Relating to India*, second edn, Oxford, Clarendon Press, 1907.

[4] This is explainable in large part as due to the absence of any other judicial machinery. The Muslim courts had become corrupt and fallen into disuse. Hindus, even during the times of the Mughal rulers were left to their own devices.

their respective laws and where only one of the parties should be a Mahomeddan or Hindu by the laws and usages of the defendant'.[5]

In the 1772 and 1781 laws, there were only two common provisions, that of contracts and inheritance. Even though in these regulations only a few topics were mentioned the courts gradually assumed the responsibility of applying the natives' personal laws in most family matters.[6] So too in the Cornwallis Code of 1793, it was mentioned that 'in suits regarding succession, inheritance, marriage and caste, and all religious usages and institutions, Mahomeddan law with respect to Mahomeddans and Hindu law with respect to Hindus are to be considered as the general rules by which judges are to form their decisions'.[7] It is not evident whether the British administrators intended the native laws of Hindus and Muslims to refer to their religious laws or to customary usages or both.

The reason why this exception in favour of laws regulating certain personal matters was considered as saving of Hindu and Muslim religious laws perhaps lies in the language used. The two major communities in India were identified by the religions they followed and the personal laws that the English administrators had decided to save were also in turn understood as religious. In this way, the categories 'religious laws' and 'personal laws' became interchangeable, but in the process, it was forgotten that before the arrival of the British administrators all aspects of the laws of Hindus and Muslims were religious. Moreover, even in the British regulations what constituted 'personal' matters to be governed by 'religious' laws changed from time to time. British policies determined what was designated as a personal matter and the final shape of the laws governing such personal matters when administered by the English courts became far removed from the religious laws of the people.

III. CONTACT BETWEEN THE RELIGIOUS LAWS AND THE STATE LEGAL MACHINERY

In the successive charters and regulations, not only was the corpus of personal laws arbitrarily determined but also the content of such rules was modified in various ways. Even after it was determined that 'personal laws' were applicable in any instance, there were still many ways in which such laws became modified in the process of their adoption by the legal system. The judicial role in this regard was significant even if unintentional. Gradually, legislative changes were also introduced but despite these changes the idea persisted that the RPLs are immutable religious laws.

The courts in moffusil towns were initially manned by the Company's servants, rather than by judges with legal training. These judges relied on the Muslim qazi or the Hindu pandit to ascertain the Islamic and Hindu laws. The reliance on the qazis and pandits inevitably led to the scriptural rules gaining prominence at the expense of local customs. As a consequence, the continued development of customs was retarded but more significantly even when the courts did recognize custom, it had to meet the artificially laid standards of proof of English law. Moreover, customs once recognized judicially, became part of the body of precedent and this in turn hindered the continuing adaptation of personal laws to the changing conditions of society.

---

[5] Rankin, G. C., *Background to the Indian Law*, Cambridge, Cambridge University Press, 1948, p. 9.

[6] Jain, M. P., *Outlines of Indian Legal History*, second edn, Bombay, N.M. Tripathi, 1966, p. 11.

[7] Ibid., p 710.

It was in 1790 that the English trained judges were brought to the Indian courts. These judges, even when applying the rules of Hindu or Muslim laws, interpreted them according to their understanding and training. Moreover, as these judges were trained in another system, their standards of proof, rules of evidence and other procedural rules transformed the Hindu and Muslim laws in unforeseen ways. Another factor that led to inevitable changes in the local laws was that the courts were enjoined to use the formulas of 'justice, equity and right' or 'justice and right' to resolve a dispute if no identifiable rule was available. This resulted in the English common law notions of 'justice equity and right' finding expression in the precedents set by Indian courts. Most of these precedents were set in the matters of RPLs and thus the content of such laws became modified further. More specifically, the Privy Council held that these formulae implied the application of English law if found applicable to Indian circumstances.[8] However, where the English law did not provide a parallel, the judges used their own sense of justice to resolve disputes in accordance with these formulae. Very often the courts used these formulae to decide cases when two religious laws were claimed to be applicable to a dispute. In these ways, the judges' own notions of right and justice found their way into the corpus of personal laws of the natives.

Further and more direct changes were introduced when the British administrators started legislating for the local conditions. Unlike the exercise of judicial power, no limits were placed on the authority of the legislatures to enact laws with regard to personal matters. However, the legislative history shows that the early administrators considered it politically expedient to make universal laws only where possible and allow diversity if it was necessary.[9] While the First Law Commission recommended that the Hindu and Muslim personal laws should be codified, the Second Law Commission forcefully argued that such laws should not be codified. Their reason for saying so was that the Hindu and Muslim laws derive their authority from the Hindu and Muslim religions respectively and since the British legislature does not have the authority to legislate religion, it does not have the authority to legislate for these laws either. However, what was forgotten in this process was that it was not only the personal laws that were religious laws but all aspects of laws of Hindus and Muslims were equally religious. The Second Law Commission had simultaneously recommended that all other aspects of civil laws ought to be codified and the English law was to provide the model for such codification. The Fourth Law Commission appointed in 1879 repeated the same sentiments with regard to the family laws of natives.[10]

Even a cursory look at the legislative history during the colonial period shows that some matters that were initially considered personal were later legislated upon and some of them were transformed into territorial laws. For instance, contracts were originally allowed to be regulated by the native laws but were subsequently regulated by a separate code. Moreover, with the attainment of greater political stability, the English administrators openly regulated activities that were considered religious by the natives. The example

[8] See *Waghela Raysanji* v. *Sheikh Masludin* (1887) LR 14 IA 89.

[9] Stokes, W., *The Anglo Indian Codes*, vol. I, Oxford, Clarendon Press, 1887, p. X.

[10] Jain, M. P., *Outlines of Indian Legal History*, second edn, Bombay, N.M. Tripathi, 1966, pp. 643, 657.

of the regulation of sati illustrates this change well.[11] Initially, the practice of sati was regulated by the successive orders passed in 1813, 1815 and 1817. The main idea behind these regulations was to ensure that unwilling women were not forced to commit sati and to that end, a policeman had to be present at the performance of sati. It was only in 1829 that Governor-General Lord William Bentinck abolished the practice completely or more precisely, made it a criminal act. While he was aware of the possible political ramifications of abolishing the practice of sati, he was also confident that the moral goodness of the act was backed by his power to enforce such a law.[12]

This pattern of legislatively modifying various practices that were initially considered religious continued in the name of humanitarian considerations, public policy, and demand by the public, etc. For instance, the Caste Disabilities Removal Act, 1850; the Hindu Widows Remarriage Act, 1856; the Native Converts Remarriage Act, 1866; the Hindu Inheritance (removal of Disabilities) Act, 1928, and the Child Marriage Restraint Act, 1929, all modified practices that were considered an integral part of their religion by the local populations.

IV. CONSTITUTION, EQUALITY AND THE RELIGIOUS PERSONAL LAWS

The government of the newly independent Indian state inherited this legacy of RPLs. The issue of RPLs came to be discussed immedi-ately after independence when the Constituent Assembly was deliberating upon the shape of the Constitution for the new state. The question whether the RPLs formed a special category of laws that was outside the purview of the Constitution was discussed but not resolved satisfactorily. The subsequent legislative history of independent India shows an uneven development of reforms. The judicial activity is similarly uneven.

Immediately after gaining independence, the Constituent Assembly was given the task of formulating a draft Constitution. In the process of drafting the fundamental rights the issue of RPLs came to be discussed at various stages of the process.[13] Initially the Constituent Assembly had appointed an Advisory Committee to formulate the articles. The Advisory Committee had three sub-committees on fundamental rights, minorities as well as tribal and excluded areas. The sub-committee on fundamental rights drafted the clause on freedom of religion and that was subsequently commented upon by the sub-committee on minorities and eventually debated in the Constituent Assembly. At all these stages, the inter-relationship between the right to freedom of conscience and the right to be governed by RPLs was a topic of debate. The sub-committee on fundamental rights initially proposed a clause that 'all persons are entitled to freedom of conscience and the right freely to profess and practice religion in a manner compatible with public morality and health'. The objections to this formulation were primarily directed at the possibility of reforming personal laws in as much as all the social reform measures would touch upon areas governed,

[11] Mani, L., 'Production of an Official Discourse on Sati in early Nineteenth Century Bengal' *Economic and Political Weekly*, 21, 1986, WS32-Ws38.

[12] Phillips, C.H., *The Correspondence of Lord William Cavendish Bentinck*, Oxford, Oxford University Press, 1977, pp. 335–345.

[13] For the following account, see Shiva Rao, B., *The Framing of India's Constitution*, vol. II, New Delhi, Indian Institute of Public Administration, 1968, pp. 56, *et. seq.*

or claimed to be governed by religious laws. Various members, including two women members who also belonged to the All India Women's Association objected that such a clause might invalidate social reform legislation. They suggested that instead of guaranteeing 'free practice of religion', the clause should guarantee 'freedom of religious worship'. As a result the sub-committee on fundamental rights decided to delete the phrase 'practice' from the clause. However, the sub-committee on minorities insisted that the phrase should remain. The Advisory Committee decided to include the words 'practice' and 'propagate' in the clause despite some members' objections that it would defeat social progress and perpetuate communal disharmony.

The Constituent Assembly discussed the clause in this form but the compromise with the minorities was considered more important than articulating whether the clause would preclude social reform legislation. A Muslim member wanted a clarification that their RPL would not be affected by the state's power to modify the secular matters associated with any religion. When the clause on the Uniform Civil Code was discussed some Muslim members voiced similar concerns and they argued that personal laws should be expressly excluded from the purview of any future Uniform Civil Code. While no such express exclusion was articulated in the eventual Constitution, it could be said that the government was fully cognizant of the potential conflict between the fundamental rights to freedom of religion and equality and the claims of the inviolable nature of the RPLs, yet, no effort was made to make unambiguous the status of RPLs.

Since the adoption of the Constitution the courts have refrained form declaring the RPLs as unconstitutional and various suits to declare the RPLs as contravening the Constitution have not discussed the issue directly. Meanwhile the legislative history of reforms of RPLs since the adoption of the Constitution has been extremely uneven. While the Hindu law has been extensively reformed, and aspects of Christian and Parsi laws have been modified but Islamic law has been considered to be outside the purview of the Parliament. In the following section a brief overview of the legislative history of RPLs is provided in order to problematize the claim that a secular state does not have the authority to reform 'religious' laws.[14]

The Hindu law was extensively reformed in 1955–1956. Although the reforms were initiated by the state and often claimed to be necessary to make the Hindu law conform to the Constitution they did not give women the same rights as men. Undeniably Hindu women gained very significant rights but the reforms were not even designed to give them radical equality. Most significantly the Hindu Succession Act, 1956 left the Mitakshara coparcenary intact and that meant that only the male members of a family could be the coparceners and the joint owners of property of the joint Hindu family. The Hindu Succession Act 1956 has been amended in 2005 to make daughters coparceners in the Joint Hindu Family and thus remove a major source of inequality between Hindu men and women's property rights. However, many differential rights still remain part of this law.

In the case of Islamic laws the Shariat Application Act, 1935, and the Dissolution of Muslim Marriage Act, 1939, had been enacted before the country became independent and

[14] For a detailed discussion of these issues see Parashar, Archana, *Women and Family Law Reform in India*, New Delhi, Sage, 1992, *passim.*

the Constitution was adopted. However, since the adoption of the Constitution reform of Islamic law has been discussed indirectly. In the Constituent Assembly when the clause on the Uniform Civil Code was being discussed some Muslim members did demand (as it turned out unsuccessfully) that the Constitution should embody a guarantee that Muslims would be allowed to be governed by their personal laws. When the Parliament was debating the Special Marriage Act, 1954, several Muslim members argued that no Muslims should be allowed to marry under it. The suggestion that an enabling law could also be seen as anti-RPLs was repeated many times subsequently.

The Criminal Procedure Code, 1973, was initially formulated to apply the maintenance provisions to every one irrespective of their RPLs but at the insistence of Muslim leaders their community was made exempt from this social welfare measure under certain circumstances. Most notably the effort of the central government to enact a uniform adoption law was thwarted with the argument that such a law would allow Muslims to avoid the application inter alia, of Shariat rules of inheritance. An initial adoption bill was introduced in 1972 but it lapsed. Another bill was introduced in 1980 but with the explicit exclusion of Muslims from its purview although not enacted. However, the exclusion of Muslims even from this bill signalled a change in the government's position. While in 1954 it had refused to accept the argument in 1980 it was willing to accept the Muslim community leaders' position that their RPL is immutable and even an enabling law should not be enacted if it would allow some Muslims to avoid being governed by their religious laws. The eventual enactment of the Muslim Women's (Protection of Rights on Divorce)

Act, 1986, signified the governments assent to the proposition that not only the Muslims are exempt from any social reform measures but also that the government should enact laws to 'enforce' Muslim law.[15] In all these instances the government has accepted some Muslim religio-political leaders as the sole spokesmen for the community. As a direct consequence of that the interests of women have suffered.

The Christian personal laws are essentially a number of state enacted laws of marriage, divorce and succession. The Indian Divorce Act, 1869, was followed by the enactment of the Indian Christian Marriage Act, 1872. These two enactments continued to apply unmodified until 2001 when the Divorce Act was amended substantially to give women the same rights as men in the matter of divorce. The succession matters were governed by the Indian Succession Act, 1925 and this Act continues to apply.[16] The Law Reform Commission had

[15] For the controversy that resulted in the enactment of this Act see, Engineer, A.A., Ed. *The Shah Bano Controversy*, Hyderabad, Orient Longman, 1987. On 23 April 1985, the Supreme Court of India in *Mohammed Ahmed Khan* v. *Shah Bano Begum* AIR 1985 SC 945, gave divorced Muslim women the right to lifelong maintenance under section 125 of the Code of Criminal Procedure 1973. Mohammed Khan, Shah Bano's ex-husband had contested her claims for maintenance insisting that he had, according to Muslim personal law, supported her for three months after their divorce. The Supreme Court stressed that there was no conflict between its verdict and the provisions of Muslim personal law, which in its view, also entitled women to alimony if they were unable to maintain themselves. The court further advised that the Muslim community take 'a lead in the matter of reform of their personal law' and that a Uniform Civil Code be formulated to 'help the cause of national integration'. The decision sparked of a nationwide controversy on the question of religious personal law and the desirability or otherwise of a Uniform Civil Code.

[16] The celebrated decision of the Supreme court in the case of Mary Roy caused a major upheaval as the

prepared two reports on the reform of Christian law in 1960 and 1983. The government had introduced a bill in 1962 to amend the Marriage and Matrimonial Causes but it lapsed without ever being discussed in Parliament. Eventually a number of Christian Women's organizations backed the changes that were eventually enacted as the Divorce Act, 1869.

The Parsi Marriage and Divorce Act, 1865 was reformulated in 1936. After independence a reform bill was introduced into Parliament in 1986 and enacted in 1988. However, most of the provisions discriminating against women remained part of the enacted law. The provisions of the Indian Succession Act, 1925, that govern Parsis were reformed in 1991. The impetus for change came from the community and it removed the differences between the rights of inheritance of the daughter and son.

V. CONCLUSION

The above account demonstrates that the state has adopted a politically expedient attitude to the claims of religious sanctity and thus the inviolability of the RPLs. It has chosen to reform some RPLs ostensibly to make them conform to the Constitution, while leaving other RPLs unreformed. It is primarily women's right to equality that has been differentially recognized and at times denied. The political aftermath of the Shah Bano controversy and the rise of Hindu communal politics has made feminists wary of demanding a Uniform Civil Code. In this context it is important that the issue is re-conceptualized as one about justice for all members of a family. One way of proceeding is to disassociate religion from family law and for the state to enact a uniform family law and enforce it.

While it might be argued that diversity and cultural autonomy are important rights in a democratic polity, the history of politicization of RPLs shows that women can always be disadvantaged in the name of cultural autonomy.[17] Obviously, a secular state allows freedom of conscience but it also cannot take upon itself the responsibility of enforcing any religion. If RPLs are not enforced by the state, the devout religious members of any community, Hindu, Muslim, Christian, Parsi or anyone else can still choose to live by their religious rules. However, in a democratic and plural polity no one should expect the state to enforce one version of religion to the detriment of some members of society.[18] Thus it is suggested that a general family law that ensures fair and just outcomes for all members of the family would be more conducive to a plural polity than the RPLs enforced in their present form.

[17] See for a similar argument Okin, Susan Moller, *Is Multiculturalism Bad for Women*, Princeton University Press, 1999.

[18] This is not a novel or extreme idea as the example of Roman Catholicism shows. Most states in Europe allow the Roman Catholics to be bound by the rules of their church for marriage and divorce. However, the Roman Catholic Church does not recognize dissolution of a valid marriage but no state law allows that argument to prevent it from enacting general, secular divorce laws. The devout Christians are of course free to abide by their religious rules, but they cannot expect the state to enforce their religion for them.

Supreme Court made the Indian succession Act applicable to all Christians and did so retrospectively. Prior to this decision The Travancore Succession Act, 1916, had given daughters a lesser share than the sons. In the aftermath of the decision a Christian member of parliament tried to introduce a bill in Parliament making the decision only prospective. See *Mary Roy* v. *State of Kerala and others* AIR 1986 SC 1011.

Environmental Law

VISHNU KONOORAYAR

A consumer is the most important visitor in our premises. He is not dependent on us. We are dependent on him. He is not an outsider in our business. He is part of it. We are not doing a favour by serving him. He is doing us favour by giving us an opportunity to do so

Mahatma Gandhi

I. INTRODUCTION

Consumer protection laws have originated and developed as a natural response to the recognition of the rights of every consumer to be protected against exploitation and abuse by manufacturers, suppliers and of goods or service providers. Traced with care, the idea of consumer protection can be found to have existed in every kind of social order and judicial mechanism, whether primitive or modern. However, the extent to which it has been emphasized and developed has varied depending on the circumstances. In the pre-industrialization period there was no consumer as we see in modern times. There was no manufacturing for sale. There were no services and no purchase system. The growth of the market economy created an increase in the requirements of men and women, who were not in a position to fulfil all their requirements

themselves. They were under compulsion to purchase goods and services. Fortunately this incapability on man's part to produce all the goods and services that was required turned out to be the major reason for the economic growth of the society. The labour was divided and specialization became the rule of the day. Wealth was distributed among the members of the society[1]. In this process of selling and buying, both the seller and buyer have a right to legitimate expectation. The sellers' right is to get the value for the goods or service sold by him in terms of money or otherwise. The buyer's (consumer's) expectation is to get the value for money which he pays. This will include an expectation for right quality, right quantity, right prices, information about the mode of use, etc. The right to legitimate expectation about the merchantable quality of goods and services the consumer purchases may be violated. In such situations, it is the duty of law to come forward to help the exploited. This paper analyses the various attempts by law to protect the consumers in India in the light of the Consumer Protection Act, 1986.

[1] But the proportion in which it was distributed continues to be a major concern through out the centuries.

II. HISTORY OF CONSUMER PROTECTION LAWS

The unresolved question throughout the development history of consumer jurisprudence was regarding the allocation of legal liability among the different players from the manufacturing stage to the distribution stage. The answer always depended on the changing economic and political policies of each state. An example would be the shifting of legal liability from the buyer to the seller by applying the doctrines of *caveat emptor*[2] and *caveat venditor*.[3]

The doctrine of *caveat emptor* says that the buyer cannot recover from the seller for the defects in the goods sold. The basic underlying principle is that the buyer had the chance to use his knowledge to be careful before buying the goods. Once he buys it and finds the goods to be defective he has to accept the loss as the cost of his carelessness. This principle has been prevalent in England in the medieval period and was followed by the courts for many centuries. The main reason for the emergence of this doctrine was that during those days the market was small and the consumer could personally inspect the goods before buying.[4] In case of defects the only option was either to sue for fraud or breach of contract. But to sue for fraud the seller should have intentionally concealed any defects in the goods sold and to sue for breach of contract the buyer should have held a written warranty. The buyer had no remedy when there was no written contract, which gave a warranty, or when the seller could prove that there were no efforts

on his part to intentionally conceal any patent or latent defects in the goods sold.

By the early part of the sixteenth century the courts in England started deviating from the above said principle. In a case the court considered the breach of the contract as an *assumpsit* and unwritten warranties were implied to a certain extent.[5] Things started changing when the policies of the governments changed from that of a strict father to that of a liberal manager. This shift in policies was to an extent a result of industrial revolution and great technological advancements in the methods of production. The above said factors increased the competition among the manufacturers. When the competition among the manufacturers grew, the consumers started getting variety of options. These changes reflected in the policies of the courts also. For example, in *John* v. *Bright*,[6] the court finally accepted that there is an implied contract of warranty regarding the quality of the goods sold. The concept of the merchantability of the goods was also introduced in this case for the first time. Another case in this aspect is *Randall* v. *Newson*,[7] where the court said that if there was a contract of sale by description there was an implied warranty that the goods were not only in conformity with the description but also merchantable quality. These changes in the approach of the courts lead to the enactment of the (English) Sale of Goods Act, 1893. The Act specifically says that the goods sold must be of merchantable quality.[8] It also says that if the buyer makes the seller known about the purpose for which he buys the goods there is an implied condition that

---

[2] A Latin term which means 'let the buyer beware'. *Emptor* in Latin is the buyer and the verb *cavere* is a verb of caution.

[3] A Latin term, which means 'let the seller beware'.

[4] See Bradgate Robert, *Commercial Law*, London, Edinburgh, Dublin, Butterworths, 2000, p. 273.

[5] See *Jordan's Case* (1528) YB 27 Hen VIII, f.24, p 1.3.

[6] (1829) 5 Bing 533.

[7] [1877] 2 QBD 102.

[8] (English) Sale of Goods Act, 1893, section 14(3).

the goods sold are fit for that purpose.[9] In fact this was the first step towards the death of the principle of *caveat emptor*.[10]

Another common law development relating to the rights of the ultimate consumers was the decision of the House of Lords in *Donoghue v. Stevenson*.[11] In this case the court extended the principle of general duty of care towards a neighbour to give justice to the ultimate consumers. The court asserted the liability of the manufacturer towards the ultimate consumers.

These developments gave way to the emergence of another principle known as *caveat venditor* which means 'let the seller beware. The shift from the principle of *caveat emptor* to the principle of *caveat venditor* was not an overnight change. It is the result of many policy changes by the state and the reflection of these policies in the decisions of the legislatures and the judiciary. *Caveat venditor* is still a developing principle. The judiciary and legislatures in different parts of the world make attempts to protect the consumers by giving more and more rights to them. The reason is that in today's mass production economy where there is little contact between the producer and consumer, sellers very often make exaggerated claims and advertisements that they do not intend to fulfil. This leaves the consumer in a difficult position with very few avenues for redressal.

In India, the legislative attempts in this regard are provisions the Indian Contract Act, 1872, Sale of Goods Act, 1930, Prevention of

Food Adulteration Act, 1954, the Standards of Weights and Measures Act, 1976, etc. These laws protect consumer interests to some extent. But they require the consumer to initiate action by way of a civil suit involving lengthy legal process, which is very expensive and time consuming. So the Consumer Protection Act was enacted in 1986.

III. THE CONSUMER PROTECTION ACT, 1986

The Consumer Protection Act, 1986[12] was enacted to provide simpler and quicker redressal of consumer grievances. The Act for the first time defined the word consumer[13] and conferred express additional rights on him. It is interesting to note that the Act does not seek to protect every consumer.[14] The protection is given only to those who come within the definition of the Act. The Act seeks to promote and protect the interest of consumers against deficiencies and defects in goods or services. It also seeks to secure the rights of a consumer against unfair or restrictive trade practices, which may be practiced by manufacturers and traders. This Act aims at establishing consumer councils[15] and other authorities for the settlement of consumers'

---

[9] Ibid., section 14(4).

[10] The attempts by law and its machinery to protect the consumers are a continuing process. The reasons for this is the emergence of faceless business corporation and the inability of the individual consumers to enforce their rights against them

[11] [1932] All ER Rep 1.

[12] Act No. 68 of 1986. It was passed on 24 December 1986.

[13] Infra.

[14] The word consumer is defined in many ways.It can be 'He who or that which *consumes*, wastes, squanders or destroys' or 'He who or that which *consumes*' or'*consumer*, buyer, buyer of labour, client, customer, leaser, lessee, obtainer, patron, procurer, purchaser, purchaser of goods, shopper, transferee, vendee'. All these definitions qualifies persons to be consumers only when they consumes something.

[15] Consumer Protection Councils are established at the Central, state and district levels. They are the advisory bodies established under the Act.

disputes, which includes consumer dispute redressal forums at the district level, state commissions in every state and a national commission at the national level.[16] These forums are vested with special powers so that action can be taken against erring suppliers, and possible compensation may be awarded to the consumer for the hardships he has undergone. The consumer, under this law, is not required to deposit huge court fees, which earlier used to deter consumers from approaching the courts. The rigors of court procedures have been dispensed with and replaced with simple procedures as compared to the normal courts, which helps in quicker redressal of grievances. The provisions of the Act are compensatory in nature. The Act applies to all goods and services unless specifically exempted by the Central Government. It covers all the sectors whether private, public or cooperative. The provisions of this Act are in addition to and not in derogation of the provisions of any other law for the time being in force. The consumer himself need not necessarily file a complaint. Any recognized consumer association can espouse his cause. Where a large number of consumers have a similar complaint, one or more of them can file a complaint on behalf of all. Even the Central Government or state government can act on behalf of the consumers.

ADVANTAGES OF CONSUMER PROTECTION ACT, 1986

The Consumer Protection Act, 1986 has many advantages over other laws related to consumer. It is simple, easy to understand even for a common man. It aims at a speedy disposal of cases and provides simple procedure to be followed. The following are some of the advantages of the Act.

[16] Preamble to the Act.

(a) Physical presence in the consumer redressal forums

When compared to an ordinary civil suit, in an action under Consumer Protection Act there is very rare need to appear before the consumer dispute redressal forums. An aggrieved consumer may enforce his right with the following simple procedures.

(i)   Complaint can be sent through registered post.
(ii) Instead of appearing himself the complainant authorizes some person to appear on his behalf.
(iii) Witness can give his evidence through affidavit without appearing in court.
(iv) Even the person against whom complaint is made can authorize someone else to appear on his behalf in the court instead of appearing himself.

(b) Simple procedure

The procedures are based on principles of natural justice and are easily understandable even by a layman. Lengthy and complicated procedures of civil courts are excluded.

(c) No need of advocate

There is no need of engaging an advocate for proceedings before Consumer Courts. One can appear himself or authorize someone to appear in Consumer Court on his behalf.

(d) Nominal fee

The fee is minimum for matters before the consumer dispute forums. As of now it is Rs. 100 for matter involving less than Rs. one lakh and maximum Rs. 5,000 for matter involving more than Rs. one crore that is payable as court fee. This fee is almost 50 times less in comparison with civil courts.

(e) Cost to complainant

A Consumer Court, as a routine, allows cost to complainant for expenses incurred by him for filing complaint, court proceedings, etc, while in other courts, this is done in very few cases.

(f) Time bound proceedings

The Consumer Protection Act provides time bound proceedings for disposal of cases. Though many times, practically, it is not possible to dispose the case in fixed time period Consumer Courts are empowered to extend such period but it is also true that Consumer Courts take much less time to decide a case in comparison with other courts.

(g) Court atmosphere

Finally, Consumer Court has a different atmosphere when compared to other ordinary courts. Its presiding officers are not required to wear uniforms like their counterparts in other courts. This is to create an atmosphere of openness so that the common man is not discouraged from complaining before these forums.

WHO IS A CONSUMER?

The definition given by Act is somewhat different from the literal meaning of the term. It also specifically excludes some kind of consumers from its preview. The definition of 'consumer[17] is given in two parts:

1. Consumer of goods
2. Consumer of services

The basic features of this definition are:

a) The goods or services must not be free. Some price should be paid for them. It includes purchase on credit or part payment or in installments.

b) It is not necessary that only the buyer can be a consumer. Definition of consumer clearly states that, any person, who, though consideration is not paid by him but uses goods with the consent of the buyer is also a consumer. For example, A purchased a watch and gifted to B. Here, B is also a consumer.

c) It excludes commercial dealings or goods purchased for resale from the definition of consumer with exception of goods and services purchased for self-employment. It means reseller and commercial dealings except for self-employment cannot take benefit of the Consumer Protection Act.

WHO IS NOT A CONSUMER?

As per the Act, the following persons are not consumers.

i) Free Goods and Services: A person enjoying goods and services free of cost

---

[17] According to the Consumer Protection Act, 1986, section 2 (1)(d), 'Consumer' means any person who,
(i) Buys any goods for a consideration which has been paid or promised or partly paid and partly promised, or under any system of deferred payment and includes any user of such goods other than the person who buys such goods for consideration paid or promised or partly paid or partly promised or under any system of deferred payment when such use is made with the approval of such person but does not include a person who obtains such goods for resale or for any commercial purpose; or
(ii) [Hires or avails of] any services for a consideration which has been paid or promised or partly paid and

partly promised, or under any system of deferred payment and includes any beneficiary of such services other then the person who [hires or avails of] the services for consideration paid or promised, or partly paid and partly promised, or under any system of deferred payment, when such services are availed of with the approval of the first mentioned person [but does not include a person who avails of such services for any commercial purpose];
[*Explanation.* For the purposes of this sub-clause "commercial purpose" does not include use by a consumer of goods bought and used by him and services availed by him exclusively for the purposes of earning his livelihood, by means of self-employment].

is not a consumer and cannot benefit from this Act.

ii) Reseller: A purchaser of goods for resale cannot take benefit of this Act.

iii) Commercial Purpose: A person purchasing goods and services for commercial purpose will also not come under the purview of this Act.

iv) Personal Services: Definition of service excludes services from the purview of this Act, where employer-employee relation exists.

v) Statutory Services: The various services provided by state like registration of documents, approval of construction plan, etc., do not fall under service as the fees paid for them is not consideration.

RELEVANT TERMS

Goods

Section 2(1)(i) of the Act[18] imports the definition of goods from the Sale of Goods Act, 1930, which defines goods as every kind of movable property other than actionable claims and money; and includes stock and shares, growing crops, grass, and things attached to or forming part of the land, which are agreed to be severed before sale or under the contract of sale.[19]

Service

Section 2(1)(o) of the Act provides that service means service of any description which is made available to potential users and includes the provision of facilities in connection with banking, financing, insurance, transport, processing, supply of electrical or other energy, board or loading or both, housing construction, entertainment, amusement or the purveying of news or other information, but does not include the rendering of any service free of charge or under a contract of personal service.

The definition provides a list of 11 sectors to which service may pertain in order to come under the purview of the Act. The list of these sectors is not an exhaustive one. Service may be of any description and pertain to any sector if it satisfies the following criteria:

1. Service is made available to the potential users, i.e., service not only to the actual users but also to those who are capable of using it.

2. It should not be free of charge, e.g., the medical service rendered free of charge in Government hospital is not a service under the Act;[20]

3. It should not be under a contract of personal service. The expression contract of personal service is not defined under the Act. In common parlance, it means: a contract to render service in a private capacity to an individual. For example, where a servant enters into an agreement with a master for employment, or where a landlord agrees to supply water to his tenant, these are the contracts of personal service. The idea is that under a personal service relationship, a person can discontinue the service at any time according to his will, he need not approach the Consumer Forum to complaint about deficiency in service.

It does not make a difference whether the service provider is a government body or a private body. Thus even if a statutory

---

[18] 'Goods' means goods as defined in the Sale of Goods Act, 1930.

[19] Consumer Protection Act, 1986, section 2(7).

[20] For details see, *Indian Medical Association* v. *V.P. Santha* (1995) 6 SCC 651.

corporation provides a deficient service, it can be made liable under the Act.[21] Since the enactment of the Act in 1986, the main question before the adjudicatory bodies, from the District Consumer Redressal Forums to the Supreme Court, was regarding the inclusion of various services available in the market within the purview of the definition under section 2(1)(o). The question of inclusion of medical, insurance, banking, construction services, etc, was frequently raised before the courts in India. In *Indian Medical Association* v. *V.P. Shantha,*[22] the Supreme Court held that doctors are subject to the Consumer Protection Act, if fee is charged for services rendered by the doctor. The court laid down the following legal propositions. (i) Where services are rendered free of charge to every one the Act does not apply; (ii) But, where fees charged are required to be paid by every one availing of the services then the Consumer Protection Act applies; (iii)Where charges are required to be paid by persons availing of services, but certain categories of persons(who cannot afford to pay) are not charged for services, then also the Act applies. Later the same court in *Jacob Mathew* v. *State of Punjab and Anor*[23] decided the issue in favour of medical professional. The court laid down a few restrictions for entertaining complaint against a doctor and arresting him. It seems by these two approaches, the court was trying to balance two conflicting interests, namely delivering justice to the consumers and upholding the nobility of the medical profession in manner so as to not shake the confidence of the doctors.

Defect

Section 2(1)(f) of the Act provides that defect means any fault, imperfection or shortcoming in the quality, quantity, potency, purity or standard which is required to be maintained by or under any law of the time being in force under any contract, express or implied or as is claimed by the trader in any manner whatsoever in relation to any goods. But despite this provision being very clear, difficulties are faced at the practical level due to a variety of reasons like illiteracy, ignorance, carelessness or negligence of the buyer. In spite of the various campaigns advocating consumer vigilance by the Department of Consumer Affairs of the government and various other civil society groups, the consumers fail to collect bills when they purchase goods.

DEFICIENCY IN SERVICE

Section 2(1)(g) of the Act provides that, deficiency means any fault, imperfection, shortcoming or inadequacy in the quality, nature and manner of performance which is required to be maintained by or under any law for the time being in force or has been undertaken to be performed by a person in pursuance of a contract or otherwise in relation to any service. In normal course, if the service is found deficient as per the above criteria, it is held deficient and the compensation is awarded. However, there may be abnormal circumstances beyond the control of the person performing service. If such circumstances prevent a person from rendering service of the desired quality, nature and the manner,

---

[21] Some other sectors/professionals/services which are not specified in the definition of service but which have been considered by the Consumer Forums as service sectors from time to time are, advocates, airlines, chartered accountants, couriers, chit funds, education, gas cylinder/LPG services, medical services, postal services, railways, investment related services, and telephone services.

[22] Supra note 20.

[23] 2005(3) CPR 70 (SC).

such person should not be penalised for the same. An illustration of deficiency of services would be *Navata Road Transport Regular Parcel Services and Ors* v. *Tirumala Fertilizers.*[24] In this case, the parcel company did not inform Tirumala Fertilisers about the arrival of the consignment for a long period. The court held it to be a clear case of deficiency of services and awarded compensation.

SPURIOUS GOODS AND SERVICES

Section 2(1)(oo) says 'Spurious goods and services' mean such goods and services which are claimed to be genuine but they are actually not so. Sale of such duplicate goods and services are actionable at the behest of both the consumer and the trader of genuine goods and services. The consumers can take up the matter to a consumer forum under the Consumer Protection Act, 1986 or under other civil and criminal laws. The trader of genuine goods and services can seek his remedy under the law of tort or for violation of his intellectual property rights.

CONSIDERATION

Consideration is something that is done or promised in return for a contractual promise. For example, in a promise between A and B for the sale of A's car to B, B's payment of the price of the car (or promise to do so) is the consideration for A's promise. The Consumer Protection Act defines consideration in the same manner as in Indian Contract Act, 1872, which defines consideration as: When, at the desire of the promisor, the promisee, or any other person has done or abstained from doing, or does or abstains from doing, or promises to do or to abstain from doing, something, such act or abstinence or promise is called a consideration for the promise.

[24] 2005(1) CPR 90 (NC).

The basic meaning of the above definition is that if as a consumer one promises to pay or do anything that can be reasonably construed as a payment or part of a payment (for a good or a service) then one has given adequate consideration for the good you wish to buy or the service you wish to avail of. The same is true for lending one's goods to a third party or letting a third party avail of the services for which one has paid.

TRADER AND MANUFACTURER

Section 2(1)(q) of the Act states that trader in relation to any goods means 'a person who sells or distributes any goods for sale and includes the manufacturer thereof, and where such goods are sold or distributed in package form, includes the packer thereof'. The term manufacturer is defined by section 2(1)(j) to mean a person who (i) makes or manufactures any goods or parts thereof; or (ii) does not make or manufacture any goods but assembles parts thereof made or manufactured by others and claims the end-product to be goods manufactured by himself; or (iii) puts or causes to be put his own mark on any goods made or manufactured by any other manufacturer and claims such goods to be goods made or manufactured by himself. This definition indicates that a manufacturer is a person who either himself manufactures goods, or assembles any goods manufactured by others, or puts his own mark or trademark on the goods manufactured by others. The Act entitles a consumer to approach a Consumer Redressal Forum against a trader and a manufacturer for any defect in goods and services purchased. However, purchases enabled through the internet and e-commerce pose a challenge since traders and manufacturers outside India cannot be made to appear before the Forums established by the Act.

HAZARDOUS GOODS

The term 'hazardous goods' have not been defined in the Act. The dictionary meaning of the term is dangerous or risky. However, the term is used in context of goods only, i.e., a person can make a complaint if he is not informed about the hazardous nature of the goods but the same is not true in case of hazardous services. The law seeks to ensure that those responsible for bringing goods to the market, in particular, suppliers, exporters, importers, retailers and the like should ensure that while in their care these goods are not rendered unsafe through improper handling or storage. Consumers should be instructed in the proper use of goods and should be informed of the risks involved in intended or normally foreseeable use. Vital safety information should be conveyed to consumers.

UNFAIR TRADE PRACTICE

Section 2(1) (r)[25] of the Act defines an unfair trade practice as a trade practice, which, for

[25] Consumer Protection Act, 1986, section 2(1)(r) reads: "Unfair trade practice" means a trade practice which, for the purpose of promoting the sale, use or supply of any goods or for the provision of any service, adopts any unfair method or unfair or deceptive practice including any of the following practices, namely:

(1) The practice of making any statement, whether orally or in writing or by visible representation which, –

(i) Falsely represents that the goods are of a particular standard, quality, quantity; grade-composition, style or model;

(ii) Falsely represents that the service of a particular standard, quality or grade;

(iii) Falsely represents any re-built, second-hand, renovated, reconditioned or old goods as new goods;

(iv) Represents that the goods or service have sponsorship, approval, performance, characteristics, accessories, uses or benefits which such goods or service do not have;

(v) Represents that the seller or the supplier has a

the purpose of promoting the sale, use or supply of any goods or for the provision of any service, adopts any unfair method or unfair or deceptive practice. This would also include the practices like making a false oral or written or by any other visible representation about

sponsorship or approval or affiliation which such seller or supplier does not have;

(vi) Makes a false or misleading representation concerning the need for, or the usefulness of, any goods or service;

(vii) Gives to the public any warranty or guarantee of the performance, efficacy or length of life of a product or of any goods that is not based on an adequate or proper test thereof

Provided that where a defence is raised to the effect that such warranty or guarantee is based on adequate or proper test, the burden of proof of such defence shall lie on the person raising such defence;

(viii) Makes to the public a representation in a form that purports to be -(i) A warranty or guarantee of a product or of any goods or service; or (ii) A promise to replace, maintain or repair an article or any part thereof or to repeat or continue a service until it has achieved a specified result, if such purported warranty or guarantee or promise is materially misleading or if there is no reasonable prospect that such warranty, guarantee or promise will be carried out;

(ix) Materially misleads the public concerning the price at which a product or like products or goods or service, have been or are, ordinarily sold or provided, and, for this purpose, a representation as to price shall be deemed to refer to the price at which the product or goods or service has or have been sold by sellers or provided by suppliers generally in the relevant market unless it is clearly specified to be the price at which the product has been sold or services have been provided by the person by whom or on whose behalf the representation is made;

(x) Gives false or misleading facts disparaging the goods, services or trade of another person;

Explanation. For the purposes of clause (1), a statement that is (a) Expressed on an article offered or displayed for sale, or on its wrapper or container; or (b) Expressed on anything attached to, inserted in, or accompanying an article offered or displayed for sale or on anything on which the article is mounted for display or sale; or (c) the standard, quality, grade, composition, style or model. The main intent of this provision is the trader or manufacturer should not be allowed any false statement as to the goods and services that he sells.

Contained in or on anything is sold, sent, delivered, transmitted or in any other manner whatsoever made available to a member of the public, Shall be deemed to be a statement made to the public by, and only by, the person who had caused the statement to be so expressed, made or contained;

(2) Permits the publication of any advertisement whether in any newspaper or otherwise, for the sale or supply at a bargain price, of goods or the services that are not intended to be offered for sale or supply at the bargain price, or for a period that is, and in quantities that are, reasonable, having regard to the nature of the market in which the business is carried on, the nature and size of business, And the nature of the advertisement.

Explanation.– For the purposes of clause (2), "bargaining price" means (a) A price that is stated in any advertisement to be a bargain price, by reference to an ordinary price or otherwise, or (b) A price that a person who reads, hears or sees the advertisement, would reasonably understand to be a bargain price having regard to the prices at which the product advertised or like products are ordinarily sold:

(3) Permits-(a) The offering of gifts, prizes or other items with the intention of not providing them as offered or creating impression that something is being given or offered free of charge when it is fully or partly covered by the amount charged in the transaction as a whole; (b) The conduct of any contest, lottery, game of chance or skill, for the purpose of promoting, directly or indirectly, the sale, use or supply of any product or any business interest;

[(3A) withholding from the participants of any scheme offering gifts, prizes or other items free of charge, on its closure the information about final results of the scheme.

Explanation: for the purposes of this sub-clause, the participants of a scheme shall be deemed to have been informed of the final results of the scheme where such results are within a reasonable time published, prominently in the same newspapers in which the scheme was originally advertised.

(4) Permits the sale or supply of goods intended to be used, or are of kind likely to be used, by consumers,

RESTRICTIVE TRADE PRACTICE

Restrictive trade practice means a trade practice which tends to being about manipulation of price or its conditions of delivery or to affect flow of supplies in the market relating to goods or service in such a manner as to impose on the consumers unjustified costs or restrictions and shall include:

(a) delay beyond the period agreed to by a trader in supply of such goods or in providing the services which has led or is likely to lead to rise in the price;

(b) any trade practice which requires a consumer to buy, hire or avail of any goods or, as the case may be, services as condition precedent to buying, hiring or availing of other goods or services.

An analysis of above definition reveals that where sale or purchase of a product or service is made conditional on the sale or purchase of one or more other products and services, it amounts to restrictive trade practice.

CONSUMER COURTS

The Consumer Protection Act, 1986 provides three tier courts for the adjudication of Consumer Disputes. The lowest level courts

---

knowing or having reason to believe that the goods do not comply with the standards prescribed by competent authority relating to performance, composition, contents. Design, constructions, finishing or packaging as are necessary to prevent or reduce the risk of injury to the person using the goods;

(5) Permits the hoarding or destruction of goods, or refuses to sell the goods or to make them available for sale or to provide any service, if such hoarding or destruction or refusal raises or tends to raises or is intended to raise, the cost of those or other similar goods or services.

(6) Manufacture of spurious goods or offering such good for sale or adopting deceptive practices in the provision of services.

are constituted at District level, which are called District Forums.[26] Above them state level Consumer Courts are constituted, which are called State Commission[27] and at the national level there is National Commission.[28]

DISTRICT FORUM

The District Forums are constituted in all the districts of India. They can hear the cases where the value of the goods or services and the compensation if any, claimed does not exceed Rs. 20 lakhs.[29] Usually every District Forum is situated in the district head quarters.

Composition of the District Forum[30]

The District Forum consists of one president and two other members (one of whom is to be a woman). The president of the Forum is a person who is, or has been qualified to be a District Judge, and other members are persons of ability, integrity and standing, and have adequate knowledge or experience of, or have shown capacity in dealing with, problems relating to economics, law, commerce, account-ancy, industry, public affairs or administration. A person can be disqualified for appointment as member on the following grounds:

1. If he is sentenced to imprisonment for an offence which involves moral turpitude;
2. Is an undischarged insolvent;
3. Is of unsound mind;
4. Has been removed or dismissed from the service of the government or a body corporate owned or controlled by the government;
5. Has financial or other interest as is likely

to affect prejudicially the discharge by him of his functions as a member.

The government may also prescribe other disqualifications for a person to become a member.

STATE COMMISSION

A State Commission has jurisdiction in whole of the state for which it is constituted. It can hear cases involving the amount more than Rs. 20 lakhs and up to rupees Rs. one crore. It has also jurisdiction to hear appeal against the orders of District Forum of that particular state. It is situated in the capital of the state.

State Commission consists of a president and two members one of whom is to be a woman. The president is a person who is or has been a judge of a High Court, and the members are persons of ability, integrity and standing and have adequate knowledge or experience of, or have shown capacity in dealing with, problems relating to economics, law, commerce, accountancy, industry, public affairs or administration.

NATIONAL COMMISSION

The National Commission is on the top of the hierarchy of Consumer Courts. It is the only one for whole of India and situated in Delhi, the capital of India. It can hear cases involving amount above Rs one crore. It can also hear appeals against the order of a State Commission.

The National Commission consists of a President, and four other members (one of whom is to be a woman). The president should be the one who is or has been a judge of the Supreme Court, and the members should be the persons of ability, integrity and standing and have adequate knowledge or experience of, or have shown capacity in dealing with, problems relating to economics, law,

---

[26] Consumer Protection Act, 1986, section 9(a).
[27] Ibid., 9(b).
[28] Ibid., section 9(c).
[29] Substituted by Act 50 of 1993 for Rs. one lakh.
[30] Consumer Protection Act, 1986, section 10.

commerce, accountancy, industry, public affairs or administration.

COMPLAINT

An aggrieved consumer seeks redressal under the Act through the instrumentality of complaint. It does not mean that the consumer can complain against each and every problem. The Act has provided certain grounds on which complaint can be made. Similarly, relief against these complaints can be granted within the set pattern.

What Constitutes a Complaint?

A complaint[31] is a statement made in writing to the National Commission, the State Commission or the District Forum by a person competent to file it, containing the allegations in detail, and with a view to obtain relief provided under the Act.

Who Can File a Complaint[32]

At the outset it is clear that a person who can be termed as a consumer under the Act can make a complaint. To be specific on this account, following are the persons who can file a complaint under the Act:

(a) a consumer; or

(b) any voluntary consumer association registered under the Companies Act, 1956 or under any other law for the time being in force, or

(c) the Central Government or any state government,

(d) one or more consumers, where there are numerous consumers having the same interest.

(e) in case of death of a consumer, his legal heir or representative.

In addition to the above, the following are also considered consumers and may file a complaint:

1. Beneficiary of the goods and services: the definition of consumer itself includes beneficiary of goods and services.

2. Where a young child is taken to the hospital by his parents and the doctor treats the child, the parents of such a minor child can file a complaint under the Act.[33]

3. Legal heirs of the deceased consumer: A legal heir of the deceased consumer can well maintain a complaint under the Act.[34]

4. Husband of the consumer: in conditions where a woman may be illiterate, or an educated women may be unaware of her legal rights, the husband can file and prosecute complaint under the Consumer Protection Act on behalf of his spouse.[35]

5. A relative of consumer: When a consumer signs the original complaint, it can be initiated by his/her relative.[36]

6. Insurance company: Where an insurance company pays and settles the claim of the insured and the insured person transfers his rights in the insured goods to the company, it can file a complaint for the loss caused to the insured goods by negligence of goods/service providers. For example, when loss is caused to such goods because of negligence of a transport company, the insurance company can file a claim against the transport company.[37]

[31] Ibid., section 2(1)(c).

[32] Ibid., sections 2(b) and 12.

[33] *Spring Meadows Hospital* v. *Harjot Ahluwalia* JT (1998) 2 SC 620.

[34] *Joseph Alias Animon* v. *Dr Elizabeth Zachariah* (1997) 1 CPJ 96.

[35] *Punjab National Bank, Bombay* v. *K.B. Shetty* (1991) 2 CPR 633.

[36] *Motibai Dalvi Hospital* v. *M.I. Govilkar* (1992) 1 CPR 408.

[37] *New India Assurance Company Ltd.* v. *Green Transport Co.* II (1991) 1 CPJ 1 (Delhi).

APPEAL

Appeal is a legal instrumentality whereby a person not satisfied with the findings of a court, has an option to go to a higher court to present his case and seek justice. In the context of Consumer Forums:

1. An appeal can be made with the State Commission against the order of the District Forum within 30 days of the order, which is extendable for further 15 days[38].

2. An appeal can be made with the National Commission against the order of the State Commission within 30 days of the order or within such time as the National Commission allows.[39]

3. An appeal can be made to the Supreme Court against the order of the National Commission within 30 days of the order or within such time as the Supreme Court allows.[40]

V. CONCLUSION

The Consumer Protection Act is a beneficial legislation enacted for the protection of the interests of consumers by providing inexpensive, speedy and efficacious remedy. It was enacted for making the redressal of the grievances of the poor consumers who are not in a position to enforce their rights in case of a violation the right to receive goods or services that are of merchantable quality. The consumer courts very often take a view in favour of poor consumers[41] to make them the real kings of the markets. The following figures show the statistics of cases disposed of by the consumer courts all over India till 20 April 20 2007.[42]

These figures show that the performance of the consumer dispute redressal mechanism in India has been satisfactory, especially when compared to the ordinary courts in India where the delay is comparatively very high.

Cases disposed of by the Consumer Courts – All India

Sl. No	Name of Agency	Cases filed since inception	Cases disposed of since inception	Cases Pending	Per cent of total Disposal
1	National Commission	47110	38156	8954	80.99%
2	State Commissions	400418	290845	109573	72.64%
3	District Forums	2387388	2160022	227366	90.48%
	TOTAL	2834916	2489023	345893	87.80

[38] Consumer Protection Act 1986, section 15.

[39] Ibid., section 19.

[40] Ibid., section 23. Now after the 2002 amendment, the appellant has to deposit 50 per cent of the amount which he is required to pay in terms of an order of consumer court or Rs. 25,000 with the State Commission/Rs. 50,000 in National Commission whatever is less.

[41] *Narayani Devi* v. *Post Master General* (1997) 2 CPJ 34 Haryana.

[42] National Consumer Disputes Redressal Commission, Table showing total number of complaints filed and cases disposed of since the enactment of consumer protection law. Available at http://ncdrc.nic.in/ , visited on 1 May 2007.

Cyber Laws

RAMAN MITTAL

I. INTRODUCTION

Cyberspace has become a platform for a galaxy of human activities which converge on the Internet. Internet is increasingly being used for communication, commerce, advertising, banking, education, research and entertainment. There is hardly any human activity that is not touched by the Internet. It has something to offer to everybody and in the process it only increases and never diminishes.

If you have access to a computer and a modem, you are licensed to drive on the information superhighway. And you are one of a growing number of online participants. As the crowd of humanity gathers in the cyberspace, we need laws to regulate it. The laws that regulate conduct in cyberspace are termed as cyber laws.

Many believe that as the Internet has developed in the absence of laws, so no laws should apply to the Internet. Since the Internet defies geographical boundaries, national laws can no longer apply in the Internet sphere. Way back in 1996 John Perry Barlow[1] made a declaration addressing the governments of the world:

[1] Fellow with the Berkman Center for Internet and Society at the Harvard Law School.

…you weary giants of flesh and steel, I come from Cyberspace, the new home of Mind. On behalf of the future, I ask you of the past to leave us alone. You have no sovereignty where we gather. Where there are real conflicts, we will identify them and address them by our means. We are forming our own Social Contract. This governance will arise according to the conditions of our world, not yours. We will create a civilization of the Mind in Cyberspace. May it be more humane and fair than the world your governments have made before.

He was hailed as 'Thomas Jefferson' of cyberspace for his declaration. But a decade later, as more physical locations go online, the greater the potential for physical manifestation of electronic misdeeds. What do we do when someone electronically turns off the hospital lights? Or someone unauthorizedly gathers and misuses someone's credit card information from the Internet? Or someone releases copyrighted material on the Internet? These and a myriad of other problems are confronting the international community which definitely need our attention.

There is another school of thought which says that it is impossible to govern and regulate the Internet. There is no doubt that the technologies like anonymity and cryptography make traditional kinds of regulation extremely difficult. 'The Internet treats censorship as damage and routes around it. The fundamental end to end nature of the Internet means that even if one mode of communication is shut down, another method can be used'.[2]

Given the Internet's unique situation, with respect to geography and identity many believe that it becomes necessary for the Internet to govern itself. Instead of obeying the laws of a particular country, Internet citizens will obey the laws of electronic entities like service providers. Instead of identifying as a physical person, Internet citizens will be known by their usernames or email addresses. Instead, an entirely new set of laws will be created to address the above cited concerns.

However, there is also substantial literature and commentary that the Internet is not only 'regulable,' but is already subject to substantial regulation, both public and private, by many parties and at many different levels. Law as a regulator of human behaviour is as much applicable to online human activities as it is applicable to the offline activities. So, the question is not 'whether law applies to the Internet'—rather it is—'how law is applicable on the Internet'.

Though 'cyber laws' encompass a host of legal issues, an attempt is made in this chapter to highlight some of the important ones.

II. PRIVACY ISSUES IN CYBERSPACE

The new technologies have enhanced the possibilities of invasion into the privacy of individuals and provided new tools in the hands of eavesdroppers. Individual privacy is at a greater stake than ever before. Computers and the Internet can be used to amass huge amount of data regarding people, profile it in various ways, commodify it and deal with it in a manner which could violate individual's privacy.

In today's world there is a great reliance on computers in all walks of life. We store our personal and business communications, credit card information, health and financial details, etc., on computers. In fact the dependence on computers is increasing and the personal computer (PC) has become a storehouse of all important and confidential data. In this situation any unauthorized access to a person's PC would violate his privacy.

RIGHT TO PRIVACY

The term 'privacy' has been described as the rightful claim of the individual to determine the extent to which he wishes to share of himself with others. It means the individual's right to control dissemination of information about himself. The concept of privacy is used to describe not only rights purely in the private domain between individuals but also constitutional rights against the state.

Earlier, law afforded protection only against physical interference with a person or his property. But with radical changes in the means of communication and communication networks, the need for privacy and its recognition as a 'right' has come to the forefront. Keeping in view all modern developments in information and communication revolution (ICR), privacy in cyberspace can be described as the desire of every individual for virtual space where one can be free of interruption and intrusion and where one can control the time and manner of disclosures of personal information.

---

[2] John Gilmore, one of the founders of the Electronic Frontier Foundation, the Cypherpunks mailing list, and Cygnus Solutions.

LEGAL FRAMEWORK FOR PROTECTION OF PRIVACY

Analysing the development of privacy laws in India, one can note that these laws evolved basically from two sources: the common law of torts and the constitutional law. In common law, a private action for damages for unlawful intrusion of privacy is maintainable. Under the constitutional law, the right to privacy is implied in the fundamental right to life and liberty.[3]

Protecting one's privacy means protection of right to control how personal information is collected and promulgated. Protection of privacy also includes protection against identity theft, or the use of an individual's personal information for fraudulent purposes. The provisions of the IT Act have a bearing on the right to privacy. The Act talks about unauthorised access, damage to computer through computer contaminants, hacking, breach of privacy and confidentiality and publishing false digital signature certificate for fraudulent purposes.

CYBER PRIVACY: TECHNOLOGICAL INSECURITIES

A cookie is information that a website puts on one's hard disk so that it can remember something about him at a later time. A cookie is a mechanism that allows the server to store its own information about a user on the user's own computer. The user can view the cookies that have been stored on his hard disk (although the content stored in each cookie may not make much sense). In general, cookies help websites to serve users better. However, the existence of cookies and their use is generally not concealed from users, who can also disallow

access to cookie information. Nevertheless, to the extent that a website stores information about you in a cookie that you do not know about, the cookie mechanism could be considered a form of spyware. Cookies can be used to track people to gain statistics as they go through the website. Because every time we visit a website, we leave a footprint of personal information about ourselves like our preferences, the websites we visit, our financial details, etc. This rather simple capability has profound implications for the privacy of website visitors. While cookies do have uses for both the user and web providers and are even helpful, they can be misused. Beneficial to the user when dealing with a company that has a good privacy policy in place, it is of questionable value when left open and available to the world at large. The real problem is with aggregation of data from multiple sources resulting in a user profile. Collected personal information is now being treated as a commodity belonging to the collectors. Many users do not go beyond the knowledge that cookies exist and websites take advantage of the user's inexperience and collect, catalogue and commodify information totally unwarranted. The Information Technology Act, 2000 (IT Act) does not deal with cookies directly but section 43(b) says that if any person, without permission of the owner or any other person who is incharge of a computer, computer or computer network, downloads, copies or extracts any data, computer data base or information from such computer, computer system or computer network including information or data held or stored in any removable storage medium, he shall be liable to pay damages by way of compensation not exceeding one crore rupees to the person so affected.

Spamming is another area of concern where cyber privacy is at stake and has become a

[3] The Constitution of India, Article 21 states: 'No person shall be deprived of his life or personal liberty except according to procedure established by law'.

major problem for all Internet users. Spam is unsolicited e-mail on the Internet and is the Internet version of 'junk mail'. Spamming is a weapon to help abusers, who repeatedly bombard an e-mail message to a particular address or addresses. Potential target lists are created by scanning usernet postings, lifting Internet mailing lists, or searching the web for addresses. Suppose, a person wants to buy a washing machine, so he visits a website selling washing machines. Suddenly, a few days later when he browses the web, he gets e-mails containing advertisements for washing machines. So, there is somebody sitting on the other side collecting information about a person without him knowing that. The low cost of e-mail spamming offered for sale with millions of e-mail addresses, coupled with the fact that the sender does not pay extra to send e-mail, has resulted in the current explosive growth of junk e-mail. The issue of spamming has not been directly dealt with in any Indian statute. The law of nuisance under tort law can be used for bringing the spammer to books. Under the law of torts, nuisance is supposed to have been caused by an act or omission, whereby a person is unlawfully annoyed, prejudiced or disturbed in the enjoyment of property. Continuous spam could also cause disruption, damage or denial of service to a computer. In case any person is receiving a voluminous, regular supply of spam messages, recourse could be had to section 43(d), (e) and (f) of the IT Act which make damage, disruption to any computer or data or programme illegal.[4]

Technological Protections Against Technological Insecurities

With the recent development of commercially available technology based systems, privacy protection has also moved into the hands of

[4] Information Technology Act, 2000, section 43.

individual users. Users of the Internet and of some physical applications can employ a range of programs and systems that provide varying degrees of privacy and security of communications. One of these technologies is digital signature. All electronic documents can be signed digitally and once signed, their secure communication on the Internet is guaranteed as the message gets encrypted. It cannot be read in transit by any third party and only the addressee will be able to decipher it. Firewall, another network based technology, is frequently used by computer networks to ward of attempts to breach the privacy of a network. A firewall is a set of related programs, located at a network gateway server that protects the resources of a private network from users from other networks. A firewall is a hardware and software combination used to create security checkpoints at the boundaries of private networks. Suppose, there is network of 50 computers, it must have one point from which the information comes in and goes out. At that point a firewall is created in the form of a checkpoint. It can block traffic to and from suspicious destinations.

III. DOMAIN NAMES

A domain name is the address of a website like www.tata.com is the address of the famous business house, Tata. The purpose of a domain name is to locate a webpage on the Internet. Every webpage has a unique address just in the same manner as every telephone has a unique number. Since websites are very many, it is inconvenient to remember them by numbers, a system evolved under which a name is mapped to the concerned number or IP address. So, simply put, a domain name is the linguistic counterpart of what is known as an Internet Protocol (IP) address.

TYPES OF DOMAIN NAMES

Broadly, domain names are of two types: (1) generic top-level domain (gTLD), and; (2) country code top level domains (ccTLD).

A gTLD is a top-level domain used by a particular class of organization. These are three or more letters long, and are named for the type of organization that they represent (for example, .com for commercial organizations, .int for international organisations). But some of these gTLDs have become unrestricted, that means they no longer represent any particular type of organization and anyone could get a domain name under it. Like .com which can be registered by anyone even if the purpose is not commercial activity, gTLDs are governed directly under a centralised system by ICANN which means all terms and conditions are defined by ICANN with the cooperation of the gTLD registries.

ccTLD is used and reserved for a country. These are two letters long, and most of them correspond to the ISO 3166-1 standard for country codes. The administration of a ccTLD is left to the specific country concerned and thus each ccTLD policy setting out the rules for allocating domains is distinct from the other. The administration of domain names within the .in (Indian) category is overseen by Center for Development of Advance Computing, Mumbai (C-DAC), a scientific R&D institution under the Ministry of Communications and Information Technology.

DOMAIN NAME DISPUTES— CYBERSQUATTING

Any business entity, for example, would prefer its own trade mark to be used as domain name since people recognize the trade mark. So Bata would prefer www.bata.com for the purpose of marketing its products and, even the consumers would relate www.bata.com with the famous company Bata that deals in shoes. But, as opposed to the physical world where two or more trademarks are capable of co-existence, the medium of the Internet does not allow for more than one domain name registration. Domain names have become akin to trade marks but the process of registration of a domain name is not the same and as stringent as that of registration of a trademark. The system is based on first-come-first-serve basis. Anyone can approach a Domain Name Registrar and register any available domain name. So, it becomes important for business entities to procure domain names that correspond with their trade marks. But there is another problem. There are various top level domains and various combinations thereof under which you could register your trademark. Like Bata could register as www.bata.com or www.bata.org or www.bata.net or www.bataindia.com. So, there could be numerous combinations that have a relation to a trademark and it is not possible for a business entity to procure all those combinations.

The practice of registering and claiming rights over Internet domain names that are not for the taking is known as cybersquatting. The cybersquatter then could offer the domain to the person or company who owns a trademark contained within the name at an inflated price. Some cybersquatters use such domain names in competition with the company which the domain is meant to represent. All this and much more is aimed at taking an unfair advantage of someone's trademark.

DISPUTE RESOLUTION

For resolving disputes which arise out of cybersquatting in relation to gTLDs there exist two separate routes—first, the normal court litigation route and second, the arbitration route.

One has to litigate domain name disputes before a court of law; the cause of action would be one in passing off or trademark infringement, depending on whether the trademark was registered or not. If one is successful in obtaining a court order, then one could furnish a copy of such order to the registrar who would transfer the domain name.

One of the earliest and most significant cases in the Indian context has been *Yahoo! Inc.* v. *Akash Arora & Anr.,*[5] where the Internet search engine Yahoo! Inc. sued a cybersquatter who had not only copied the domain name 'www.Yahooindia.com' but had used Yahooindia as a trademark in a similar script on its website by offering directory services with information specific to India, and was passing itself off as an extension of Yahoo. The Delhi High Court granted an injunction restraining him from using Yahoo as a part of his domain name or as a trade mark. Specifically, the court held that trademark law applies with equal force on the Internet as it does in the physical world. The courts in India had occasions to decide many other cases on similar reasoning.

The *Satyam Infoway Ltd.* v. *Sifynet Solutions (P) Ltd.*[6] case is the first one from the Supreme Court of India dealing with legal protection of domain names and has given seal to the law laid down by the High Courts in various cases that the domain names are entitled to legal protection equal to that of a trademark.

Domain name disputes are typically resolved using the Uniform Domain Name Resolution Policy (UDRP) developed by ICANN. Under UDRP, most types of trademark-based domain-name disputes must

be resolved by agreement, court action, or arbitration before a registrar will cancel, suspend, or transfer a domain name. The policy offers an expedited administrative proceeding for trademark holders to contest 'abusive registrations of domain names'. UDRP currently applies to all .biz, .com, .info, .name, .net, and .org top-level domains, and some country code top-level domains. The intention is to create a process that is faster and cheaper than the legal system.

Under the policy, currently, the following four are the only authorized providers:

1. World Intellectual Property Organization (WIPO);
2. National Arbitration Forum (NAF);
3. CPR Institute for Dispute Resolution;
4. Asian Domain Name Dispute Resolution Centre (ADNDRC).

Each provider has a list of panellists from which either one or three are chosen to decide a particular dispute. The policy is incorporated by reference into the registration agreement that the registrant had with the registrar at the time of registering its domain name. By virtue of the incorporation of the UDRP into the registration agreement, the registrant submits itself to the jurisdiction of the approved dispute resolution providers and binds itself to the UDRP.

Three elements that have to be established by a complainant to obtain relief are:

1. Respondent's domain name is identical or confusingly similar to a trademark or service mark in which the complainant has rights;
2. Respondent has no right or legitimate interest in respect of the domain name; and
3. Respondent's domain name has been registered and is being used in bad faith.

---

[5] 1999 PTC 201.
[6] 2004 (28) PTC (SC) 566.

Apparently, the main requirement under the policy is that the domain name of the complainant 'should have been registered and used in bad faith'.

Thousands of cases have been decided by the dispute resolution providers using the UDRP. It is neither possible nor desirable to list all those cases here but it would suffice to discuss a few.

IV. COPYRIGHT PROTECTION IN CYBERSPACE

Copyright protection in cyberspace involves a plethora of legal issues. In this part one of the important copyright issues relating to P2P networks has been examined.

Peer-to-peer (P2P) technology, with which users can use the Internet to exchange files with each other directly or through a mediating server, is seen as a threat to copyright industry. Recently, P2P networks such as Napster, Gnutella and Kazaa have led to massive reproduction and distribution of copyrighted works. On the information superhighway this loss of control over their own digital products has sent the digital product industry into shock and panic.

P2P NETWORKING

P2P is defined as two or more computers connected by software which enables the connected computers to transit files or data to other connected computers. In recent usage, P2P has come to describe applications in which users can use the Internet to exchange files with each other directly. The P2P connection means that it is a direct link, the file is being directly transferred from one computer to the other, it is not going through any mediating server.

VARIOUS P2P NETWORKS AND THEIR LEGAL IMPLICATIONS

Napster was created in 1999 and it quickly became popular around the world and pioneered the concept of P2P file sharing. With Napster, individual people stored files that they wanted to share (typically mp3 music files) on their hard disks and shared them directly with other people.

In order to download a free music file, first of all, one had to become a member of Napster service by downloading the Napster software on one's computer which was available for free at the Napster's Web site 'www.napster.com'. After implementing the Napster software the computer became a small server, able to make files available to other Napster users. Then the computer connected to Napster's central servers. The Napster software that a member downloaded on his computer automatically told Napster central servers that these were the music files on his computer. So, the Napster central servers had a complete list of every shared song available on every hard disk connected to Napster at that time. A Napster user could send a request to the Napster server for a particular piece(s) of music. Now, the Napster server did not contain any music on its own server but had a list of all the music that was available on the Napster members' computers. The list was dynamic in nature as the music files available depended on which member was online at a particular time. The entire user community could be searched for artists or titles in seconds.

Napster became so popular so quickly because it offered a unique product–free music that anybody could obtain nearly effortlessly from a gigantic database.

But for the music industry Napster was a big, automated way to illegally copy copyrighted material. The industry sued Napster under a claim of copyright infringement. The court, while deciding in favour of music industry, said that putting the list on the website was akin to running a huge distribution network. The central database for song titles was Napster's Achilles' heel. The court[7] ordered Napster to stop listing the music files which were under copyright protection and there was no means with Napster to segregate copyrighted music files from those that were in public domain. The only option with Napster was to shut down the database and the absence of a central database killed the entire Napster network.

One distinguishing feature of the P2P services that came after Napster was that they had no central server maintaining direct file listings of all the files. The other distinction was that Napster was related to music files and that too specifically mp3 files. But most of these new softwares, Gnutella, Kazaa, etc., allow any type of files to be transmitted and downloaded.

Given that there is no central server to store the names and locations of all the available files first, one has to install a version of any P2P network say, Gnutella on one's computer and type in the name of the song/film or any other file one wants to find. The machine knows of at least one other Gnutella machine somewhere on the network because it has been told the location of the machine by typing in the IP address. The machine sends the file name typed in to the Gnutella machine(s) it knows about. These machines search to see if the requested file is on the local hard disk. If so, they send back the file name (and machine IP address) to the requester. At the same time, all of these machines send out the same request to the machines they are connected to, and the process repeats. After getting all of the search results the machine directly contacts the computer that has the desired file.

Most of these post Napster P2P networks have also faced litigation. The latest in the series of legal battles against the P2P file sharing softwares is *MGM Studios, Inc.* v. *Grokster, Ltd.*,[8] which is a United States Supreme Court case in which the court unanimously held that defendant P2P file sharing companies Grokster and Streamcast could be sued for inducing copyright infringement for acts taken in the course of marketing file sharing software. The plaintiffs were a consortium of 28 of the largest entertainment companies (led by Metro-Goldwyn-Mayer studios). The case has been called the most important intellectual property case in decades.

The court unanimously concurred that Grokster could be liable for inducing copyright infringement. The principle laid down by the court is that it has to be shown that the distributors of the file sharing program have advertised and/or otherwise induced its use for copyright infringement; if this intent can be shown, additional contributory aspects may be relevant.

DAMAGE BY P2P NETWORKS AND REACTION OF COPYRIGHT INDUSTRY

Millions of people around the world have downloaded various P2P softwares and are increasingly using them to exchange music, movie and software files. The copyright industry has been giving figures that go to show the decline in the sales of copyrighted products and they cite the reason as Internet

---

[7] *A&M Records* v. *Napster, Inc.*, 239 F.3d 1004 (9th Cir. 2001).

[8] 545 U. S., 125 S. Ct. 2764 (2005).

piracy. The industry points the finger directly at the Internet.

Shocked and dismayed, the industry, in the last couple of years, has been fighting this menace of 'piracy' on all possible fronts that include, lobbying, litigation, legislation and technological measures. The industry is starting to prosecute not only companies like Napster but also individuals who download copyrighted content and the persons who make it possible, namely the Internet service providers.

In the past there has been pressure from the industry for stronger protection of their rights in the digital context. In 1996, two treaties were concluded at WIPO: the WIPO Copyright Treaty (WCT) and the WIPO Performances and Phonograms Treaty (WPPT) (commonly referred to as the 'Internet treaties'). These treaties address the issues of the definition and scope of rights in the digital environment, and some of the challenges of online enforcement and licensing. As a continuation of this process, in many countries laws have emerged in this direction.

Indian Legal Landscape vis-à-vis P2P Networks

Let us examine a network like Napster functioning in India which allows people to share and distribute music, films and computer software. Section 51 of the Copyright Act, 1957 says that in case anyone does anything the exclusive right to do which is by this Act conferred upon the owner of the copyright, his Act amounts to infringement of copyright. Section 14 of the Copyright Act, 1957, which governs the domain of exclusive rights granted to copyright owners says that making copies of any work by using whatever medium, communicating the work to the public or issuing copies of the work to public fall within the domain of exclusive rights of a copyright owner. So, if any person is running a network like Napster in India he could be liable for encroaching upon the exclusive rights of the copyright owner as he is essentially facilitating the communication of the work to the public.

As for the persons who actually make available and download copyrighted works, the law is very clear. Section 14 says that issuing copies of work or communicating the same to the public amounts to infringement. So, a person who downloads a software like Napster and implements the same on his machine is making the copyrighted work available to any member of the public who has the corresponding software installed on his machine.

Now for networks akin to Gnutella or Kazaa, where there is no central server brokering the requests of people, it is rather hard to stop the system in one go. There is no one person or entity that is managing the affairs. The entire thing is managed by a software and that is already out and lakhs of people have made copies of the same. You cannot really outlaw the installation and use of that software as it could legally be used for sharing files which are not protected by copyright. But individuals who use such software for sharing copyrighted works remain guilty under the above stated provisions of Copyright Act, 1957. Catching them is rather difficult.

Copyright Law and Digital Technology: Need for Balance

Technology is copyright industry's best friend and worst enemy. Our challenge is to ensure that the laws of copyright adapt to the new technological environment in a way that feeds and encourages creative activity rather than in a way that inhibits or overwhelms it. The proprietary aspect of copyright law is only one side of the matter, which is to be considered in close relation with its cultural-economic aspect. In other words, the right of copyright owners to equitable remuneration should always be balanced with the interests of society at large. The key is to balance which has always to be interpreted and reinterpreted considering varying interests from time to time along with the advancement of technology.

V. CYBER CRIMES

'Technological progress is like an axe in the hands of a pathological criminal.' So, said Albert Einstein. New technologies create new criminal opportunities but few new types of crime. What distinguishes cyber crime from traditional criminal activity? The difference lies in the fact that in case of cyber crimes the criminal uses a digital computer or network. So, technology is the only distinguishing factor that might exist between different realms of criminal activity.

Criminals do not need a computer to commit fraud, traffic in child pornography and intellectual property, steal an identity, or violate someone's privacy. All these criminal activities existed before mankind came to know about cyberspace. Therefore cyber crime represents an extension of traditional criminal behaviour in cyberspace, of course, alongside some novel illegal activities. Therefore any kind of criminal behaviour done through computers, Internet, etc., is termed as cyber crime. Let us discuss a few important kinds of cyber crimes here.

HACKING

Hacking is 'unauthorized access' to a computer and refers to access to the whole or any part of a computer system without permission. Hackers worldwide attempt to hack into remote computer systems for multiple purposes like eavesdropping, data theft, fraud, destruction of data, causing damage to computer systems, or for mere pleasure or personal satisfaction.

At the basic level, hackers[9] are considered to be learners and explorers who want to help rather than cause damage, and who often have very high standards. But the term hacking has acquired dual meaning today and a hacker may variably mean a cyber burglar or vandal, an individual or group who believes in causing malicious harm to a network or computer, or to steal information like passwords, credit card numbers, names and address, financial information, and in short, anything stored on a computer.

One example of a hacking software is a 'Trojan Horse' program, in which malicious or harmful code is contained inside apparently harmless programming or data in such a way that it can get control and do its chosen form of damage, such as ruining the file allocation table on a hard disk.[10] Trojan Horse is a snooping software, which may come as an e-mail borne virus. The Trojan Horse may even be able to record each and every keystroke one makes, save the information to a hidden file and then when one goes online, upload the file to the hacker's computer. This means that even if you do not keep personal information or passwords on your computer the hacker can still obtain them from the keystroke log he uploaded.[11]

Hacking has been made a punishable offence under the IT Act. Section 66 of the IT Act that deals with 'hacking', states:[12]

[9] Many call those who break into (crack) computer systems 'crackers'.

[10] See, http://searchsecurity.techtarget.com/sDefinition/0,,sid14_gci213221,00.html.

[11] Supra note 32, p 286.

[12] Information Technology Act, 2000, section 66(1).

(1) Whoever with the intent to cause or knowing that he is likely to cause wrongful loss or damage to the public or any person destroys or deletes or alters any information residing in a computer resource or diminishes its value or utility or affects it injuriously by any means, commits hacking.

(2) Whoever commits hacking shall be punished with imprisonment up to three years, or with fine which may extend up to two lakh rupees, or with both.

The emphasis for committing 'hacking' under the IT Act is on the effect on the information residing in the computer and any subsequent wrongful loss due to access rather than mere access to a computer itself. Hacking of a protected system is punishable under section 70 of the IT Act.[13]

CYBER TERRORISM

'The terrorist of tomorrow may be able to do more with a keyboard than with a bomb'.[14]

As criminals, terrorists, and foreign intelligence services learn to exploit the power of cyber tools and weapons the world becomes a more dangerous place to live. Terrorists could use information technologies and global network posing a dangerous threat to humanity in the 21st century. Moreover, cyber terrorism could be conducted remotely and anonymously, it would be cheap, and it would not require handling of explosives or a suicide mission.

The Internet presents terrorists exclusive opportunities. It serves as a source of easy access to almost all data without drawing any significant attention. Knowing about potential arms dealers comes handy. Necessary manuals detailing how to make bombs and how to deal with explosives can be easily acquired from the Internet. Recruiting mercenaries and indoctrinating them could also be arranged easily on the Internet. Recent news suggests that terrorists have begun to use the Internet with ease and comfort. They use it as it presents maximum organizational and assaulting capabilities. The free mailing facilities like Yahoo and Hotmail could be used by anyone from anywhere on earth in order to keep in touch with the remote organisers and exchange messages without any significant risk of being intercepted.

It seems improbable that national utilities such as water, electricity and gas, airplanes, space satellites and other critical infrastructure could be brought down by cyber terrorists, without using some physical assistance and insider help.

PORNOGRAPHY

The *Encyclopaedia of Ethics* defines pornography as 'the sexually explicit depiction of persons, in words or images. created with the primary, proximate aim, and reasonable hope, of eliciting significant sexual arousal on the part of the consumer of such materials'. The question of what constitutes pornography is extraordinarily complex. Standards that are applied in each society or country in defining

---

[13] Ibid., section 70, states:

(1) The appropriate Government may, by notification in the Official Gazette, declare that any computer, computer system or computer network to be a protected system.

(2) The appropriate Government may, by order in writing, authorise the persons who are authorised to access protected systems notified under sub-section (1).

(3) Any person who secures access or attempts to secure access to a protected system in contravention of the provision of this section shall be punished with imprisonment of either description for a term which may extend to ten years and shall also be liable to fine.

[14] Dorothy E. Denning, 'Activism, Hacktivism, and Cyberterrorism: The Internet as a Tool for Influencing Foreign Policy', http://www.crime.vl.ru/docs/stats/stat_92.htm.

pornography are highly subjective and are contingent upon differing moral, cultural, social, and religious beliefs. Legal definitions of 'pornography' differ globally.

Censorship of pornographic material is not a new phenomenon and has been debated nearly every time a new medium of distribution has emerged. The Internet has been no exception in this regard. Given that the issue has been around for a while, it is undesirable to go into the general arguments made for and against the censorship of pornography—the object being to discuss the specific challenges brought about by the Internet.

Pornography on the Internet is available in different formats. These range from pictures and short animated movies, to sound files and stories. Most of this kind of pornographic content is available through World Wide Web pages. There are also sex related discussions on the Internet Relay Chat channels where users in small groups or in private channels exchange messages and files. Individuals can easily view pornographic materials from the privacy of their own home or office. The Internet has decreased the hurdle of shame that comes with purchasing pornographic materials or the embarrassment of being caught with it.

Computer alteration of images and the potential for creating computer generated pornography pose formidable challenges for courts and law enforcement officials throughout the world. Section 67 of the Information Technology Act, 2000 deals with the issue of cyber pornography whereby the publication or transmission of lascivious material has been made an offence.[15]

---

15 Information Technology, 2000, section 67, 'Whoever publishes or transmits or causes to be published in the electronic form, any material which is lascivious or appeals to the prurient interest or if its effect is such as

JURISDICTION

An important aspect of cyber crime is its non-local character—criminal activities could occur in jurisdictions separated by vast distances. This poses severe problems for law enforcement, since previously more or less local crimes now require international cooperation. For example, if a person accesses pornography located on a computer in a country that does not ban pornography, is that individual committing a crime in a nation where such materials are illegal? Where exactly does cyber crime take place?

The jurisdictional principle of IPC based on territoriality and nationality has been widened by the IT Act, 2000. Section 1(2) states that the Act:[16]

[s]hall extend to the whole of India and, save as otherwise provided in this Act, it applies also to any offence or contravention thereunder committed outside India by any person.

Further, section 75 says:[17]

(1) Subject to the provisions of sub-section (2), the provisions of this Act shall apply also to any offence or contravention committed outside India by any person irrespective of his nationality.

(2) For the purposes of sub-section (1), this Act shall apply to an offence or contravention committed outside India by any person if the act or conduct constituting the offence or

---

to tend to deprave and corrupt persons who are likely, having regard to all relevant circumstances, to read, see or hear the matter contained or embodied in it, shall be punished on first conviction with imprisonment of either description for a term which may extend to five years and with fine which may extend to one lakh rupees and in the event of a second or subsequent conviction with imprisonment of either description for a term which may extend to ten years and also with fine which may extend to two lakh rupees'.

16 Information Technology Act, 2000, section 1(2).

17 Ibid., section 75.

contravention involves a computer, computer system or computer network located in India.

For the offences and contraventions contained within the IT Act, any person whether or not he is a citizen of India can be made liable for his act whether committed within or outside India provided the effect of the same is felt on any computer[18], computer system[19] or computer network[20] located in India. Therefore, even if a foreigner outside the territorial limits of India commits an offence or contravention under the IT Act, the courts in India would have the jurisdiction over him. The extra-territorial operation of the IT Act has been put in place considering the ease with which anybody actually present anywhere in the world can commit a cyber crime having an impact in India. In this way the legislature in India has been influenced by the effect

[18] Ibid., section 2(i) states: 'computer' means any electronic, magnetic, optical or other high-speed data processing device or system which performs, logical, arithmetic and memory functions by manipulations of electronic, magnetic or optical impulses, and includes all input, output, processing, storage, computer software or communication facilities which are connected or related to the computer in a computer system or computer network.

[19] As per the Information Technology Act, 2000, section 2(j): 'computer network' means the interconnection of one or more computers through – (i) the use of satellite, microwave, terrestrial line or other communication media; and (ii) terminals or a complex consisting of two or more interconnected computers whether or not the interconnection is continuously maintained.

[20] As per the Information Technology Act, 2000, section 2(l): 'computer system' means a device or collection of devices, including input and output support devices and excluding calculators which are not programmable and capable of being used in conjunction with external files which contain computer programmes, electronic instructions, input data and output data that performs logic, arithmetic, data storage and retrieval, communication control and other functions.

theory, whereby the jurisdiction is determined by examining where the effect of a particular offence is felt.

INVESTIGATION OF CYBER CRIMES

As a global network, the Internet offers criminals multiple hiding places in the real world as well as in the network itself. However, just as individuals walking on the ground leave marks that a skilled tracker can follow, cyber criminals leave clues as to their identity and location, despite their best efforts to cover their tracks. On the one hand, we need skilled investigators to nab those criminals who are traversing through the cyberspace. No doubt, cyber forensics is emerging as a new branch of study and practice. On the other hand, in order to follow such clues across national boundaries more international cooperation is required. This cooperation has to result in international treaties and conventions.

VI. CONCLUSION

After conquering land, water, air and outer space, cyberspace becomes the fifth frontier where man has unfurled his eternal flag. Though a product of technological innovation, cyberspace has thrown and continues to pose newer challenges to mankind. These challenges include issues of business, crime, intellectual property and civil rights among others. For cyberspace to play a meaningful role in our society we must counter these challenges and find answers to the problems that technology has posed.

Cyber law as a new aspect of law is still emerging as the dynamic forces of law and technology continue to intersect. Therefore it has become a subject of considerable interest where lawyers, social scientists and law and policy makers have exhibited curiosity.

Anti-terror Laws and Human Rights in India

UJJWAL KUMAR SINGH

The Indian Parliament has so far enacted three anti-terror laws, the Terrorist and Disruptive Activities (Prevention) Act (TADA) 1985, 1987,[1] the Prevention of Terrorism Act (POTA), 2002, and the Unlawful Activities Prevention Act, 2004. TADA lapsed in 1995 and POTA was repealed in 2004. The repeal of POTA was followed by the amendment of an existing law–the Unlawful Activities Prevention Act, 1967 (UAPA)–to include POTA provisions pertaining to punishment for terrorist activities and organisations. UAPA (2004) may then well be considered the third anti-terror law in India. The question that one must necessarily ask at this point, before examining the provisions of the acts, is, what is meant by 'terrorism' and 'terrorist activity' that these laws propose to 'prevent'. The concept of terrorism is complex and defies an accepted definition. It has been looked at differently from various ideological, political and historical vantage points. Moreover, a sifting or selective labelling is noticed in the way in which a particular act and event, e.g.,

Bombay blasts in 1993 and 2006, and the blasts in Delhi in 2005, and the attack on the Parliament building on 13 December 2001 get described as 'acts of terror', and the killing of Muslims in Gujarat in 2002 and lynching of dalits in Duleena, Jhajjar, Haryana do not get described as such. In the sections that follow, we shall examine in the following section the exceptional provisions pertaining to remand, bail, investigation procedures and trial under anti-terror laws, and the implications of such extraordinary laws for human rights.

I. ANTI-TERROR LAWS IN INDIA: TADA AND POTA

THE TERRORIST AND DISRUPTIVE ACTIVITIES (PREVENTION) ACT, 1985

TADA was brought in May 1985 in the context of the separatist movement for Khalistan. The act was initially brought for two years. It was, however, re-introduced in 1987, through an ordinance and made more stringent through the conferment of special powers to the central government to make rules for carrying out the provisions of the ordinance and also to constitute designated courts to try TADA cases. The Statement of Objects and Reasons of the act declared, 'on the basis of experience,

---

[1] The Terrorist Affected Areas (Special Courts) Act, 1984 empowered the central government to declare an area to be terrorist affected, and to constitute special courts for the speedy trial of suspected terrorists.

it was felt that in order to combat and cope with terrorist and disruptive activities effectively, it is not only necessary to continue the said law but also strengthen it further'. The act which replaced the ordinance, i.e., TADA 1987, therefore, introduced two changes: (a) persons in possession of arms and ammunitions as specified in the Arms Rules 1962 or other explosive substances, shall be punishable with imprisonment for a term not less than five years, but which could extend to imprisonment for life with fine, and; (b) confessions made by a person before a police officer not lower in rank than the Superintendent of Police were made admissible in the trial of the person for an offence under the act. TADA 1987 was extended every two years, the last being the two-year extension in 1993.[2] During the course of the extensions, the act not only became stringent, it also assumed a more general application, as its area of operation, which began with just one state and two union territories, covered most of the country by 1993.[3] After TADA expired in 1997, there was no central law to deal with terrorism till the Prevention of Terrorism Ordinance was promulgated in 2001.

[2] It is significant that TADA, at this penultimate stage of its journey, became so much 'routine' that only eight members of Parliament (excluding the minister presenting/defending the Bill) participated in the discussion which lasted merely an hour and ten minutes. See People's Union for Democratic Rights, 'Lawless Roads: A Report on TADA 1985-1993', Delhi, September, 1993, p. 5.

[3] In 1985, the government cited two union territories and four states in its statement of objects in reasons. Two years later, two more were added. In 1991 the total states became 17. In 1993, TADA was in force in 22 out of the 25 states and two out of the seven union territories. The exceptions were Kerala, Orissa, Sikkim, Andaman and Nicobar, Dadra and Nagar Haveli, Daman and Diu, Lakshadweep, and Pondicherry. Ibid., p. 4.

PREVENTION OF TERRORISM ACT, 2001 (POTA)

The Prevention of Terrorism Ordinance (POTO) was promulgated on 24 October 2001 for 'the prevention of and for dealing with terrorist activities'. In the years intervening the expiry of TADA and the promulgation of POTO, successive governments had wanted to bring in an anti-terror law in order to plug what they called a 'legal vacuum' in dealing with terrorism. The immediate justification of POTO, however, was the 11 September 2001 bombings in the USA and the United Nations Security Council resolution seeking a worldwide concerted effort in confronting global terrorism. The debates in Parliament—from October 2001 through March 2002—show that POTA was being justified as part of the international effort to fight terrorism. The 'statement of objects and reasons' stated in the text of the act clearly identify the 'global dimensions' of challenges to 'internal security'. The Prevention of Terrorism (Second) Ordinance was promulgated on 31 December 2001, following the adjournment of the Parliament after a terrorist attack on the Parliament building on 13 December 2001. Amidst fractured political support, and the rejection of the Prevention of Terrorism Bill in the Rajya Sabha, the act to replace the Ordinance was passed in an extraordinary joint sitting of the two Houses of Parliament on 26 March 2002.

The repeal of POTA figured prominently in the Common Minimum Programme (CMP) of the Congress Party led United Progressive Alliance (UPA) government that replaced the National Democratic Alliance (NDA) led by the Bharatiya Janata Party (BJP) in May 2004. The repeal of POTA happened through an Ordinance in September 2004, and was a rare occasion when an extraordinary law was repealed. While the CMP conveyed that the repeal was a result of the 'gross misuse' of the act in the two years of its existence, it also committed itself to continue its fight against terrorism by strengthening existing laws. The repeal of POTA took place, therefore, with the simultaneous promulgation of an ordinance amending the UAPA 1967.

THE UNLAWFUL ACTIVITIES PREVENTION ACT, 2004 (UAPA, 2004)

While the repeal of POTA has done away with provisions relating to bail and confessions, POTA provisions pertaining to definition of terrorist acts, banning of terrorist organisations and interception of electronic communication have been retained through importation into the UAPA A comparison of the provisions of TADA, POTA and UAPA will be undertaken later. The box below identifies the ways in which terrorism and terrorist activities have been defined in the different acts. It must be pointed out that TADA identified 'spreading communal disharmony' as a significant constituent of a terrorist and disruptive offence. Amidst widespread criticism that the clause was especially amenable to abuse and was used to target specific minority communities, it was dropped in POTA. The unfolding of POTA showed, however, that irrespective of the clause, the act was used in a way that discriminated between religious communities. Also significant is the way in which the UAPA while defining commission of a terrorist offence assumes extra-territoriality.

Defining Terrorism: A Comparison of Provisions under TADA, POTA and UAPA

TADA[4]	POTA	UAPA 2004
Section 3(1): Whosoever with the intent to overawe the government as by law established or to strike terror in the people or any section of the people or to alienate any section of the people or to adversely affect the harmony among different sections of the people does any act or thing by using bombs, dynamite, or other explosive substance or inflammable substances or	Section 3(1) Whoever, – (a) with the intention to threaten the unity, integrity or sovereignty of India or to strike terror in the people or any section of the people does any act or thing by using bombs, dynamite or other explosive substances or inflammable substances (whether biological or otherwise) of a hazardous nature or by any other	Section 15: Whoever with the intent to threaten the unity, integrity, security or sovereignty of India or to strike terror in the people or any section of the people in India or in any foreign country, does any act by using bombs, dynamite or other explosive substances or inflammable substances or firearms or other lethal weapons or poisons or noxious gases or other chemicals or by any other substances (whether biological or otherwise)

(Continued on next page)

[4] Terrorist Affected Areas (Special Courts) Act 1984, section 2(h), defined a 'terrorist' as a person who indulged in wanton killings of persons or in violence or in the disruption of services or means of communication essential to the community or in damaging property with a view to: (i) putting the public or any section of the public in fear, or (ii) affecting adversely the harmony between different religious, racial, language or regional groups or castes or communities; or (iii) coercing or overawing the government established by law; or (iv) endangering the sovereignty and integrity of India.

(Continued from previous page)

TADA[4]	POTA	UAPA 2004
fire-arms or other lethal weapons or poisons or noxious gases or other chemicals or any other substances (whether biological or otherwise) of a hazardous nature in such as manner as to cause, or as is likely to cause, death of, or injuries to, any person or persons or damage to, or destruction of property or disruption of any supplies or services essential to the life of the community, or detains any person and threatens to kill or injure such persons in order to compel the government or any other person to do or abstain from doing any act, commits a terrorist act.	whatsoever, in such a manner as to cause death, injury, or destruction of property or equipment, used or intended to be used for the defence of India; (b) is or continues to be a member of an association declared unlawful under the Unlawful Activities (Prevention) Act, 1967, or voluntarily does an act aiding or promoting in any manner the objects of such association…commits a terrorist act.	of a hazardous nature, in such a manner as to cause, or likely to cause, death of, or injuries to any person or persons or loss of, or damage to, or destruction of, property or disruption of any supplies or services essential to the life of the community in India or in any foreign country or causes damage or destruction of any property of equipment used or intended to be used for the defence of India or in connection with any other purposes of the Government of India, any state government or any of their agencies, or detains any person and threatens to kill or injure such person in order to compel the Government in India or the government of a foreign country or any other person to do or to abstain from doing any act, commits a terrorist act.

Conspiracy and 'supporting terrorism'

3(3) Whoever conspires or attempts to commit, or advocates, abets, advises or incites or knowingly facilitates the commission of, a terrorist act, shall be punishable with imprisonment…(4) Whoever harbours or conceals, or attempts to harbour or conceal, any terrorist shall be punishable with imprisonment…	3(3) Whoever conspires or attempts to commit, or advocates, abets, advises or incites or knowingly facilitates the commission of, a terrorist act or any act preparatory to a terrorist act…(4) Whoever voluntarily harbours or conceals, or attempts to conceal any person knowing that such person is a terrorist…(5) Any person who is a member of a terrorist organisation,	Same as POTA Section 17 (punishment for raising funds for terrorist act) Section 18 (punishment for conspiracy) Section 19 (punishment for harbouring) Section 20 (punishment for being member of terrorist gang or organisation) Section 21 (punishment for holding proceeds of terrorism) Section 22 (punishment for threatening witness).

(Continued on next page)

(Continued from previous page)

TADA[4]	POTA	UAPA 2004
	which is involved in terrorist acts…(6) Whoever knowingly holds any property derived or obtained from commission of any terrorist act or has been acquired through the terrorist funds… (7) whoever threatens any person who is a witness or any other person in whom such witness may be interested, with violence, or wrongfully restrains or confines the witness.	

II. HOW ARE ANTI-TERROR LAWS 'EXTRA-ORDINARY' OR DIFFERENT FROM ORDINARY LAWS?

If one were to identify some of the characteristic features of extraordinary laws, or alternatively, respond to the question, 'what makes laws like TADA and POTA extra-ordinary?,' the following features could perhaps be listed:

(i) These laws come with objects and intents proclaiming the need to respond to specific problems of an extraordinary nature. It follows from the fact of extra-ordinariness that these laws will be temporary and that their lives would be coterminous with the extra-ordinary events they intend to overturn

(iii) Since they are extra-ordinary measures in response to extra-ordinary events/situations, they consist of extra-ordinary provisions pertaining to arrest, detention, bail, investigation, evidence, trial, and punishment. They bring in, therefore, a parallel system of investigation and trial, and hand out enhanced punishments for offences, aiming thereby to make anti-terror acts deterrent.

Anti-terror laws, thus, are premised on the idea of 'terror' being an 'extraordinary crime', requiring 'extraordinary measures' of investigation and trial. They provide for a legal and judicial procedure where the provisions of bail, admissibility of specific evidence in courts and punishment are changed substantially by providing exceptions in the ordinary law. Let us now examine specific provisions of TADA and POTA to see how they set in motion extraordinary measures of investigation and trial.

EXTRAORDINARY MEASURES OF INVESTIGATION AND TRIAL

Both TADA and POTA laid down extra-ordinary measures pertaining in particular to bail, admissibility of confessions made to the police, and setting up of special courts with greatly enhanced powers. Most of these measures come explicitly as exceptions to provisions that exist in ordinary law.

Bail

Bail under Criminal Procedure Code (CrPc)	Bail under TADA	Bail under POTA
Sections 436 to 450 of chapter XXXIII of the CrPC, provide the framework for granting bail to the accused. The provisions draw a distinction between bailable and non-bailable offences. Bailable and non-bailable offences are listed in the Indian Penal Code, 1860 (IPC), and indicated in the First Schedule of the CrPC. Bailable offences are relatively lesser offences like causing simple hurt, being a member of an unlawful assembly, etc., and any person committing a bailable offence has a legal right to be released on bail. A non-bailable offence is of a more serious nature like murder, rape, dacoity, etc. While a person accused of non-bailable offences cannot get bail as a matter of right, it does not mean that the accused cannot get bail at all. Apart from bailable and non-bailable offences, section 2(c) of the CrPC divides offences as cognizable and non-cognizable. Cognizable offences like murder, rape, dacoity, are those for which a police officer can arrest a person without a warrant from a magistrate. In non-cognizable offences e.g., cheating, causing hurt, bigamy etc., a warrant from a magistrate is required for making arrest. The First Schedule of the CrPC lists cognizable and non-cognizable offences. For offences under laws other than the IPC, offences under which three years or more punishment is handed down is a cognizable offence.	Section 8 of TADA made granting of bail subject to the public prosecutor having been given the opportunity to oppose the application for release [section 8(a)], and the satisfaction of the court that there are reasonable grounds for believing that the applicant is not guilty of such offence and not likely to commit such an offence while on bail [section 8(b)].	Section 49(6) of POTA lay down that 'no person accused of an offence under the act, if in custody, be released on bail or on his own bond unless the court gives the public prosecutor the opportunity of being heard' [section 49 (6)] 'until the court is satisfied that there are grounds for believing that that he is not guilty of committing such offence' [section 49 (7)]. Due to the ambiguous wording of a proviso in section 49 (7), which stated that the provisions of section 49(6) would apply after the expiry of a period of one year from the date of detention of the accused under the act, it came to be commonly believed and assumed in judgments, that bail under POTA was not possible before the expiry of one year.

Prolonged Period of Remand/Detention

Both TADA and POTA prescribed exceptions to the ordinary law facilitating prolonged detention, by providing for arrests without warrant, extending the period of police and judicial custody and the period within which the charge sheet could be drawn.

Remand provisions under CrPC	Remand provisions under TADA	Remand provisions under POTA
Under article 22(2) of the Constitution of India, every person who is arrested and detained should be brought before the nearest Magistrate within a period of 24 hours of arrest, excluding the time required for travelling from the place to arrest to the magistrate's court.	Section 20(4)(b) of TADA laid down exception to section 167(2) of CrPC providing that the references to '15 days', '90 days' and '60 days', wherever they occur be construed as '60 days', 'one year', and 'one year', respectively.	Section 49 (a) of POTA laid down exception to section 167(2) of CrPC providing that the references to '15 days', '90 days' and '60 days', wherever they occur, shall be construed as references to '30 days', '90 days', respectively.
Under section 167 of the CrPC, the magistrate is authorised to extend the period of detention for a maximum period of 15 days, if the investigation cannot be completed within 24 hours. At the end of 15 days, the accused must be produced before the magistrate, who can, if there are adequate grounds for further detention in judicial custody, extend the detention further for 15 days. The total period of detention cannot exceed 60 days, whether the investigation of the offence has been completed or not.		Section 49 (b) provided further that in case it was not possible to complete the investigation in 90 days, the special court could, on the basis of the report of the public prosecutor, extend the period to 180 days.

Confessions Made to Police Officers

Along with the 'right to speedy trial', 'protection against self-incrimination' is a fundamental principle of the criminal justice system. More often than not, confessions are seen with suspicion, and governed therefore by exclusionary rules, which basically means that any confession is seen as suspect, unless it is unquestionably established that pre-trial procedures and safeguards have been adhered to. While the evidentiary value of confessions as mentioned above, is suspect, confessions made to the police have an even lower credibility as legal evidence, since the police is normally also the investigating agency, and more often than not, such a confession is extracted under varying degrees of repression and coercion. Most constitutions assure protection against self-incrimination, or provide the right to remain silent and the laws of evidence exclude confessions made to police officers as primary evidence of guilt.

In the *Kartar Singh* v. *State of Punjab*,[5] the Supreme Court affirmed the admissibility of confessions as it existed under TADA, and

---

[5] *Kartar Singh* v. *State of Punjab* Writ petition no. 1833 of 1984 (decided on 11 March 1994), (1994) 3 SCC 569.

Provisions pertaining to confession under the ordinary law and the Constitution of India	Provisions under TADA	Provisions under POTA
(i) Article 20(3) of the Constitution of India declares that 'no person accused of any offence shall be compelled to be a witness against himself' embodying thereby the principle of protection against compulsion of self-incrimination. (ii) Sections 26 and 27 of the Indian Evidence Act 1872: Section 26 lays down that 'No confession made by any person whilst he is in the custody of a police officer, unless it be made in the immediate presence of a Magistrate, shall be proved as against such person. Section 27 lays down that 'Provided that, when any fact is deposed to as discovered in consequence of information received from a person accused of any offence, in the custody of a police officer, so much of such information, whether it amounts to a confession or not, as relates directly to the fact thereby discovered, may be proved'.	The admissibility of confession to a police officer as legal evidence was first permitted in India under TADA. Section 15 of TADA lay down, 'notwithstanding anything in the Code or in the Indian Evidence Act 1872 (1 of 1872), but subject to the provisions of this section, a confession made by a person before a police officer not lower in rank than a Superintendent of Police and recorded by such police officer either in writing or on any mechanical device like cassettes, tapes or sound tracks from out of which sounds or images can be produced, shall be admissible in the trial of such person for an offence under this Act or rules made thereunder' [15(1)]. 'The police officer shall before recording any confession under sub-section (1), explain to the person making it that he is not bound to make a confession and that, if he does so, it may be used as evidence against him and such police officer shall not record any such confession unless upon questioning the person making it, he has reason to believe that it is being made voluntarily' [15(2)].	Section 32(1) of POTA lays down that 'notwithstanding anything in the Code or in the Indian Evidence Act 1872 (1 of 1872), but subject to the provisions of this section, a confession made by a person before a police officer not lower in rank than a Superintendent of Police and recorded by such officer either in writing or on any mechanical or electronic device like cassettes, tapes or sound tracks from out of which sound or images can be reproduced, shall be admissible in the trial of such person for an offence under this act or the rules made thereunder'. The guidelines suggested by the Supreme Court in the *Kartar Singh case* were included in POTA as safeguards.

also lay down specific guidelines as safeguards, to ensure that 'confession obtained in the pre-indictment interrogation' by a police officer is 'not tainted with any vice, but is in strict conformity with the well-recognised and accepted aesthetic principles and fundamental fairness'. The guidelines were as follows:

(i) The confession must be recorded in a free atmosphere in the same language in which the person is examined and as narrated by him;

(ii) The person from whom a confession has been recorded under section 15(1) of the act, should be produced before the Chief Metropolitan Magistrate or the Chief Judicial Magistrate to whom the confession is required to be sent under rule 15(5) along with the original statement of confession, written or recorded on mechanical device without reasonable delay;

(iii) The Chief Metropolitan Magistrate or the Chief Judicial Magistrate should scrupulously record the statement, if any, made by the accused so produced and get his signature and in case of any complaint of torture, the person should be directed to be produced for medical examination before a medical officer not lower in rank than of an assistant civil surgeon;

(iv) Notwithstanding anything contained in the Code of Criminal Procedure, 1973, no police officer below the rank of an Assistant Commissioner of Police in the metropolitan cities and elsewhere of a Deputy Superintendent of Police or a police officer of equivalent rank, should investigate any offence punishable under this Act of 1987;

(v) The police officer if he is seeking the custody of any person for pre-indictment of pre-trial interrogation from the judicial custody, must file an affidavit sworn by him explaining the reason not only of such custody but also for the delay, if any, in seeking the police custody;

(vi) In case the person, taken for interrogation, on receipt of the statutory warning that he is not bound to make a confession and that if he does so, the said statement may be used against him as evidence, asserts his right to silence, the police officer must respect his right of assertion without making any compulsion to give a statement of disclosure.

Interception of Electronic Communication (C-LEVEL)

TADA had no provision for telephone tapping. POTA allowed electronic interceptions, which are otherwise not admissible as evidence, to be presented in the Special Court as evidence of guilt against the accused. The UAPA 2004, as amended after POTA's repeal included the provision.

Telephone tapping

TADA	POTA	UAPA 1967	UAPA 2004
No provision	Chapter V of POTA (sections 36 to 48) lay down the specific provisions pertaining to 'Interception of Communication in Certain Cases', giving its definition (section 36); appointment of competent authority (section 37); the procedure for application and authorisation of interception (sections 38 and 39); the safeguards, including a review procedure (sections 40 and 46); and submission	No provision	Section 46: Notwithstanding anything contained in the Indian Evidence Act 1872 or any other law for the time being in force, the evidence collected through interception of wire, electronic or oral

(Continued on next page)

(Continued from previous page)

TADA	POTA	UAPA 1967	UAPA 2004

of annual report of interception (section 48).

Section 38 (1): A police officer not below the rank of Superintendent of Police supervising the investigation of any terrorist act under POTA could submit an application in writing to the competent authority for an order authorising or approving interception. The application shall include the identity of the investigating officer and a statement of the facts and circumstances relied upon by the applicant, the type of communication to be intercepted, and the identity of the person whose communications are to be intercepted. The order by the competent authority must specify the identity of the person whose communication is to be intercepted, the nature and location of communication facilities, the agency authorised to intercept and the period or time during which interception is authorised. The competent authority shall, immediately after passing the order under sub-section (1) of section 39, shall submit a copy of the same to the review committee with all the relevant papers. Section 45: Notwithstanding anything in the Code or in any other law for the time being in force, the evidence collected through the interception of wire, electronic or oral communication under this chapter shall be admissible as evidence against the accused in the court during the trial of a case:; provided that the contents of any wire, electronic or oral communication intercepted pursuant to this chapter or evidence derived therefrom shall not be received in evidence or otherwise disclosed in any trial, hearing or other proceedings in any court unless each accused has been furnished a copy of the order ten days before trial. Section 46: The review committee shall review every order passed by the competent authority. Section 47: Interception and disclosure of wire, electronic or oral communications is prohibited except as otherwise specifically provided in section 39. Section 48: Annual reports of interceptions are to be prepared giving full accounts of interceptions, under the instructions of the central or state governments.

communication under the provisions of the Indian Telegraph Act, 1885 or the Information Technology Act, 2000 or any other law for the time being in force, shall be admissible as evidence against the accused in the court during the trail of a case: Provided that the contents of any wire, electronic or oral communication intercepted or evidence derived therefrom shall not be received in evidence or disclosed in a trial unless the accused has been furnished with a copy of the order. Unlike POTA, however, there is no provision of recourse to the review committee or legislative review.

Review Procedure and Committees

Under TADA	Under POTA	Under UAPA 2004

TADA did not have initially a provision for setting up a Review Committee. In the *Kartar Singh* v. *State of Punjab*,[6] the Constitution Bench of the Supreme Court suggested that a 'higher level of scrutiny and applicability of TADA' should be ensured by setting up a screening or review committee. The committee consisting of the Home Secretary, Law Secretary and other Secretaries was to review all TADA cases instituted by the central government, as well as to have a quarterly administrative review, reviewing the application of TADA provisions in the respective states. Similar screening or review committees were suggested at the state level as well.

POTA provided for central and state review committees as safeguards against misuse of the act. Section 60 of POTA lays down that (1) The central government and each state government shall, whenever necessary, constitute one or more review committees; (2) Every such committee shall consist of a chairperson and such other members not exceeding three and possessing such qualifications as may be prescribed; (3) A chairperson of the committee shall be a person who is, or has been, a judge of a High Court, who shall be appointed by the central government, or as the case may be, the state government, so however, that the concurrence of the Chief Justice of the High Court shall be obtained in the case of a sitting judge: Provided that in the case of a union territory, the appointment of a person who is a Judge of the High Court of a state shall be made a chairperson with the concurrence of the concerned High Court.

Amendments in the Review Procedure: from administrative to quasi-judicial powers: Amidst several complaints, some of which came from the review committee itself about the lack of cooperation from state governments, an ordinance was promulgated on 28 October 2003 to amend section 60 of POTA to give more 'teeth' to the review committee. Thus on an application from an 'aggrieved party', the central and state review committees could now decide, whether there existed a *prima facie* case for proceeding against the accused arrested under POTA 'and issue directions accordingly' [section 60(4)]. This

6 (1994) 3 SCC 569.

(Continued on next page)

(Continued from previous page)

Under TADA	Under POTA	Under UAPA 2004
	amendment not only made the direction binding on the central and state governments and police officers investigating the case [section 60(5)], it also provided that the direction issued by the Central Review Committee would prevail over any order passed by a state committee in any case of review relating to the same offence under POTA [section 60 (6)].	No provisions.

Review procedure in the POTA Repeal Act:
The Prevention of Terrorism (Repeal) Act, 2004, provided the guidelines for dealing with the cases that have accumulated over the act's short span of life. Section 3 of the repeal act directed that the legal-judicial process set in motion in cases under POTA would be put on hold until the review committee gave its approval. Under its new and enhanced powers, the review committee was entrusted with the task of reviewing all cases registered under the Act, to see whether or not a *prima facie* case for proceeding against the accused could be made, whether or not an appeal for review had been made to the review committee under section 60(4) of the Act. The task of review had to be completed within a year. While reviewing cases, the review committee had the powers of a civil court, and could order the production of specific documents or requisition public records from any court or office. If the review committee felt that there was no *prima facie* case against the accused, then even if the court had taken cognizance in the case, it shall be deemed to have been withdrawn. Similarly cases still in the process of investigation would be closed. Further, in cases in which trial had not begun, the Act provided that no court could take cognizance of an offence under the repealed POTA one year after the commencement of the repeal ordinance.

(f) Special Courts with Enhanced Powers

TADA and POTA empowered the central and state governments to set up parallel courts referred to as designated courts (as in TADA) and special courts (as in POTA) with over-riding powers. In instances where the central government set up such a court where one constituted by the state government was already in place, all cases pending before the latter, would be transferred to the designated/special court constituted by the central government.[7]

(i) Enhanced Jurisdiction of Parallel Courts: The jurisdiction of designated and special courts constituted under TADA and POTA, respectively, was especially enhanced so that it superseded the jurisdiction of all local courts in its area, in respect of offences committed under the act(s). Moreover, all cases relating to such offences pending immediately before the date of issue of such notification before such local courts would stand transferred on that date to the specified court.[8]

(ii) Power of Designated Courts with respect to other offences: When trying an offence under TADA and POTA, the designated and special courts could also try any other offence with which the accused may be charged at the same trial if the offence was connected with the offence under the acts. Moreover, if in the course of the trial it was found that the accused had committed any other offence under the act (TADA or POTA) or under any other law, the special court could convict the person of the offence and pass a sentence under the act.[9]

(iii) Trial by Designated/Special Courts to have preference: Section 17 of TADA laid down that the trial under the act of 'any offence by the Designated Court shall have precedence over the trial of any other case against the accused in any other court (not being a Designated Court) and shall be concluded in preference to the trial of such other case and accordingly the trial of such other case shall remain in abeyance'.

(iv)Appeal against the Designated/Special Courts: Appeals against decisions made by the Designated Court under TADA could be made only to the Supreme Court. Section 19 of TADA laid down that while an appeal against any judgment or order of the designated court would lie as a matter of right before the Supreme Court, no appeal against any judgement, sentence of order of the designated court could be made to any other court. Every appeal, moreover, had to be made within a period of 30 days from the date of the judgment, unless the Supreme Court was satisfied that the appellant had sufficient cause for not making an appeal within the stipulated period.

III. ANTI-TERROR LAWS: PERSPECTIVES AND POSITIONS

THE OFFICIAL /GOVERNMENT'S PERSPECTIVES: NECESSARY CORRECTIVES

While both the supporters of anti-terror laws and its detractors agree that these laws are draconian, the official position through different regimes has emphasized the necessity

[7] Terrorist and Disruptive (Prevention) Act, 1987, section 9(2); Prevention of Terrorism Act, 2002, section 23(2).

[8] Terrorist and Disruptive (Prevention) Act, 1987, section 11.

[9] Ibid, section 12; Prevention of Terrorism Act, 2002, section 26.

of such laws. The various arguments put forward may be broadly divided into:

(a) *Necessary correctives framework*: Supporters of anti-terror laws often argue that these laws have to be brought in to control the 'extra-ordinary situations' that emerge primarily because of the openness and freedom which democracy allows. In other words, they argue that these laws are not inimical to democracy, but integral to the functioning of democracy. As necessary and crucial correctives, they serve important restorative, curative and corrective purposes, working towards the preservation of 'legitimate' political authority.

(b) *Plugging the legislative vacuum*: In the interlude between the lapsed TADA and enactment of POTA, when there was no anti-terror law in India, there was a constant lament of a legislative vacuum in dealing with crimes of extraordinary nature. The Law Commission, for example, in its 173th Report (April, 2000), pointed at the necessity of plugging this vacuum by putting in place a law to deal with terrorism.

(c) *Crisis of national security and institutional erosion*: Certain arguments pointed at the imperatives of national security legislation in India, emphasizing that: (a) there was a chronic crisis of national security in India epitomised by terrorism, organised crime, criminalisation of politics, the growing numbers of the poor and rootless, pressures of population and consumerism on the limited natural resources; (b) that matters worsened by the fact that civil and judicial administration abdicated their responsibilities; while the judiciary took recourse to arid legal formalism the civil administration suspended their activities in the face of mass violence; (c) that a gradual pro-cess of erosion had set into all institutions of governance in the country; in order to redeem the crisis in national security and check institutional erosion, it was important that such laws be enacted.

(d) *Building a strong state*: Anti-terror laws are increasingly associated with the idea of a strong state. Absence of such a law is often seen as a manifestation of a soft / weak state by those advocating anti-terror laws.

(e) *Cooperating with the international effort against terrorism*: All anti-terror laws brought into statute books after 9/11 have lofty claims, drawing from the so-called 'international consensus' over 'making the world safe for democracy'. Moreover, the United Nations Security Council Resolution 1373 adopted on 28 September 2001 has often been cited as a justification for anti-terror laws.[10]

THE SUPREME COURT'S AFFIRMATION OF ANTI-TERROR LAWS

Upholding the validity of TADA and POTA, the Supreme Court took up questions of

[10] On 28 September 2001, the Security Council unanimously adopted 'a wide-ranging anti-terrorism resolution' number 1373, calling for international cooperation for suppressing and combating international terrorism through specific with steps and strategies. The resolution also established a committee of the council to monitor the resolution's implementation and called on all states to report on actions they had taken to that end, no later than 90 days from its adoption. Based on the resolution, the Counter-Terrorism Committee set up under the resolution, asked for specific measures from member countries viz., legislation or measures for prohibition of recruitment to terrorist groups, and the supply of weapons; steps being taken to prevent the commission of terrorist acts, procedures for denying safe haven to terrorist, steps taken to establish terrorist acts as serious criminal offences, and procedures and mechanism in place to assist other states.

'legislative competence' and on its basis justified the acts as addressing an 'overwhelming need' and 'supreme necessity', rather than principles of constitutionality, especially questions of derogation of fundamental rights.

In its judgement in *PUCL* v. *Union of India* (2003), upholding the constitutional validity of POTA, the Supreme Court concluded that: (a) in deciding the legislative competence of the central government on legislating on the matter it was necessary to understand the context which made the enactment of POTA necessary. It was 'clear to Parliament that terrorism was not a usual law and order problem', and the court could not 'go into and examine the 'need' for POTA. It is a matter of policy'. Arguing that the mere 'possibility of abuse could not be counted as a ground for denying the vesting of [extraordinary] powers' the Supreme Court emphasized, however, that 'the fight against terrorism must be respectful to human rights'.

The Supreme Court's position on POTA was congruous and continuous with its decision in 1994 upholding the constitutionality of TADA in *Kartar Singh* v. *the State of Punjab* where the Supreme Court maintained that, 'terrorism' cannot be classified as a mere disturbance of 'public order' disturbing the 'even tempo of the life of community of any specified locality' but it is much more—'a grave emergent situation created either by external forces particularly at the frontiers of this country or by anti-nationals throwing a challenge to the very existence and sovereignty of the country in its democratic polity'.[11]

THE NATIONAL HUMAN RIGHTS COMMISSION OF INDIA (NHRC)

In the discharge of its statutory function of reviewing safeguards for the protection of human rights under section 12 of the Protection of Human Rights Act, 1993, the NHRC set out to adopt 'a well-informed and unambiguous position on TADA', from what it identified as its non-negotiable 'central preoccupation' of 'protection of civil liberties'.[12] It conducted from this premise, a 'full-fledged examination of all aspects of TADA' especially as reports and complaints of its arbitrary and abusive use 'began flooding the Commission within weeks of its establishment'.[13] Inscribing the question of TADA on its regular agenda, the Commission 'invited periodic meetings' with officers of the central and state governments, and visited various states on its own fact-finding investigations. As early as 6 June 1994, the Commission admitted in Srinagar that it had 'learnt enough to have serious doubts about the worth and terms of the act', and began contemplating seeking a review of the Supreme Court judgement which had upheld the constitutional validity of TADA. It followed, thereafter, a 'three pronged strategy', whereby it continued to monitor the implementation of the act, prepared a dossier for possible recourse to the Supreme Court, and as the date for the renewal of the act drew near, it resorted to a 'direct approach' of sending letters on 20 February 1995 to parliamentarians recommending that the life of the act should not be renewed when it expired on 23 May 1995.[14] The letter made it clear that the act made 'considerable deviations from the normal law' was 'draconian in effect and character', and, 'incompatible with (India's) cultural traditions, legal history and treaty obligations'. The NHRC concluded with the crucial observation that that it found it difficult

---

[11] (1994) 3 SCC 569, p. 572.

[12] NHRC, Annual Report 1994-95, p. 8.
[13] Ibid., p. 9.
[14] Ibid.

to maintain human rights—a charge with which the Parliament entrusted it—'unless the draconian law was removed from the statute books'.[15]

Consistent with its stand on TADA, while considering the Prevention of Terrorism Bill, the NHRC addressed two questions: was there a need for the enactment of the proposed law (POTA) and, if there was, what was the kind of new law that needed to be enacted. The NHRC's 'considered unanimous opinion' as stated in its annual report (2001-2002) was that there was 'no need' to enact POTA, since the kind of actions that the Prevention of Terrorism Bill, 2000, set out to identify in section 3, were 'substantially taken care of under the existing laws'.[16] Moreover, the 'avowed justification for the new law' viz., the difficulty of securing convictions under the criminal justice system, and delay in trials, were not, in NHRC's opinion, addressed by the proposed law. The problem, which the criminal justice system in India faced, according to it, related to: (a) proper investigation of crimes, (b) efficient prosecution of

criminal trials and (c) delays in adjudication and punishment in courts. None of these problems, however, could be solved 'by enacting laws that did away with the legal safeguards that were designed to prevent innocent persons from being persecuted and punished', nor by 'providing for a different and more drastic procedure for prosecution of certain crimes'.[17] The NHRC also concluded that the Bill would 'hinder rather than enhance, the effective implementation of treaties and other international instruments on human rights' and that, in particular, the provisions of the Bill 'would not be in consonance with many provisions of the International Covenant on Civil and Political Rights (ICCPR) to which India was party.[18]

IV. ANTI-TERROR LAWS AND IMPLICATIONS FOR HUMAN RIGHTS

(1) Anti-terror laws bypass constitutional safeguards that are provided in the Constitution in cases of detention (Article 22) and principles of fair trial as laid down in the criminal procedure. As a result these laws facilitate long-term detention of large numbers of accused/suspects, without charges being brought against them, or proven / disproven in a court of law.

(2) The above, combined with provisions that made confessions to a police officer admissible, opens up immense possibilities of torture in custody. Significantly, admission of confessions to police officers as evidence is prohibited in ordinary law because the law makers recognized the prevalence of torture and coercion by police, reinforced by custodial deaths reported to the NHRC. In the Supreme Court judgment in *State* v. *Mohd. Afzal and*

[15] Ibid., pp. 55-56.

[16] In its opinion on the Prevention of Terrorism Bill, the NHRC pointed out that 'any action which threatens the unity, integrity, security or sovereignty of India' was already covered by section 153-B of the Indian Penal Code, 1860 (IPC). 'Offences against the State' was dealt with in chapter VI of IPC, especially sections 121-A (conspiracy to overawe by means of criminal force or show of criminal force), 122 (collecting arms and ammunitions with the intention of waging war against the Government of India), 124-A (sedition). Chapter XVI likewise dealt with 'Offences against the Human Body'. Apart from the IPC, the Arms Act, 1959, Explosives Act, 1884, Explosive Substances Act, 1908, and the Armed Forces (Special Powers) Act, 1958 were other existing laws that were available to deal with specific situations: Annual Report 2001-2002, pp. 322–323.

[17] Ibid., pp. 323–324.

[18] NHRC, Annual Report 2000, Annexure 4.

others, known as the Parliament attack case, delivered in August 2005, the court expressed 'serious doubts whether it would be safe to concede the power of recording confessions to the police officers to be used in evidence against the accused making the confession and the co-accused'.

(3) Certain provisions, especially section 21 of POTA, assume a civil society founded on suspicion and distrust. The act squeezes out spaces of freedom and liberty, stifling voices of political dissent. It aims at ushering in a depoliticised mass society, where elements of publicness, freedom and democratic deliberation are absent. The narrowing of democratic spaces of dialogue and deliberation, moreover, breeds a politics of fear and intimidation, the hallmark of the days before and during the emergency.

(4) The unfolding of anti-terror laws the world over has shown that they are usually used in a way so as to spin a web of suspicion around specific communities, especially religious and racial minorities, immigrants, and radical political groups. The wide powers of arrest and detention under the acts, combined with stringent bail conditions, lead to indiscriminate arrests.

(5) Moreover, there is a more permanent effect that the acts have on ordinary legal procedures, leading to what has been termed as the 'permanence of the temporary'. Extraordinary laws have a general tightening effect on the law, whereby their provisions become standards of measuring efficiency of law. As seen in the case of UAPA 2004, they get absorbed into ordinary laws, leading to a permanence of what was originally construed and justified as temporary measures. We have

noted already that the repeal of POTA was accompanied by amendment in the Unlawful Activities (Prevention) Act, 1967, to bring in specific features of the repealed POTA in UAPA, which was a 'permanent' law. When POTA was repealed, and its extraordinary provisions pertaining to bail, confessions to a police officer, and the period of police and judicial remand were dropped, the provisions giving evidentiary value to telephone tapping were retained through the amended UAPA 2004, without, however, the safeguards that POTA provided. Moreover, unlike POTA, there is no provision in UAPA of recourse to the Review Committee. Further, the inclusion of extraordinary measures into an 'ordinary' law, not only gives them a permanent place in law, it simultaneously excludes them from periodic legislative review, which was necessary for extraordinary laws for their extension, e.g., TADA had to be reviewed every two years and POTA every three years by the Parliament.

(6) The unfolding of TADA and POTA showed that they were primarily political laws, with a strong ideological content which was demonstrated most starkly in their selective application in Gujarat. Both TADA and POTA came in response to and were used against people's movements, against tribals in some states, and against political opponents in others. They mark a trend where the scope of terrorism and terrorist activity is broadened to include a wide range of political activity ranging from armed secessionist movements to expressing support to political groups and political ideologies, which are at variance with those in power.

Alternate Dispute Resolution Mechanisms

JAYA V.S.

I. INTRODUCTION

Equal justice for all is a cardinal principle on which the entire system of administration of justice is based. It is so deep-rooted in the body and spirit of common law as well as civil law jurisprudence, that the very meaning which we attribute to the word 'justice' embraces it. The greatest challenge to the justice delivery system is the delay in the disposal of cases and prohibitive cost of litigation. Experience has shown that adjudication of disputes through courts, while unavoidable, does not, in every case, provide a satisfactory or amicable solution.

Alternate Dispute Resolution or ADR mechanisms evolved to provide a solution to legal disputes and to do complete justice to the persons in conflicts. It is a voluntary process that is gradually gaining legal recognition. The ADR is at present a movement all over the world to find an answer to the never-ending litigation, where solutions are almost never reached. The society, state and the parties to the dispute are equally under an obligation to resolve the dispute before it disturbs the peace in the family, business community, society or ultimately humanity as a whole. In a civilized society, the rule of law should prevail and principles of natural justice should apply and complete justice should result. Arbitration, mediation and conciliation are accepted modes of alternative dispute resolution mechanisms. Certain kinds of disputes such as matrimonial disputes, family disputes, disputes with neighbours and several other categories of petty civil and criminal cases, which form a substantial percentage of pending litigation, can be better and more satisfactorily resolved by organized and institutionalized processes of mediation or conciliation through intervention of public spirited, respected and senior citizens. These processes may often allow for a greater consideration of local sensitivities and customs.

II. HISTORICAL BACKGROUND

Arbitration, an alternative dispute resolution mechanism, was very popular and prevalent in ancient India and awards were known as decisions of Panchayat, which were binding in nature. During the British rule in India, the Panchayat system was not abrogated. In West Bengal Regulation of 1772, a provision for arbitration was made and subsequent regulations also provided for arbitration in certain matters. The legislative council for

India came into existence in 1834 and the Civil Procedure Code, 1859 was enacted which also dealt with law of arbitration. The Code of Civil Procedure, 1882 repeated the same provisions concerning arbitration. The first Indian Arbitration Act was enacted in 1899 on the lines of English Arbitration Act, 1888. The Act made provision for reference of disputes, present as well as future, to arbitration without the intervention of the court. Later on the Indian Arbitration Act, 1940 consolidated and amended the law relating to domestic arbitration very exhaustively. There were two more arbitration Acts in India in relation to foreign awards, namely—the Arbitration (Protocol and Convention) Act, 1937, and the Foreign Awards (Recognition and Enforcement) Act, 1961, which were enacted in compliance of International conventions to which India was a party. Thus, the law of arbitration was scattered in three enactments. The Arbitration and Conciliation Act, 1996 has further amended and consolidated the law of arbitration and repealed all these three enactments.

Though there used to be other methods like mediation and conciliation to settle disputes arising between parties, historical developments show that in the earlier period, only arbitration was considered to be an alternative to ordinary court procedures.

III. FORMS OF ALTERNATE DISPUTE RESOLUTIONS

Let us now examine the various forms of alternate dispute resolution mechanisms in detail:

ARBITRATION

In simple words arbitration is adjudication over disputes between parties by a judge who has been agreed upon by the contending parties to decide upon the matter. The parties are permitted to agree upon the procedure to be followed for such arbitration. In India the specific law governing arbitration is the Arbitration and Conciliation Act, 1996. Arbitration may be ad hoc or institutional.

An ad hoc arbitration is arbitration agreed to and arranged by the parties themselves without recourse to any institution. The proceedings are conducted and the procedures are adopted by the arbitrators as per the agreement or, with the concurrence of the parties. It can be a domestic,[1], international,[2] or foreign arbitration.[3] In case of disagreement on the appointment of an arbitrator under ad hoc arbitration cases, section 11 of the Arbitration and Conciliation Act empowers the Chief Justice of High Court or Chief Justice of India, as the case may be, to appoint the arbitrators. The Chief Justice is also empowered to designate any person or institution to take the necessary steps for the appointment of arbitrators. A scheme made by the Chief Justice may designate a person by name or *ex-officio*, or an institution, which is specializing in the field of arbitration. The new

---

[1] Domestic arbitration takes place in India when the arbitration proceedings, the subject matter of the contract and the merits of the disputes are all governed by Indian law, or when the cause of action for the dispute arises wholly in India, or where the parties are otherwise subject to Indian jurisdiction.

[2] International arbitration can take place either within India or outside India in cases where there are ingredients of foreign origin relating to the parties or the subject matter of the dispute. The law applicable to the conduct of arbitration and the merits of the dispute may be Indian law or foreign law, depending on the contract in this regard, and the rules of conflict of laws.

[3] A foreign arbitration is an arbitration conducted in a place outside India and the resulting award is sought to be enforced as a foreign award.

provision has really given recognition to the role of arbitral institutions in India.

Institutional arbitration is arbitration conducted under the rules laid down by an established arbitration organization.[4] Such rules are meant to supplement the provisions of Arbitration Act in matters of procedure and other details the Act permit. They may provide for domestic arbitration or international arbitration or for both, and the disputes dealt with may be general or specific in character.

Other kinds of arbitration are specialized arbitration and statutory arbitration.

Specialized arbitration is arbitration conducted under the auspices of arbitral institutions, which have framed special rules to meet the specific requirements for the conduct of the arbitration in respect of disputes of particular types including disputes as to commodities, maritime, construction, specific areas of technology, etc.

Statutory arbitration is arbitration conducted in accordance with the provisions of certain special Acts, which specifically provide for arbitration in respect of disputes arising from matters covered by those Acts. The provisions of 1996 Act generally apply to those arbitrations unless they are inconsistent with the particular provision of those Acts, in which case the provisions of those Acts are applicable.

The advantages of arbitration may be noted as follows:

1. Speedy disposal of cases;
2. More efficacious than ordinary court litigation;
3. Ensures party autonomy;
4. Procedural technicalities are absent.

[4] For example, The Indian Council of Arbitration (ICA), New Delhi.

CONCILIATION

The proceedings relating to conciliation are dealt under sections 61 to 81 of Arbitration and Conciliation Act, 1996. This Act is aimed at permitting mediation, conciliation or other procedures during the arbitral proceedings to encourage settlement of disputes. This Act also provides that a settlement agreement reached by the parties as a result of conciliation proceedings will have the same status and effect as an arbitral award on agreed terms on the substance of the dispute rendered by an arbitral tribunal.

Section 61 states that conciliation shall apply to disputes arising out of legal relationship, whether contractual or not and to all proceedings relating thereto. Unless any law excludes, these proceeding will apply to every such dispute while being conciliated. The parties may agree to follow any procedure for conciliation other than what is prescribed under the 1996 Act.

According to section 62, a party can take initiative and send invitation to conciliate under this part after identifying the dispute. Proceedings shall commence when other party accepts the invitation. If rejected, the proceeding shall stop there itself. If the other party does not reply within 30 days, the invitation can be treated as having been rejected.

CONCILIATION AND ARBITRATION

Unlike an arbitrator, a conciliator does not give a decision but his main function is to induce the parties themselves to come to a settlement. An arbitrator is expected to give a hearing to the parties, but a conciliator does not engage in any formal hearing, though he may informally consult the parties separately or together. The arbitrator is vested with the power of final decision and in that sense, it is his contribution that becomes binding. In contrast, a conciliator has to induce the parties to come to a settlement by agreement.

A party initiating conciliation can, under section 62, send to the other party a written invitation to conciliation. Conciliation commences when the other party accepts in writing this invitation. If it does not accept it, then there will be no conciliation.

The conciliator is not bound by the Code of Civil Procedure, 1908 or the Indian Evidence Act, 1872. He is to be guided by the principles of objectivity, fairness and justice. Subject to the above, he may conduct the proceedings in such manner as he considers appropriate, taking into account:

1. The circumstances of the case;
2. The wishes expressed by the parties;
3. Need for speedy settlement.

If the settlement is product of conciliation, with all the formalities of reducing it into writing and authenticated by the conciliator, on a stamped paper, it will be an award and thus a decree, which could be executed immediately. Non-compliance would lead the party affected to straight away file an execution petition.

The advantages of resolving disputes by conciliation are as follows.

1. The parties and the third neutral party (in place of judge) sit together to resolve the issue.
2. The matter settles at threshold of the first count, and for all times to come instead of resorting to all possible appeals to High Court and the Supreme Court, as many times as the Code of Civil Procedure 1908 provides.
3. The social advantage of parties going back home happily without broken relations is of high value. Bickering and enmity will not be enhanced as happens in other modes of rule-based resolutions.
4. Drastically cuts down the cost of litigation and the time it involves. The early disposal of the case will reduce the hidden and unproductive costs like travelling to courts and keeping off from working for several productive days.
5. Execution is done simultaneously with the settlement.
6. It offers a more flexible alternative, for a wide variety of disputes, small as well as large.
7. It obviates the parties from seeking recourse to the system.
8. It reserves the freedom of the parties to withdraw from conciliation without prejudice to their legal position inter se at any stage of the proceedings.
9. It is committed to maintenance of confidentiality throughout the proceedings and thereafter of the dispute, pertaining to the information exchanged, the offers and counter offers of solutions made and the settlement arrived at.
10. It facilitates the maintenance of continued relationship between the parties even after the settlement or at least during the period the settlement is attempted at. This feature is of particular significance to the parties who are required to continue their relationship despite the dispute, as in the case of disputes arising out of construction contracts, family relationships, family properties or disputes between members of any business or other organisations.
11. There is less scope for corruption or bias.

MEDIATION

Mediation is the negotiation facilitated by a third party. It is a private, voluntary, informal non-binding and cost effective process which provides an environment for constructive communication.

As per provision of order X, rule 1-A of the Code of Civil Procedure, 1908, after recording admission or denial of documents, the court is under an obligation to direct the parties to opt for any of the four modes of alternative dispute resolution including mediation. Both the parties can make the request for reference of a dispute to mediation. A wide nature of disputes, including matrimonial, labour, motor accident claims, eviction matters between landlord and tenants, complaints under section 138 of the Negotiable Instruments Act, 1881, petitions under section 125 of the Code of Criminal Procedure, 1973, or any compoundable offence can be referred for mediation. If only one of the parties makes a request and the other party is not averse to the idea of mediation, the dispute can still be referred. Any court can otherwise make a reference of a dispute as provided under section 89 of the Code of Civil Procedure, 1908. Lawyers can assist the parties in the mediation proceedings. Rather, it has been found that wherever the parties are assisted by their advocates, a settlement is arrived at a bit early, for the lawyers can explain the weakness and strength of their respective cases and the time factor which might be taken in litigation. Since the proceedings before a mediator are informal, the parties can even bring any of their relations to assist them.

Mediation is a process, facilitation, and an empowerment.[5] The core value in mediation is that the process provides the parties with an opportunity to negotiate, converse and explore options aided by a neutral third party, the mediator, to exhaustively determine if a settlement is possible. It is a process of empowerment of the parties to control their destiny in their dispute.

Mediation involves a determination of interests—the interests of the parties. A concept frequently not found in the litigator's lexicon. Interests are the needs, wants, and desires that are of importance to the parties. To get there, mediation provides a forum for principled negotiations. These negotiations may at times become frustrating and troubling, but with the mediator's help, the parties keep moving forward. Principled negotiations stimulate exploration of settlement alternatives and an opportunity to evaluate those alternatives, weighing them against the likely outcome of going to trial and viewing proposals through the lenses of reality. If the dispute settles at the mediation, it settles on a basis acceptable to the parties; the spectre of trial is removed, and, the threat of being tied up on appeal is eliminated.

Role of Mediator

Mediation is accepted as the most viable process of resolving a conflict between two parties before any legal or physical conflict is opted for settling the score for any kind of problem. The mediator facilitates, renders assistance, gives advise if necessary, presents the options available, analyses the strategies, suggests strategies to be adopted, hammers out the issues to be settled, drafts the agreement sentences so that the parties do not find any difficulty in agreeing with them and finally

---

[5] Delhi District Court Mediation Centres receive cases for mediation not only from all the four District Courts but also from the Supreme Court of India and Delhi High Court. To create awareness about the process of mediation, Delhi Mediation Centre has brought out a pamphlet. Delhi Mediation Centre has also prepared a documentary to popularise mediation.

authorizes the settlement. The mediator does not settle. He will not give an award like an arbitrator. He also does not prefer to adjudicate the issues. He will also not prescribe the procedure. He does not examine the witnesses and insist on the production of evidence, etc.

Flexible Process

There is no rigid framework of rules for mediation. It is a very flexible process. A person who is acceptable to both the parties would serve as mediator. He is perceived as neutral, capable of understanding the issues of their dispute and knowledgeable enough about the mediation processes, along with a sense of time and the attitude to resolve the problems.

It is important to decide on the cost of the mediation at the beginning itself. The mediator should indicate the possible cost and obtain the consent of parties to share the cost equally. If not, the cost of mediation would become an issue of conflict to be mediated between the mediator and the parties.

NEGOTIATION

Negotiation is a communication process. It is voluntary and non-binding. It offers control over procedure and outcome since there is wide range of possible solutions. It aims at maximum joint gains, which are quick, inexpensive, private, and less complicated. Negotiation is possible where parties must cooperate to meet these goals. Parties can influence each other to act in ways that provide mutual benefit or avoidance of harm. Parties are affected by time constraints and they can identify and agree on issues.

The negotiation works when:

1. The parties are willing to cooperate and communicate to meet their goals.

2. The parties can mutually benefit or avoid harm by influencing each other.

3. The parties know that they have time constraints.

4. The parties realize that any other procedure will not produce the desired outcome.

5. The parties can identify the issues that require to be sorted out.

6. The parties also agree that their interests are not incompatible to each other

7. The parties know that it is preferable to participate in private cooperative process rather than go through severe external constraints like loss of reputation, excessive cost, and possibility of adversarial decision.

Negotiation is a 'mixed motive' exchange. The motives of both the parties get mixed and proposed to be exchanged. Interests are combined and addressed together. The value is shared and before that additional values are also created. First the parties to the dispute understand each other, the problem, and their ultimate interests, and sit together to resolve them with maximized benefits possible.

A good negotiator should know his subject intimately, should become an expert, manifest a sense of personal integrity, and should know how to exercise power. The negotiation is a combination of several skills, and a continuous practice of skills. A good negotiator is a person who is an effective communicator and combines the skills of comprehending the whole problem, and while negotiating, keeps in mind the interests of both the parties.

LEGAL SERVICES AUTHORITIES ACT, 1987

The Legal Services Act, 1987 envisages constitution of Legal Services Authorities to provide free and competent legal services to the weaker sections of the society, to ensure that opportunities for securing justice are not denied to any citizen by reason of economic or other disabilities, and to organise Lok Adalats to see that operation of the legal system promotes justice on the basis of equal opportunity.

LOK ADALAT

The *Lok Adalats* (people's courts) were established by the government to settle disputes through conciliation and compromise. The first Lok Adalat was held in Chennai in 1986. A Lok Adalat accepts those cases which are pending in the regular courts within their jurisdiction, which could be settled by conciliation and compromise. The Lok Adalat is presided over by a sitting or retired judicial officer as the chairman, with two other members, usually a lawyer and a social worker. There is no court fee. If the case is already filed in the regular court, the fee paid will be refunded if the dispute is settled in the Lok Adalat. Procedural laws and the Indian Evidence Act, 1872 are not strictly followed while assessing the merits of the claim by the Lok Adalat.

The main condition for recourse to Lok Adalat is that both parties in dispute should agree to reach a settlement. The decision of the Lok Adalat is binding on the parties to the dispute and its order is capable of execution through legal process. No appeal lies against the order of the Lok Adalat. Lok Adalat is very effective in settlement of money claims. Disputes like partition suits, damages and matrimonial cases can also be easily settled before the Lok Adalat.

Significance of Lok Adalat

In the context of the ever-increasing number of cases, the court system is under great pressure. If there was a permanent mechanism or machinery to settle matters at a pre-trial stage, many matters would not find their way to the courts. Similarly, if there are permanent forums to which courts may refer cases, the load of cases could be taken off the courts. In order to reduce the heavy demand on court time, cases must be resolved by resorting to ADR methods before they enter the portals of the court. The significance of Lok Adalat as an ADR mechanism is evident from the large number of third party claims referred by Motor Accident Claim Tribunal (MACT) that it has settled. Except matters relating to offences, which are not compoundable, a Lok Adalat has jurisdiction to deal with all matters. Matters pending or at pre-trial stage, provided a reference is made to it by a court or by the concerned authority or committee, when the dispute is at a pre-trial stage and not before a court of law, can be referred to Lok Adalat. The concept of Lok Adalat has been gathered from system of Panchayats, which has roots in the history, and culture of India. Use of ADR mechanisms is, therefore, also an attempt for decentralization of justice.

The National Legal Services Authority constituted under the Legal Services Authorities Act, 1987, serves as the apex and nodal agency for laying down policies and principles for making legal services available under the Act. The ground level operations of Lok Adalats are handled by state-level, district-level and *taluka*-level agencies constituted in the respective States. A Lok Adalat settlement is binding like an order, decree, judgment or award of a court. It is executable and non-appealable. It brings a case or dispute to a final resolution in a single forum and stage.. It has proved inexpensive, easy, expeditious and a simple ADR mechanism, particularly, for indigent, illiterate and ignorant sections of society.

IV. CONCLUSION

In the justice delivery system, ADR is employed since the litigative journey in the court of law has become exorbitantly expensive, time-consuming, cumbersome, dilatory, complex and also stressful, for a variety of reasons. The necessity and utility of ADR is unquestionable. Resolution of disputes is an essential characteristic for societal peace, amity, comity and harmony, and easy access to justice. In the past, the privileged and powerful sections of society had performed the function of resolving dispute and dispensing justice. The emergence of modern democratic states has seen the evolution of sophisticated legal mechanisms, and courts that follow formal procedures, and are presided over by trained adjudicators entrusted with the responsibilities of resolution of disputes on behalf of the state. The procedural formalisation of justice also witnessed a rise the number of cases which are also time consuming and result in heavy amount of expenditure. Moreover in the light of India's socio-economic conditions, the state has a duty to secure that the operation of legal system promotes justice on the basis of equal opportunity. Obviously, this has led to a search for an alternative complementary and supplementary mechanism to the existing process of the traditional civil court which allows for inexpensive, expeditious and less cumbersome and, also therefore, less stressful resolution of disputes.

Suggested Further Reading[*]

GENERAL

Austin, Granville, *The Indian Constitution: Corner-stone of a Nation*, Oxford, Clarendon Press, 1996.

––, *Working a Democratic Constitution: The Indian Experience*, New Delhi, Oxford University Press, 1999.

Baxi, Upendra, *Towards a Sociology of Indian Law*, New Delhi, Satvahan, 1986.

Indian Legal System, Revised Edition, New Delhi, Indian Law Institute, 2006.

Kaul, J.L., *Human Rights: Issues and Perspectives*, New Delhi, Regency, 1995.

Seervai, H.M., *Constitutional Law of India*, Fourth Edition, New Delhi, Universal Law Publishing Co., 2005.

Singh, Mahendra P., *V.N. Shukla's Constitution of India*, Tenth Edition, Lucknow, Eastern Book Co., 2006.

Singh, S.N. (ed.), *Law and Social Change*, New Delhi, P.G. Krishnan Foundation, 1990.

South Asia Human Rights Documentation Centre, *Handbook of Human Rights and Criminal Justice*, New Delhi, Oxford University Press, 2005, Second Edition, 2007.

PUBLIC INTEREST LITIGATION

Bakshi, P.M., *Public Interest Litigations in India*, New Delhi, Ashoka Law House, 1988.

Baxi, Upendra, 'Taking Rights Seriously: Social Action Litigation in the Supreme Court of India', *Supreme Court on Public Interest Litigation: Cases and Material. The Debate over Original Intent*, Vol. 1, New Delhi, LIPS India Private Limited.

Sathe, S.P., *Judicial Activism in India: Transgressing Borders and Enforcing Limits*, New Delhi, Oxford University Press, 2002.

LAWS RELATING TO CRIMES IN INDIA

Deb, R., *Principles of Criminology, Criminal Law and Investigations*, Third Edition, Calcutta, S.C. Sarrkar, 1995.

Essays on the Indian Penal Code, Revised Edition, New Delhi, Indian Law Institute, 2005.

Pillai, P.S.A., *Criminal Law*, Ninth Edition, New Delhi, Butterworths, 2000.

OFFENCES AGAINST WOMEN

Dhanda, Amita and Archana Parashar (eds), *Engendering Law: Essays in Honour of Lotika Sarkar*, Lucknow, Eastern Book Co., 1999.

Sarkar, Lotika and B. Sivaramayya (eds), *Women and Law: Contemporary Problems*, New Delhi, Vikas, 1994.

Saxena, Shobha, *Crime against Women and Protective Laws*, New Delhi, Deep and Deep, 1995.

PREVENTING ATROCITIES AGAINST SCHEDULED CASTES AND SCHEDULED TRIBES

Agrawal, Girish and Colin Gonsalves, *Dalits and*

---

[*] References provided in the chapters of the book have been not included here.

the Law, New Delhi, Human Rights Law Network, 2005.

Kannabiran, K.G., *The Wages of Impunity: Power, Justice and Human Rights*, Hyderabad, Orient Longman, 2004.

Report on Prevention of Atrocities Against Scheduled Castes, New Delhi, National Human Rights Commission, 2004.

Suppressing the Voice of the Oppressed: State Terror on Protests against the Khairlanji Massacre, Report to the Nation by an All Indian Team, 2007.

LABOUR LAWS AND THE WORLD OF WORK

Labour Law and Labour Relations: Cases and Materials, Third Edition, New Delhi, Indian Law Institute, 2007.

Pai, G.B., *Labour Law in India*, New Delhi, Butterworths, 2001.

Report of the National Commission on Labour, Government of India, 2002.

ENVIRONMENTAL LAW

Divan, Shyam and Armin Rosencranz, *Environmental Law & Policy in India*, Second Edition, New Delhi, Oxford University Press, 2001.

Leelakrishnan, P., *Environment Law*, Lexis Nexis Student Series, New Delhi, Lexis Nexis, Butterworths, 2004.

Singh, Gurdip, *Environmental Law in India*, New Delhi, Macmillan India Ltd., 2005.

THE CONCEPT OF RELIGIOUS PERSONAL LAWS

Agnes, Flavia, *Law and Gender Inequality: The Politics of Women's Rights in India*, Delhi, Oxford University Press, 1999.

Jaising, Indira, (ed.), *Justice for Women Personal Laws, Women's Rights and Law Reform*, Goa, The Other India Press, 1996.

Parashar, A., *Women and Family Law Reforms in India*, New Delhi, Sage, 1992.

Personal Law Series, New Delhi, Indian Social Institute, 2006.

Saxena, Poonam Pradhan, 'Matrimonial Laws and Gender Justice', *Journal of the Indian Law Institute*, Vol 45, No. 3 & 4, 335-87, 2003.

CONSUMER LAW

Aggarwal, Sukhdev, *Commentary on Consumer Protection Act*, Second Edition, Delhi, Bright Law House, 2003.

Eradi, V. Balakrshna, *Consumer Protection Jurisprudence*, New Delhi, Butterworths, 2004.

Lowe, Robert and Geoffrey Woodroffe, *Consumer Law and Practice*, Sixth Edition, London, Sweet and Maxwell, 2004.

Sharma, K.M., *Key to Consumer's Law*, New Delhi, Kamal Publishers, 1994.

Verma, S.K., Afzal Wani and SS.S. Jaswal, *Treatise on Consumer Protection Laws*, New Delhi, Indian Law Institute, 2004

ANTI-TERROR LAWS AND HUMAN RIGHTS

Louis, Prakash and R. Vashum, *Extraordinary Laws in India: A Reader for Understanding Legislations Endangering Civil Liberties*, New Delhi, Indian Social Institute, 2002.

Prevention of Terrorism Ordinance: Government Decides to Play Judge and Jury, New Delhi, South Asia Human Rights Documentation Centre, 2001.

Singh, Ujjwal Kumar, *The State, Democracy and Anti-Terror Laws in India*, New Delhi, Sage, 2007.

Verma, Preeti (ed.), *The Terror of POTA and Other Security Legislation. A Report on the People's Tribunal on the Prevention of Terrorism Act and other Security Legislation*, New Delhi, Human Rights Law Network, 2004.

ALTERNATE DISPUTE REDRESSAL

Mittal, D.P., Law *of Arbitration ADR and Contract,*

Second Edition, New Delhi, Taxmann Allied Services (P) Ltd., 2001.

Kwatra, G.K., *The Arbitration and Conciliation of Law in India*, The Indian Council of Arbitration, New Delhi, 2002.

Rao, P.C. and William Sheffield (eds), *Alternate Dispute Redressal: What it is and How it Works*, New Delhi, Universal, 1997.

Glossary

Ab initio – From the beginning

Actus Reus – The elements of an offence excluding those which concern the mind of the accused.

Ad hoc arbitration – Proceedings that are not administered by others and which require the parties to make their own arrangements for the selection of arbitrators and the applicable law, rules, procedures and administrative support.

Alternate Dispute Resolution mechanisms – Dispute resolution processes and techniques that fall outside the state judicial process.

Affirmation – To confirm, ratify

Approver witness/evidence – An accomplice who turns state's evidence.

Arbitration – The hearing or determination of a dispute or the settling of differences between parties by person(s) chosen or agreed to by them.

Bailable /non-bailable offences – Bailable and non-bailable offences are listed in the Indian Penal Code, and indicated in the First Schedule of the CrPC. Bailable offences are relatively lesser offences like causing simple hurt, being a member of an unlawful assembly, etc., and any person committing a bailable offence has a legal right to be released on bail. A non-bailable offence is of a more serious nature like murder, rape, dacoity, etc. While a person accused of non-bailable offences cannot get bail as a matter of right However, it does not mean that the accused cannot get bail at all.

Binding precedent (*stare decisis*) – The doctrine that requires the courts to follow earlier decisions or precedents, when the same points arise again in litigation.

Caveat Emptor – Let the buyer beware

Caveat Venditor – Let the seller beware

Central laws – Refers to the laws that are enacted by the Central government.

Certiorari (writ of) a writ issues by a court of superior jurisdiction to an inferior tribunal to inspect the proceedings and determine whether there have been any irregularities.

Charge sheet – The record of cases and charges made at a police station.

Civil suit – A legal proceeding of a civil kind (non Criminal) brought by one person against another.

Cognizance/Cognizable – A case in which a police officer in accordance with the First Schedule of the Code of Criminal Procedure or under any other law can arrest a person without warrant/a case in which a police officer has no authority to arrest without warrant.

Cognizable/non-cognizable offences – Apart from bailable and non-bailable offences, Section 2(c) of the CrPC divides offences as cognizable and non-cognizable. Cognizable offences like murder, rape, dacoity, are those for which a police office can arrest a person without a warrant from a magistrate. In non-cognizable offences e.g., cheating, causing hurt, bigamy etc., a warrant from a magistrate is required for making arrest.

Conciliation – An alternate dispute resolution mechanism whereby the parties to a dispute agree to utilize services of a conciliator who then meets with the parties separately in an attempt to resolve their differences.

Concurrent List – List III of the Seventh Schedule of the Constitution of India.

Consensus ad idem – Agreement as to the same thing, the common consent necessary for a binding contract.

Coparcenery property – Property which consists of ancestral property or of joint acquisition or of proerty thrown into the common stock and accretions to such property.

Copyright infringement – Copyright infringement is the unauthorized use of material which is covered by copyright law, in a manner that violates one of copyright owner's exclusive rights, such as the right to reproduce or perform the copyrighted work, or to communicate the work to the public.

Court of Sessions – A court presided over by a Sessions Judge.

Custodial death – Death of a person occurring while in the charge/protection/security of the police in the lock-up or in prison.

Cryptography – Cryptography is the study of computer message secrecy which includes *encryption* i.e. the process of converting ordinary information (plaintext) into unintelligible gibberish (ciphertext). In modern times the security of ATM cards, computer passwords, and electronic commerce, all depend on cryptography.

Deem – To treat a thing as being something which it is not or having certain qualities which it does not have.

Designated Court/Special court – Courts set up to try cases under the Terrorist and Disruptive Activities (Prevention) Act [TADA] and Prevention of Terrorism Act [POTA], respectively.

Dissenting judgement – A judgement where the judge announces his dissent from the majority view of the court and gives his reasons.

District judge – Includes judge of a City Civil Court, Additional District Judge, Joint District Judge, Assistant District Judge, Chief Judge of a Small Cause Court, Chief Presidency Magistrate, Additional Chief Presidency Magistrate, Sessions Judge, Additional Sessions Judge and Assistant Sessions Judge.

Enactment – The passing of law by a legislative body.

Estoppel – A bar that prevents one from asserting a claim or right that contradicts what one has said or what has been legaly established as true.

Ex-officio – By virtue of office or official position.

Extra-ordinary laws – laws that are enacted to address special crimes not covered under ordinary law.

Federal – A political society in which several states form a unit but remain independent in their internal affairs to a considerable extent.

Grievous hurt- serious physical injury defined in the Indian Penal Code, 1860

Green Bench – The bench of the court hearing environmetal law matters.

Hanafi- A person of the Muslim faith who conforms to the tenets and doctrine s of the Hanafi School of Muslim law.

Homicide – The killing of a human being by another human being.

Illegitimate legislation – Legislation that is beyond the powers of the legislature.

Impunity – Exemption from punishment, or being free from injurious consequences of one's actions.

Incarceration – The act or process of confining someone.

Intellectual property rights – Rights granted to those who create or own that which is the product of the human intellect and its creativity.

Inter alia – Among other things

Internet Protocol (IP) address – An IP address is a unique address of a computer on the Internet which is used for identification and communication between computers—just like a street address or a phone number.

Institutional arbitration – Arbitration conducted under rules laid down by a permanent arbitral institution.

Interpellation(in a parliament) – Interruption of proceedings by the demand of an explanation from (the minister concerned).

Inviolable – Not to be violated, infringed, or broken (a rule).

Judicial custody – A person kept under custody through court orders. Usually such persons are kept in prisons. It is different from police custody, whereby, a person is kept in police lockup.

Jurisprudence – The science or theory of law.

Justiciable – Those constitutionally guaranteed rights which place an obligation on the state to provide the conditions for the exercise of rights, which means that in case the government fails in its obligation to provide for a right, the courts can intervene and instruct the government to do so. Non-justiciable rights are those rights which are recognized as human but do not have legal backing.

Legitimation – The making legitimate or lawful that which was originally not so

Litigant – A party to a lawsuit.

Lok Adalats – A lok adalat constituted under the Legal Services Authorities Act, 1987 has jurisdiction to settle by way of effecting compromise between parties, any matter which may be pending before any court.

Magistrate of First Class – Under the CrPC these Magistrates can pass sentences of imprisonment for terms not exceeding three years and/or of fines not exceeding five thousand rupees.

Magistrate of Second Class – Under the CrPC these Magistrates can only pass sentences of imprisonment not exceeding one year and/or of fines not exceeding one thousand rupees.

Monetary bail bonds – The security taken from a person arrested or imprisoned for his appearance in court when called upon to do so.

Surety – The persons who makles himself or herself responsible for the performance or payment of a sum of money to a third person.

Magna Carta – The charter originally granted by King John of England in 1215 and subsequently reenacted by Parliament to protect subjects from arbitrary arrest, imprisonment and other extortions by abuse of the royal prerogative

Mediation – Mediation is an attempt to bring about a peaceful settlement or compromise between disputants through the objective intervention of a neutral party

Mediator – A person who mediates between parties who have a dispute or differences.

Mens rea – The state of mind expressly or implicitly required by the definition of the offence charged. There is a presumption that it is an essential ingredient in every criminal offence, liable to be displaced either by the words of the statute or by the subject-matter with which it deals. Many minor statutory offences, however, are punishable irrespective of the existence of mens rea; the mere intent to do the act forbidden in sufficient.

Moffusil – Country as opposed to town; the interior of the country

Non-derogable – That which cannot be diminshed or repealed.

Novation/novatio – The renewal of an existing obligation.

Nullity (of marriage) – A marriage that is null and void.

Obligate – To impose a duty.

Ordinance – A decree or order issued under the authority of the executive.

Panchnama – A record of what a panch saw or heard.

Paralegals – One who assists a lawyer in the practice of law but who is not a trained lawyer.

Parallel court – Special or Designated Courts set up to try cases under special/extraordinary laws.

Penal custodial institutions – Jails, places where people are kept in confinement under authority of law for purposes of punishment.

Petition – An application for a court order or for some judicial action.

Plenary power – A power subject to limitations.

Primary/secondary evidence – Original or first hand evidence/that which is inferior to primary or best evidence which becomes admissible when the primary or best evidence of the fact in question is lost or becomes inaccessible.

Processual justice/Procedural justice – Abiding by rules of procedure.

Prohibition (writ of) – A writ issued by a court of superior jurisdiction to an inferior tribunal forbidding the latter to continue proceedings in excess of its jurisdiction or in contravention of the law.

Proscribe – To forbid.

Prosecutrix – A woman who institutes and carries on proceedings in a court of law especially in a criminal court.

Public prosecutor – Generic term for the government's lawyer in a criminal case whose responsibility it is to frame charges against the accused.

Qazi – A judge under Muslim law; also registrar of marriages and divorces and also has certain functions in religious worship.

Quorum – The minimum number of members of any body of persons whose presence is necessary for that body to transact its business so that its acts may be valid.

Redressal – To set right; to make amends.

Restitution (of conjugal rights) – The compelling of a husband or wife, who has withdrawn and lives separate without cause, to cohabit with the other.

Sedition – The offence of publishing orally or otherwise any words or documents with the intention of exciting disaffection, hatred or contempt against the sovereign

Self-incrimination – implicate/charge one's own self in a crime (e.g. through a confessional statement).

Shariat – The body of Islamic law.

Sine Qua Non- Essential condition.

Spyware – Spyware is a kind of computer software that is installed surreptitiously on somebody's computer with an idea to secretly monitor his behavior without his informed consent.

Statutory limitation- The period specified by a statute within which action must be brought.

Suprema Lex – Supreme law

Trade mark/trade mark infringement – A trademark is a distinctive sign which is used by a business organization to uniquely identify the source of its products/services to consumers, and to distinguish its products/services from those of other entities. The unauthorised use of someone's trademark can be described as trademark infringement.

Third party Claims – A claim by civil defendant or respondent against a party not already named in a court or other adversarial proceeding.

Undischarged Insolvent – A person who is declared to be a bankrupt by a court of law.

Vagrancy laws – Laws relating to those who wander about from place to place, who are idle and have no visible means of support.

Void – A contract, an action, an order etc that has no legal effect and cannot bind any person.

Voidable – A contract, an action, an order etc that can be avoided (held to be void and set aside).

Writ – A written command or formal order issued by a court directing a person(s) to whom it is addressed to do or refrain from doing some act specified in the command or order.

Contributors

UPENDRA BAXI Professor, University of Warwick and formerly, Vice-Chancellor, University of Delhi.

V.R. KRISHNA IYER Former Judge, Supreme Court of India.

PUNAM S. KHANNA Reader, JDM College, University of Delhi.

VISHNU KONOORAYAR Assistant Research Professor, Indian Law Institute, New Delhi.

VED KUMARI Professor, Law Centre-I, Faculty of Law, University of Delhi.

RAMAN MITTAL Reader, Campus Law Centre, faculty of Law, University of Delhi.

S MURALIDHAR Judge, Delhi High Court.

B.B. PANDE Formerly Professor, Faculty of Law, University of Delhi and presently, Consultant, National Human Rights Commission.

ARCHANA PARASHAR Division of Law, Macquarie University, Australia.

M.ROOPA International Environmental Law Research Centre, New Delhi.

ANUPAMA ROY Senior Fellow, Centre for Women's Development Studies, New Delhi.

KAMALA SANKARAN Research Professor, Indian Law Institute, New Delhi.

UJJWAL KUMAR SINGH Reader, Department of Political Science, University of Delhi.

PARMANAND SINGH Formerly Head and Dean, Faculty of Law, University of Delhi.

JAYA V.S. Assistant Research Professor, Indian Law Institute, New Delhi.